# THE
# FREEDOM WRITERS
# DIARY

## TEACHER'S GUIDE

Also by Erin Gruwell

*The Freedom Writers Diary:*
*How a Teacher and 150 Teens Used Writing to Change Themselves*
*and the World Around Them*

*Teach with Your Heart:*
*Lessons I Learned from the Freedom Writers*

# THE
# FREEDOM WRITERS
# DIARY

## TEACHER'S GUIDE

Erin Gruwell
and
The Freedom Writers Foundation

BROADWAY BOOKS
NEW YORK

PUBLISHED BY BROADWAY BOOKS

Copyright © 2007 by Erin Gruwell and the Freedom Writers Foundation

Published in the United States by Broadway Books,
an imprint of The Doubleday Broadway Publishing Group,
a division of Random House, Inc., New York.
www.broadwaybooks.com

BROADWAY BOOKS and its logo, a letter B bisected on the diagonal, are trademarks of Random House, Inc.

Page 98 Anna Quindlen article: Reprinted by permission of International Creative Management, Inc.
Copyright © 2007 by Anna Quindlen. First appeared in *Newsweek* magazine.

Book design by Chris Welch

978-0-7679-2696-6

PRINTED IN THE UNITED STATES OF AMERICA

3  5  7  9  10  8  6  4  2

THIS BOOK IS DEDICATED TO:

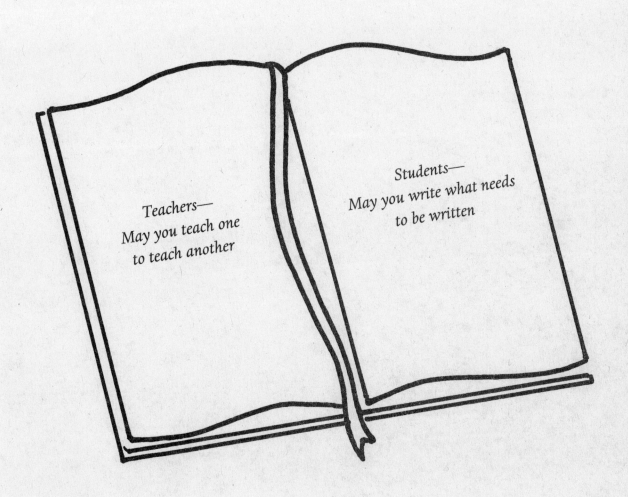

Teachers—
May you teach one
to teach another

Students—
May you write what needs
to be written

# Contents

# THE
# FREEDOM WRITERS
# DIARY

## TEACHER'S GUIDE

# Letter to the Educator

Dear Educator,

I'm so excited to have this opportunity to share *The Freedom Writers Diary Teacher's Guide* with you. The guide includes many of the original activities that I did with the Freedom Writers in Room 203 at Woodrow Wilson High School in Long Beach, California, from 1994 to 1998. Several of these activities are derived from the students' entries in *The Freedom Writers Diary*, and the Line Game and the Toast for Change were even featured in the movie *Freedom Writers*.

When I walked into my first class as a new teacher, I could not have been less prepared to deal with the harsh realities of the lives of my students or the way the outside world would crash into my classroom. These teenagers lived in a racially divided community and were already hardened by firsthand exposure to gang violence, broken homes, juvenile halls, and drugs. The obstacles these teens confronted as students became challenges for me as their teacher.

The 150 freshman who drifted into Room 203 had already been dubbed as the school's "rejects." Sure enough, that hurtful judgment was reiterated several weeks later when I was told that my students were "too stupid" to read a book from cover to cover. My students were far from stupid, but they had certainly given up on education. They felt as if they had no reason to care about school; the potential rewards of college and a career seemed remote, even alien.

After hearing, "Ms. G, this doesn't have anything to do with my life," more than once, I made it my mission to prove my students wrong by finding ways to make my lessons speak to their experiences and tap into their talents.

The students brought their histories of racial conflict into the classroom. They needed an educational philosophy that promoted tolerance and encouraged them to rethink their beliefs about themselves. I decided to assign books written by, for, and about teenagers who had lived during wars but were able to right the wrong by chronicling their own harrowing stories. To my amazement, students who had originally hated reading and writing became engrossed in reading Anne Frank's *The Diary of a Young Girl* and Elie Wiesel's *Night*. These books and others resonated with the reality of living in a dangerous urban environment, not long after the Los Angeles riots in 1992.

When one of my students exclaimed, "I feel like I live in an undeclared war zone," I realized that these young people needed to be encouraged to pick up a pen rather than a gun. Tragically, this student had lost two dozen friends to gang violence. In an attempt to connect with my class, I gave my students journals in the hopes of giving them a voice. Before long, they began to pour out their stories openly, unburdened by the anxieties associated with spelling, grammar, and grades. Journals provided a safe place to become passionate writers communicating their own histories, their own insights. As they began to write down their thoughts and feelings, motivation blossomed. Suddenly, they had a forum for self-expression, and a place where they felt valued and validated.

As sophomores, my students were inspired to write letters to Miep Gies, the courageous woman who hid Anne Frank, and Zlata Filipovic, the teenage author who penned *Zlata's Diary: A Child's Life in Sarajevo*. When Miep Gies told my students to make sure that "Anne's death is not in vain," they understood her message that writing and storytelling have the power to change the world. Following in the footsteps of extraordinary teenagers like Anne and Zlata, my students used their own diaries to share their experiences of loss, hardship, and discrimination.

As juniors, I had my students watch a documentary about the Freedom Riders, the civil rights activists who rode integrated buses across the South in 1961. The courage of the Freedom Riders inspired my class to adopt the name "Freedom Writers," reflecting the students' determination to use their journals to speak out about the racism and intolerance that surrounded them. To celebrate their newfound identity, the Freedom Writers followed in the footsteps of the Freedom Riders and took a trip to Washington, D.C. In a symbolic tribute to their namesake, they delivered a bound copy of their favorite diary entries to Richard Riley, the U.S. Secretary of Education.

As a senior class, the Freedom Writers received the Spirit of Anne Frank Award for their commitment to combating discrimination, racism, and bias-related violence. They also devoted long hours to editing their journal entries and were rewarded with a publishing contract to turn their class book into what would become a number-one-ranked *New York Times* bestseller, *The Freedom Writers Diary: How a Teacher and 150 Teens Used Writing to Change Themselves and the World Around Them* (Broadway Books, 1999). But even more meaningful to the Freedom Writers than awards or publication was the moment they collectively walked across a graduation stage and claimed their high school diplomas, a feat few had thought possible.

After the Freedom Writers graduated from Wilson High in 1998, I made the difficult decision to trade my beloved Room 203 for California State University, Long Beach, where I became a Teacher in Residence in the College of Education. My goal was to help as many students as possible by teaching future educators the importance of working with at-risk kids who had been written off by the educational system. During my time at the university, some of my college students were Freedom Writers now pursuing careers in education. One of them once commented, "The best part of Ms. G's class [at Wilson High] was how she'd start us on one of her off-the-wall activities and suddenly we were all coming up with our own ideas. It was like we were teaching the class with her. I think that's why so many of us want to be teachers." Hearing that, I began to dissect what truly happened in Room 203, in the hopes that my lesson plans could be replicated in other classrooms, regardless of age, academic ability, or socioeconomic level.

At the university, I discovered that some of the pedagogical strategies I had arrived at instinctively while teaching at Wilson High were supported by research in the field of education. I learned that educational psychologists strongly support a student-centered learning model based on "internal motivation." Students who are internally motivated feel a sense of choice in the classroom and are more likely to achieve academic success. Teachers who support "internal motivation" listen to their students, engage interest, encourage questions, and allow their students flexibility in problem solving. Encouraged by this academic validation of my student-centered methods, I drew on my classroom experiences with the Freedom Writers and began to teach future educators how to motivate their students from the inside out.

Hundreds of future teachers later, a very successful businessman challenged me to bottle my "Secret Sauce" and take my pedagogical methods to the next level. With his help, as well as crucial input from many of the original Freedom Writers, we established the Freedom Writers Foundation, a nonprofit organization devoted to replicating the success of the Freedom Writers.

Today, thanks in part to the scholarships provided by the Freedom Writers Foundation, many of the Freedom Writers have graduated from college. Some have earned their teaching credentials, while others are pursing master's degrees and Ph.D.s. In addition, there are Freedom Writers who contribute to the day-to-day running of the Foundation, help to organize and lead teacher-training workshops, and visit schools to empower youths to write their own stories.

Over the years, the outpouring of interest from teachers and students across the country who have read *The Freedom Writers Diary* has been overwhelming. By holding a mirror to their lives, the Freedom Writers were able to touch on universal truths, illuminate the lives of teenagers, and provide hope for the future. In particular, the book has motivated educators who want to have similar experiences with their students yet need a blueprint to follow. Through *The Freedom Writers Diary Teacher's Guide*, I hope to share what I have learned with you, the educator.

It is only fitting that the Freedom Writers themselves were instrumental in helping me develop this *Teacher's Guide*. Throughout the guide, you will find Freedom Writer Feedback, a collection of comments and reactions about the activities they experienced.

The next step in the development of this guide was to pilot our activities with a group of teachers, who became affectionately known as the "Freedom Writer Teachers." These dynamic individuals were among the first educators to go through the Freedom Writers Institute in Long Beach, California. They come from urban, rural, and suburban regions of the United States and Canada, and their classrooms reflect a range of socio-economic and academic levels. The Freedom Writer Teachers have a breadth of experience that includes working with at-risk students, honors students, English Language Learners, and incarcerated youth, ranging from middle school to high school. The Freedom Writer Teachers taught *The Freedom Writers Diary* in their classrooms and tested our activities with their own students. They have played an integral role in creating this guide, contributing ideas and suggestions, sharing their students' reactions to the activities, and passing along their own comments, which can be found in the "Teacher Talk" section of the *Teacher's Guide*.

*The Freedom Writers Diary Teacher's Guide* offers a standards-based curriculum that combines innovative teaching methods with an easy-to-use compilation of lesson plans that serve a variety of student needs and classroom settings. The activities collected here changed my students' attitudes toward learning and improved their academic achievement. Apathetic students developed into critical thinkers and socially aware citizens. Other benefits included significantly reduced truancy rates, fewer behavioral problems, improved reading retention, and higher test scores. I believe these outcomes are possible in any classroom.

This guide was written for dedicated teachers like you who wish to revitalize your classrooms using meaningful lessons infused with a real world context. Teaching *The Freedom Writers Diary* in conjunction with this guide will help you inspire your students to write about their own journeys, give them the confidence to reach their full academic potential, and encourage them to improve their community through the message of tolerance. My hope is that all students can learn from our unique story and pick up a pen and write what needs to be written.

May you teach one to teach another . . .

—Erin Gruwell (aka Ms. G)

# MS. G'S SECRET SAUCE

Over the years, I have been challenged more than once to "bottle my Secret Sauce." This *Teacher's Guide* attempts to do exactly that. There are several "chefs" who have helped me select the perfect ingredients, the most valuable being the Freedom Writers. After reflecting upon our work together in Room 203, the Freedom Writers and I came up with the perfect recipe. We tested it on a group of teachers (our wonderful "Freedom Writer Teachers") to see if our recipe could work in diverse classrooms across the country. It did! Student success with the Freedom Writers method surpassed our expectations. My mission is now to share my Secret Sauce with educators like you.

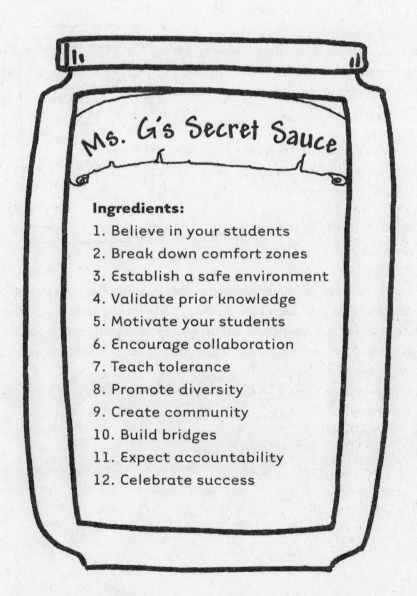

**Ms. G's Secret Sauce**

**Ingredients:**
1. Believe in your students
2. Break down comfort zones
3. Establish a safe environment
4. Validate prior knowledge
5. Motivate your students
6. Encourage collaboration
7. Teach tolerance
8. Promote diversity
9. Create community
10. Build bridges
11. Expect accountability
12. Celebrate success

Here are the ingredients of my Secret Sauce, along with a description of their importance in the recipe for success. Each ingredient is followed by my students' reactions, which were featured in *The Freedom Writers Diary*.

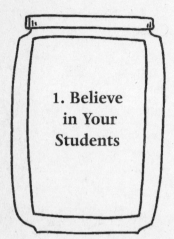

**1. Believe in Your Students**

I believed that all of my students were capable of learning. Although the Freedom Writers were deemed "unteachable" by many of the other teachers at Wilson High, I believed that every one of them could succeed, regardless of their socioeconomic status, race, ethnicity, academic record, or personal history. Because I believed in my students, they believed in themselves and success was inevitable.

*"[Ms. Gruwell] told me she believed in me. I have never heard those words from anyone . . . especially a teacher."*

—*Diary #23*

On the first day of school, my students sat in comfort zones based on race, gang affiliation, cliques, and familiar faces. The comfort zones were about self-segregation. I realized I needed to break down these barriers to create an environment that was more inclusive.

*"On the streets, you kick it in different 'hoods, depending on your race or where you are from. And at school, we separate ourselves from people who are different from us."*

—*Diary #3*

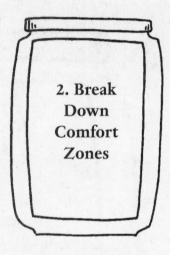

**2. Break Down Comfort Zones**

**3. Establish a Safe Environment**

I realized many of my students came from home environments that were extremely difficult, sometimes dangerous. Their home life had an adverse impact on their ability to learn. Once I realized that my students saw my classroom as a refuge, I tried to foster an environment where they felt comfortable expressing their opinions and beliefs.

*"I walk in the [class]room and I feel as though all the problems in my life are not important anymore. I am home."*

—*Diary #24*

What my students may have lacked in "book smarts," they made up for in "street smarts." It was important for me to treat the Freedom Writers as if they had a "Ph.D. of the Streets," because they were sophisticated in their own right. By making use of the knowledge they already possessed, I was able to make connections between their previous experiences and the new skills they were developing in the classroom.

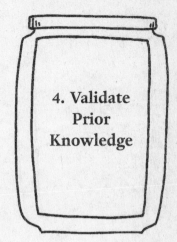

**4. Validate Prior Knowledge**

*"It's amazing how savvy they are. They're a walking encyclopedia when it comes to pop culture, quoting the lines from their favorite movies verbatim or reciting every lyric from the latest rap CD . . . I think the key is to build on what they already know."*

—Ms. Gruwell's Diary #2

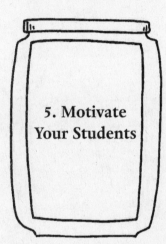

**5. Motivate Your Students**

When one of my students said, "Why do we have to read books by dead white guys in tights?" I knew that I needed to find material that would invest them in the outcome of their work. I introduced writers who pushed my students to take part in the world they were reading about.

*"This story ['The Last Spin'] is a trip. I've never read something in school that related to something that happened in my life."*

—Diary #14

I encouraged the Freedom Writers to work in collaborative groups so that they could learn to appreciate the different perspectives held by other students in the class. Collaborative groups also demonstrated to the Freedom Writers that teamwork can be more effective than working alone.

**6. Encourage Collaboration**

*"We learn together, we laugh together, we cry together, and we wouldn't have it any other way."*

—Diary #142

**7. Teach Tolerance**

Teaching tolerance and acceptance of one another was the key component of what made the Freedom Writers' experience so unique.

*"I believe that I will never again feel uncomfortable with a person of a different race."*
—Diary #116

As more of my students shared their life stories, the value inside each student became apparent to everyone in our classroom. My goal was to embrace every element of diversity, be it economic, ethnic, religious, or academic, and celebrate the richness of those differences.

*"The diversity of ideas, traditions and spirit is the true purpose of the Freedom Writers."*
—Diary #77

**8. Promote Diversity**

**9. Create Community**

The Freedom Writers treated one another as confidants and began to see themselves as a family. Instead of competing, they helped one another both inside and outside the classroom. Working as a community for a common goal made change possible.

*"Through their writing, they discovered they shared a common identity, which united them into a community that connected them, not separated them from the world."*
—Epilogue, p. 276

In order for my students to be lifelong learners, I needed to bring learning to life. They had to learn that their education was not confined to the classroom, textbooks, or even to a test. I made it my mission to bring parts of the world, to which they had never been exposed, into my classroom.

*"Ms. Gruwell can never do things the simple way. She always has some big teaching scheme even when we are nowhere near a classroom."*

—*Diary #116*

**10. Build Bridges**

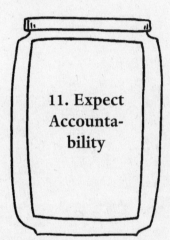

**11. Expect Accountability**

I have found that if you make students accountable and have high expectations, they will rise to meet them. My purpose-driven assignments were developed with input from the Freedom Writers, so that they had the opportunity to hold themselves and one another accountable. By including them in the teaching process, my students rose to the occasion. I expected them to succeed and they did.

*"[Ms. Gruwell] showed me that excuses will not bring about success and that adversity is not something you walk with but something you leap over."*

—*Diary #157*

Failure in my class was not an option. By developing a comprehensive curriculum that engaged, enlightened, and empowered my students, I was able to help them make valuable connections between the classroom and their lives. They became critical thinkers, which helped them succeed on standardized tests and aspire to higher education.

*"Historians say history repeats itself, but in my case I have managed to break the cycle because I am going to graduate from high school and go to college, an opportunity my parents never had."*

—*Diary #105*

**12. Celebrate Success**

# Introduction

The Freedom Writers Diary Teacher's Guide takes students through a three-stage process that will maximize their understanding of The Freedom Writers Diary while supporting the central message of tolerance. For best results, I suggest that you begin teaching the Engage Your Students activities first, following the order presented—which mirrors the timeline in The Freedom Writers Diary. The activities in Enlighten Your Students and Empower Your Students can then be taught according to what best suits your individual curricular needs and weekly schedules. There are no specific time allotments designated for the activities presented in this Teacher's Guide. Teachers can implement activities in one class period or over multiple days.

## THE ENGAGE, ENLIGHTEN, AND EMPOWER MODEL

**Engage Your Students:** This section includes lesson plans and activities for you to share with your students before they begin reading The Freedom Writers Diary. The goal is to establish a collaborative and supportive academic environment that will draw your students into the learning process, help them make connections between who they are as individuals and who they are as students, and encourage them to discover commonalities with their classmates.

**Enlighten Your Students:** This section offers lesson plans and activities that help students delve into literary themes, topics, and concepts while reading The Freedom Writers Diary, and concludes with a unit on the film, Freedom Writers (2007). Due to its range of contents, Enlighten Your Students covers various categories for ease of use: writing, vocabulary, grammar, oral communication, culminating activities, and Freedom Writers film activities. Students will practice different kinds of writing and public speaking, and become critical thinkers as they explore their own opinions, reasoning, and reactions within a "real world" context.

**Empower Your Students:** This section encourages students to achieve positive changes in themselves and in their communities by bringing the outside world into the classroom, and taking their classroom into the world. Nontraditional activities, such as inviting a guest speaker into class or taking a field trip, can expose students to new social and academic perspectives.

The *Teachers Guide* promotes a holistic approach to language arts: We integrate reading, writing, vocabulary, and grammar with a variety of learning modalities, all focused on a common theme. Each lesson plan for the Engage, Enlighten, and Empower sections of the book contains five important educational elements: implementing different learning modalities, the use of visual graphics, journal writing, adherence to academic standards, and authentic assessment. What follows are brief introductions to each of these elements.

## LEARNING MODALITIES

Many of the Freedom Writers struggled with learning disabilities (dyslexia) or behavioral challenges (Attention Deficit Disorder, Attention Deficit Hyperactivity Disorder). In addition, some were English Language Learners. As a new teacher, I desperately tried a variety of ways to engage my students and bring my activities to life.

Little did I know that my wacky idea of bringing in two sandwiches and some clumsy drawings of sandwich ingredients to teach about writing would prove successful. Later, I found out why this technique worked. Dr. Howard Gardner, a Harvard professor, advanced the theory of multiple intelligences to illustrate that all human beings have a repertoire of skills for solving different problems; within these repertoires, however, individuals have different learning modalities. By bringing in sandwiches, sketches, and other elements to teach the writing process, I managed to activate my students' linguistic, visual-spatial, bodily-kinesthetic, and interpersonal learning modalities.*

Following suit, your students will have opportunities to use different learning modalities as they move from activity to activity. Each lesson plan includes a list of materials that you will need, ranging from popular culture (music and movie clips), to food items (peanuts and Froot Loops), to art supplies (crayons and poster boards). Be sure to check ahead of time what you will need for each activity. We also suggest that you have a television and DVD player, a CD player, and a computer.

*Howard Gardner, *Frames of Mind: The Theory of Multiple Intelligence* (1983).

## VISUAL GRAPHICS

I found that traditional note taking was often a significant challenge for the Freedom Writers. Allowing my students to process information and demonstrate their comprehension through visual techniques greatly enhanced the learning process. I am not artistic by any means, but I found that admitting my lack of talent seemed to bolster my students' sense of artist confidence. Suddenly, my creative students were tempted to submit their own visual graphics.

We have included student-drawn visual graphics with each activity in this guide, as well as explanations for how to use them. Your students may think these visual graphics are corny, so play off their reaction and challenge them to do better! Your students can create their own visual graphics for an activity using a black marker and blank sheet of paper. Add their names along with a copyright symbol at the bottom of the original, photocopy, and distribute to the class. Have contributors come to class early and draw their images on the board so that you can use the new graphic while modeling the activity for the class.

## JOURNAL WRITING

To mirror the Freedom Writer experience, we recommend that you provide journals for your students prior to reading *The Freedom Writers Diary*. By keeping journals, students learn to value writing as a process. Journal writing is an avenue through which your students can respond to events in their personal lives and in their academic lives. Because all the students will keep journals at the same time, they bond as a community of writers, reflecting on their individual and shared experiences at school, at home, and in their neighborhoods.

The license to write freely, without fear of criticism or judgment, is central to the success of student journals. The Freedom Writers method allows students to voice their own truths, however painful or awkward, in honest, unvarnished prose. Too often, I believe, writing is rewarded merely on the basis of standard spelling, punctuation, and usage. Teachers should also value vivid, forceful student writing that actually says something. Encouraging students to use their own voices unleashes their potential for powerful self-expression and deeply effective storytelling.

The *Teacher's Guide* also includes activities that require students to use different writing styles in different contexts for different audiences. As students learn to edit their own and each other's prose for a specific purpose, they develop skills essential to success in the classroom and beyond. Since many educators have used *The Freedom Writers Diary* as a launching pad to discuss specific themes and inspired journal writing in their classrooms, we have provided writing prompts for every diary entry in Appendix B.

## ACADEMIC STANDARDS

*The Freedom Writers Diary* can easily be taught as literature on its own. However, using this *Teacher's Guide* will help you fulfill the requirements established by English Language Arts national standards. The current trend in education is for all curricula to be standards-based. As teachers, we must abide by the standards that our state and districts have adopted to ensure that our students are meeting their achievement goals in each academic area. We have aligned each activity in this guide with the Language Arts standards formulated by the National Council of Teachers of English (NCTE). Standards can be daunting, something imposed from the outside. However, the language of the NCTE standards does a good job of emphasizing the learner at the center of the academic process.

I understand that most states have their own specific standards, but there are also many commonalities that you will find reflected in the criteria listed in Appendix C. It is these common and interrelated themes that we address and that are specified in greater detail on the Web site for the National Council of Teachers of English: www.ncte.org.

## AUTHENTIC ASSESSMENT

Standardized tests are a reality of our educational system. Regardless of how teachers may personally feel about the effectiveness of such testing programs, there is no way around them. But it does not follow that teaching to the test is the best way to educate our students, or even to help them achieve top scores. I believe that the best teaching and the best learning happen when you teach to a student, not to a test.

This *Teachers Guide* does not include quizzes, multiple-choice tests, or standardized essays. Instead, every activity is organized around the idea of *authentic assessment*. In authentic assessment, students are asked to demonstrate their language arts skills through meaningful and relevant tasks; teachers, meanwhile, monitor the strengths and needs of their students as they progress from activity to activity.

The *Teacher's Guide* employs multiple forms of authentic assessment:

- Visual graphics: The graphics associated with each activity provide an immediate way of measuring the level of student engagement.
- Open-ended questions: Activities include open-ended language exercises that allow students to employ imagination, creativity, and critical thinking skills.
- Language arts assessment: A range of writing assignments, including interviews, letter writing, and a feature story, provide opportunities for evaluating student progress in reading and writing.
- Portfolios: We suggest that all assignments be collected in portfolios

as a way of tracking students' developmental progress and showcasing students' work at the end of the unit. Portfolios welcome multiple audiences, including the student, classmates, teachers, and even parents. (We recommend that students use a three-ring binder to organize their portfolio.)

- Self-evaluation: An integral component of authentic assessment is self-evaluation, giving students an opportunity to review their academic progress.

It is my firm belief that authentic assessment does not compete with, but rather enhances student performance on mandated tests. By honoring their reading, writing, and communication skills through meaningful activities in which they are fully engaged, students develop critical thinking skills that serve them in testing environments and in the world at large.

## NOW IT'S YOUR TURN

Within the engaging, enlightening, and empowering lesson plans in the *Teacher's Guide*, you will find the key ingredients for cooking up success in your own classroom. We want to emphasize that *The Freedom Writers Diary* and the accompanying *Teacher's Guide* are not intended to serve as a substitute for your mandated curriculum, but rather as a means of enhancing that curriculum and encouraging your students to perform at the highest level. There is no one perfect model for every classroom, so we look to you as independent educators to implement our lesson plans as you see fit.

As a teacher, I was inspired by my students' hearts, minds, and voices, which reverberate within the pages of *The Freedom Writers Diary*. In that spirit, I have tried to honor the hearts, minds, and voices of your students as they read *The Freedom Writers Diary* and engage in the activities contained in this *Teacher's Guide*.

## MANDATED REPORTING

You must make your students aware of the fact that teachers are "mandated reporters" and therefore obligated by law to report cases of child abuse or neglect when and if they become aware of such instances through their students' communications (oral or written). This does not mean students are prohibited from such communications, only that they must be made aware of possible repercussions.

# ENGAGE YOUR
# STUDENTS

The Engage Your Students lesson plans allow students to forge new friendships, create a community, and establish the foundation for a nurturing and collaborative learning environment before they begin reading *The Freedom Writers Diary*. Most students, especially those in their teens, tend to be reluctant to share their anxieties and vulnerabilities. These activities challenge students to get out of their comfort zones and utilize all of their learning modalities. In doing so, a wealth of information about your students is revealed. This information will enable you to tap into your students' experiences, sensibilities, and learning styles as a starting point for their explorations of literature and language. I highly recommend that you teach the lessons in the order presented: first you engage your students as individuals, then as partners with other students, next as collaborative groups, and finally as a cohesive community within the classroom.

**Visual Graphics:** Each activity has an original visual graphic designed to promote student participation while enhancing the particular theme of the lesson. For best results, have students clear everything off their desks except for the visual graphic and other materials integral to the activity. While students write or draw on their graphics, you will have an opportunity to walk around the room and assess their level of engagement and understanding.

**Vocabulary:** Each activity contains vocabulary words that were inspired by the specific activity. The words are brought together at the end of the section in a culminating activity called Freedom Writer Bingo. These words will familiarize your students with concepts and terms useful for reading *The Freedom Writers Diary*.

**Journal Writing:** After the inaugural *What Makes Me Unique* assignment, the journal writing prompts in this section are listed under the Assessments that conclude each activity. Journals serve as a way for students to reflect and expand upon their increasing awareness of themselves and their classmates. At the same time, teachers can use the journals to evaluate how much understanding and insight their students glean from each activity. Encourage your students to write in their journals every day about their experiences, thoughts, and feelings. This out-of-class "free writing" may yield some of your students' best stories, which they can then revise for the Class Book, the culminating project for the Enlighten Your Students section.

*Primetime Live* **DVD:** Although this activity is optional, I have learned that teachers who use this video with their students have found it to be an exceptional motivational tool. (To order this DVD, please visit www.freedomwritersfoundation.org or www.films.com.)

# LESSON PLAN FORMAT

The lesson plans for the Engage Your Students section of the *Teacher's Guide* are presented in a consistent format for ease of implementation. Each contains the following components:

- **Objective:** Describes the overall goal of the activity.
- **Backstory from Room 203:** Provides context, background, and pedagogical reasoning behind the activity derived from my classroom.
- **Ms. G's Tips:** Provides anecdotal advice from my personal experience.
- **What You'll Need:** List of required materials.
- **Process:** Step-by-step explanation of how to do each activity.
- **Visual Graphic Instructions:** Brief summary of how to use our student-generated visual graphics.
- **Vocabulary:** Lists of words that we suggest embedding into each lesson.
- **Assessment:** Journaling topics that assess student comprehension.
- **Taking It Further:** Explores ideas that go beyond the activity for further understanding.

Each lesson in the Engage Your Students section also has a sidebar that contains comments from *The Freedom Writers Diary*, the Freedom Writers themselves, and the Freedom Writer Teachers.

- **Freedom Writer Feedback:** Comments from the Freedom Writers recalling the impact these lessons had on them.
- ***Freedom Writers Diary* Quotations:** A passage from the book illustrating the Freedom Writers' experience.
- **Teacher Talk:** Comments from our Freedom Writer Teachers in the field who have implemented these lessons with their students.
- **National Council of Teachers of English (NCTE) Standards:** At the end of each lesson, you will find a list of the NCTE standards that are met by each activity.

# COAT OF ARMS

## OBJECTIVE

The Coat of Arms activity is a great way to get to know your class. Students will use arts-and-crafts supplies to decorate shields in ways that reflect different aspects of their lives. The shields are separated into four sections that express the students' goals, their favorite things, someone they admire, and something that makes them unique. Create your own Coat of Arms, so your students can get to know you as well. Use the completed shields to decorate and personalize your classroom. They will serve as a permanent reminder of what the students have in common with one another and with you, while inspiring their own sense of individual pride.

## BACKSTORY FROM ROOM 203

This activity invites students who may feel anxious or alienated at the start of the school year into a nonthreatening space of fun and creativity associated with a simpler time (a time that some students may have missed altogether). Have as many art supplies available as possible, as well as various magazines, newspapers, and other media for your students to make the Coat of Arms truly unique. To help your students grasp the concept of this project, have a couple of completed shields to show as examples. The activity is especially reassuring for English Language Learners who can use visual elements to express themselves. By fostering creativity and self-expression in the classroom, you lay the groundwork for your students' journey toward finding their voices through writing.

## MS. G'S TIPS

If possible, take pictures of your students before you introduce this activity. Have the photos ready for your students before you begin. One option is to use a Polaroid camera to take pictures of your students as they enter the classroom. Another option is to use a digital camera and print the pictures in your classroom as you take them. Remember to get the students involved by asking them to bring in pictures of their families, friends, pets, or favorite places.

## WHAT YOU'LL NEED

- Coat of Arms visual graphic (see page 25)
- Poster board (recommended) or white paper

- Scissors
- Glue or tape
- Markers
- Magazines
- Newspapers
- Miscellaneous art supplies
- Photographs

## PROCESS

**Step 1:** Introduce the activity by showing students your completed Coat of Arms or examples from previous classes. Pass out the accompanying Coat of Arms visual graphic. Distribute supplies, or create a supplies station where your students can easily access all the available materials.

**Step 2:** Using the Coat of Arms visual graphic as a guide, ask the students to draw a shield on a large piece of poster board or on a clean sheet of white paper. Alternatively, create a template out of cardboard for them to trace. (See Visual Graphic Instructions on page 22.)

**Step 3:** Ask your students to draw a picture or glue a photo of themselves to the center of the shield.

**Step 4:** Ask your students to fill in the shield using the following guidelines:

Box 1: Goals
This box represents the students' immediate and future goals. These could include personal, school, career, or family-related goals.

Box 2: Favorite Things
This is a place for students to show their favorite things, including sports, pets, entertainers, and hobbies.

Box 3: Someone You Admire
Have the students draw or paste in a picture of someone they admire. They can also use different cut-out words that describe why they admire that particular individual. Possible options: a family member, an activist, a sports hero, a religious leader, a celebrity.

Box 4: What Makes You Unique
Students can use words, pictures, or drawings to show the rest of the class what makes them unique. Be sure to tell them to describe their personalities, talents, or special characteristics, such as a "good cook," "good at basketball," or a "good dancer."

The Ribbon Across the Bottom of the Shield: Motto
Students will write their own personal motto across the bottom of the shield. This is a great time to ask them to define the word

"motto" and share examples of mottos that were used by historical figures, such as Gandhi's "Be the change you wish to see in the world" or Anne Frank's "In spite of everything, I still believe that people are truly good at heart." The Freedom Writer Teachers suggested, "What doesn't kill you, will make you stronger," or the Freedom Writers original "When diverse worlds come together, beauty is inevitable."

**Step 5:** When the students are done with their shields, ask for volunteers to stand up and share what their shields mean with the class.

**Step 6:** When the shields are complete, hang the projects around the classroom. This is a very quick and easy way to convert an ordinary classroom into a fun place to learn, full of life and color. Students will be proud of their creations and happy to see their work on the wall. Hanging the work on the wall allows each student to get a better idea of their classmates' (and their teacher's!) backgrounds and future goals.

## VISUAL GRAPHIC INSTRUCTIONS

Your students can use the Coat of Arms visual graphic to brainstorm their ideas before transferring them to a poster board. (If a poster board is not available, simply have your students use the graphic to illustrate their work.)

## VOCABULARY

Each of the following vocabulary words relates to the lesson plan and should be incorporated into your description of the activity and class discussion that follows:

- Aspiration
- Credo
- Motto
- Personify
- Symbolize

Sample sentence: For the motto inscribed on your Coat of Arms shield, choose a favorite saying that expresses a principle, goal, or idea.

## ASSESSMENT

As the students present their shields to the rest of the class, have them respond to some of the following questions:

- Was it hard to pick something to represent who you are?
- Did you learn anything about yourself while you created your shield?

• Have you learned anything surprising about one of the other students in the class?
• How is your shield different from the others?
• Do you have anything in common with anyone else in the class?

## TAKING IT FURTHER

Some of the Freedom Writer Teachers encourage their students to use art supplies to create a Coat of Arms on the front cover of their journals. If they wish, students can create their own categories for self-expression.

### Freedom Writer Feedback

"The Coat of Arms helped me share my personality with the whole class. The best part was hanging our shields in our classroom, which helped me see how much I had in common with everyone else, even Ms. G."

### *Freedom Writers Diary* Quotation

"*I can't believe that someone I don't even know . . . could have so much in common with me.*"
—*Diary #38*

### Teacher Talk

"The students began working on their Coat of Arms activity in class and I later assigned it as homework. They were given a 'no holding back' guideline, which meant that they could design, color, and create their Coat of Arms in any way. No grades, no judgments. This created a sense of ownership and pride over their work."

NCTE Standards: 4, 5, 6, 9, 10, 11, 12

## COAT OF ARMS (TEMPLATE)

**Box 1: Goals**
This box represents your immediate and future goals. These can include personal, school, career, or family-related goals.

**Box 2: Favorite Things**
This is a place for your favorite things such as sports, pets, hobbies, entertainers, etc.

**You:**
Draw a picture or glue a photo of yourself in this box.

**Box 3: Someone You Admire**
Draw or paste in a picture of someone you admire.

**Box 4: What Makes You Unique**
Use words, pictures, or drawings to show the rest of the class what makes you unique.

**Motto:** Write your own personal motto in this ribbon.

Name: _____ Class: _____

## COAT OF ARMS

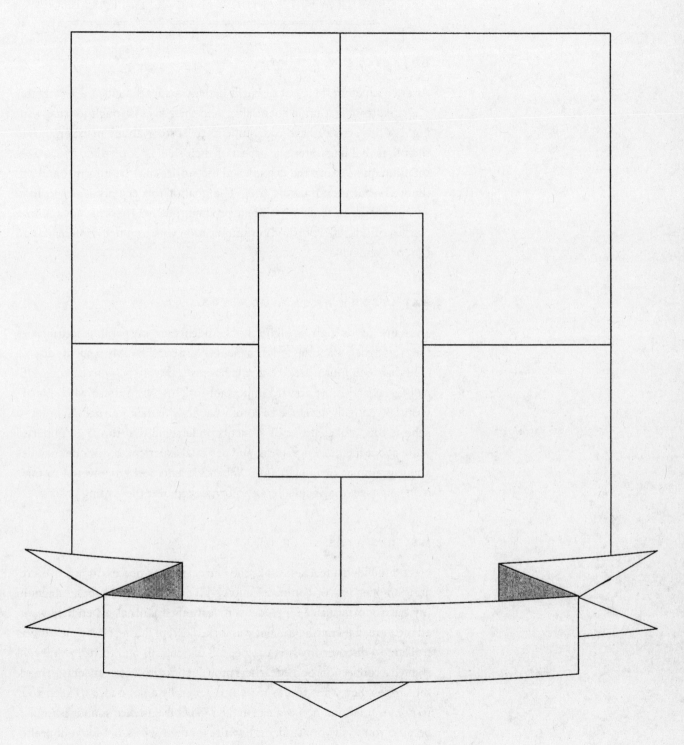

# JOURNAL WRITING KICKOFF:
# WHAT MAKES ME UNIQUE

## OBJECTIVE

After completing the Coat of Arms activity, your students are now better prepared to reflect upon themselves and their lives through journal writing. For this activity, have your students tell a story about an experience in their lives that illustrates one aspect of their shields: something that makes them unique. Assure the class that these stories may be informal and off-the-wall—but they must be true. The goal of this activity is *not* to have your students produce a polished product, but for them to engage in a process of self-reflection and communication with as much confidence and candor as possible.

## BACKSTORY FROM ROOM 203

So many junior high or high school students are on perilous journeys as they forge their identities amid challenges and conflicts. My students discovered that their journals became safe havens, a private place to explore difficult issues and move toward important insights. Even those who "hated" writing eventually developed a comfort zone with their journals. In order to achieve this, make sure your students understand that this is an outlet to write about their feelings, ideas, and personal experiences without anxieties about grammar or punctuation. When students feel empowered to their own language, they gain a sense of ownership over the writing process.

## MS. G'S TIPS

I recommend that teachers make the journal writing process interactive, creating an open line of communication with each student. I kept a cabinet in my classroom available for students to leave their journals when they wanted me to read them (the cabinet was locked except during class time). It was thrilling to discover my first cabinet-full of journals and to realize they all wanted a connection. Some teachers provide sticky notes for students to mark the entries they want you to read. It is generally a good idea to keep your responses brief and non-evaluative (i.e., "That experience sounds painful"), because you want your students to write for themselves, not for your praise. When appropriate, teachers may ask students to use certain journal entries as springboards into more formal assignments that are developed on separate pieces of paper and submitted for grades.

## WHAT YOU'LL NEED

- Journal
- Pen or pencil
- Journal visual graphic

## PROCESS

Discuss ground rules with your students about the importance of journaling. Journals will not be graded on spelling, grammar, or content, and will not be shared with classmates.

**Step 1:** Distribute the Journal visual graphic to your students and explain that they are going to write about something that makes them unique. As a strategy for loosening up your students and their creativity, try playing some music while the group tosses out ideas for things that make a person "unique." You might, for example, get students to think about characters from books they have read in class or popular movies: What made these characters unique? How was their uniqueness conveyed through certain events or details?

**Step 2:** Now have your students use their Journal visual graphics.

**Step 3:** Students write their "What Makes Me Unique" stories in their journals. This can be in-class or out-of-class writing.

## VISUAL GRAPHIC INSTRUCTIONS

On one blank page, they should write the phrase "What Makes Me Unique" and list possibilities. On the other blank page, students should brainstorm ideas for stories (anecdotes, events, and experiences) that convey what makes them unique.

## ASSESSMENT

When this activity (in class or at home) has been completed, go around the room and have students read aloud the part of their entry that will most surprise their classmates. This can be a terrific icebreaker as students inspire one another to share what they have written. Then engage your students in a discussion about their first experiences writing in the journals. What aspects of this activity did they enjoy? What did they find difficult? (I suggest that you keep a journal to write in along with your students and often share your own entries as an example.)

### Freedom Writer Feedback

"I think that journal writing can be a life-saving experience. Before Ms. G gave me a journal, I used to walk around with everything bottled up inside. I didn't even care about school because I was always worrying about something else. Journaling was the outlet I needed to express myself and unload, which gave me the opportunity to pay attention to other things, like school."

### Freedom Writers Diary Quotation

"[My diary] became a friend, the paper that it was made of was ready and willing to accept anything and everything I had to say; it could handle my fear, my questions, my sadness. I discovered the beauty of writing—when one can pour oneself onto a great white emptiness and fill it with emotions and thoughts and leave them there forever."
—(Zlata's Diary, foreword, p. xiv)

### Teacher Talk

"I always have students test me to see if I am true to my word about not penalizing them for using whatever language they want [in their journals]. So I sometimes get a lot of cursing. When these students realize they aren't going to end up at the principal's office, the cursing goes away and their writing opens up. Trust is crucial to this process."

NCTE Standards: 4, 5, 6, 11, 12

## TAKING IT FURTHER

Invite students to illustrate their entries and, if they have not already done so, decorate their journal covers. Provide markers, magazines, construction paper, glue for collages, and anything else you can think of. Then arrange all the journals on desks for a "gallery" walk. Students willing to share what's inside their journal—their entry and illustrations—can mark those pages with sticky notes.

JOURNAL

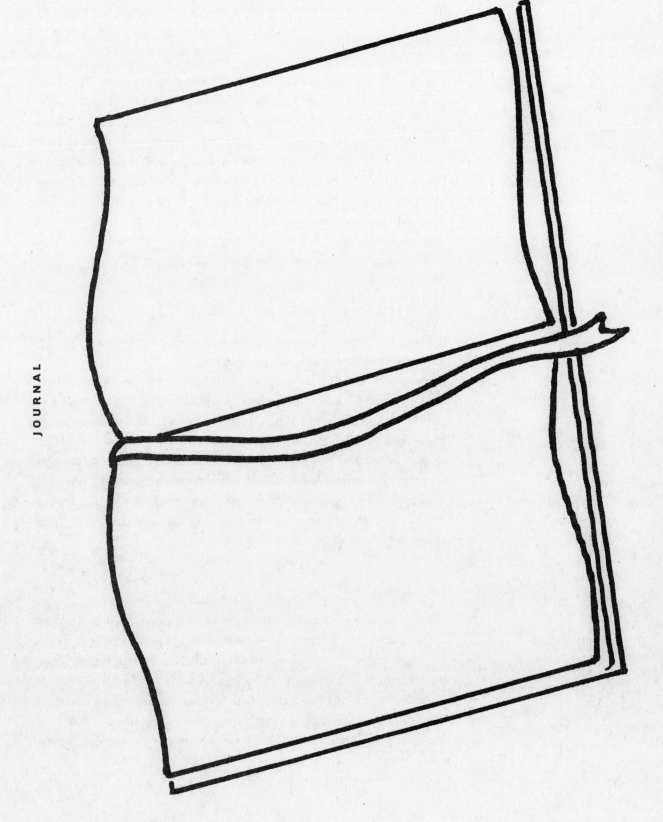

# GETTING TO KNOW YOU BINGO

### OBJECTIVE

Students tend to segregate themselves on the basis of superficial yet socially powerful factors, such as ethnicity. This exercise forces the students to step out of their comfort zones and see past their perceived differences. On the first day of the game, students identify one of their own unique qualities and write it down on a note card. The next day, students must match each classmate with one of the anonymous attributes typed onto a "bingo board" by the teacher (each square on the board is filled in with an attribute). Suddenly, the students in the room are looking at one another through new eyes. Instead of making judgments based on stereotypes, they are wondering, for example, who can speak four languages.

### BACKSTORY FROM ROOM 203

It is extremely challenging to get students who are convinced that they have zero in common with other students to interact with one another. No one wants to be the first to make an overture. By having students look into their own lives for something unique, you disrupt their habit of relying on cliques to express identity. When students rush around the classroom trying to figure out which statement corresponds to whom and having their squares initialed by that person, they cross invisible borders, at least temporarily. This activity provides a lively and entertaining way of preparing your students to grasp one of the most serious themes in *The Freedom Writers Diary*, the importance of looking beneath the surface to see other people for who they truly are.

### MS. G'S TIPS

I like to make things a little more fun by playing music in the background as the students match statements to classmates, and I occasionally announce that there are only "a couple of minutes" left. The sense of urgency spurs the students to talk to as many people as possible, as quickly as possible. Consider introducing this activity with a video clip that relates to cliques. You can find such scenes in a myriad of films, such as *The Breakfast Club*, *Clueless*, *Mean Girls*, or *The Outsiders*. Be sure to have the clip cued up and ready to go.

## WHAT YOU'LL NEED

*Day 1*
- 5" × 7" index cards

*Day 2*
- Bingo board visual graphic
- Music (optional)
- Portable stereo (optional)
- Video clip (optional)
- VCR or DVD player (optional)
- Prizes (optional)

## PROCESS

*Day 1*

**Step 1:** Distribute one index card to each student.

**Step 2:** Ask your students to write down one unique trait about themselves on the index card. Be sure to explain that the statements need to be *personal*, so simply stating that their "favorite food is pizza," will not be enough. The statements must be brief and unique, such as "Speaks four languages" or "Was born in Costa Rica."

**Step 3:** Type or write the students' statements onto the bingo board. Make sure that each student has a corresponding statement. If there are extra spaces, include a couple of interesting things about yourself or create a "free space."

*Day 2*

**Step 4:** After the students move all desks and chairs to the side of the room, they should walk around and try to match statements to classmates. When they guess correctly, that person should initial their corresponding box. Whoever gets all their boxes initialed first wins!

**Step 5:** You can offer a prize to the "winner," if you'd like. After the game is finished, read the boxes to the class and have each student stand when you read their statement out loud. Allow them to elaborate, if they wish.

## VISUAL GRAPHIC INSTRUCTIONS

Using the Getting to Know You Bingo visual graphic, fill in the unique information that your students provided. Once it is filled in, photocopy a class set of the graphic and use it for the interactive bingo activity.

### Freedom Writer Feedback

"Getting to Know You Bingo was really fun because it gave us a chance to introduce ourselves. The game allowed us to do this as a whole class, which is always better than having to do it individually in front of everyone. Plus, doing this activity with the intention of winning made it really exciting."

### Freedom Writers Diary Quotation

"We spend so much time trying to figure out what race a person is when you could just get to know them as individuals." —Diary #47

### Teacher Talk

"How wonderful it was to find out more about my kids. I have a bungee jumper . . . what a risk taker! My students love learning these cool facts about each other. An immediate camaraderie surfaces. To see their excitement interacting with each other, laughing and smiling, was the highlight of my day."

NCTE Standards: 4, 5, 11, 12

## VOCABULARY

Each of the following vocabulary words relates to the lesson plan and should be incorporated into your description of the activity and class discussion that follows:
- Affiliation
- Anonymous
- Association
- Distinct
- Inconspicuous

Sample sentence: Some students enjoy feeling anonymous when they enter a new classroom, but some want everyone to know who they are.

## ASSESSMENT

In their journals, have your students each make a quick list of the thoughts, emotions, and memories triggered by their bingo square, and then turn that list into a poem or reflective piece. Students should then copy their creative work and/or lists onto separate pieces of paper to be posted in rows on the wall as your class's bingo board.

## TAKING IT FURTHER

Have your students draw maps showing how their school lunch room or their own community is divided into certain groups and subcultures.

**GETTING TO KNOW YOU BINGO**

**Directions:** Circulate around the room and guess which classmate contributed each statement. Once a match has been made, that person should print his/her initials in the corresponding box. Keep moving around the room until every box is filled in.

Find a person who . . .

| | | | | |
|---|---|---|---|---|
| | | | | |
| | | | | |
| | | | | |
| | | | | |
| | | | | |

# LINE GAME

## OBJECTIVE

It can be difficult for students to open up in front of their peers and their teacher, but the Line Game gives students an opportunity to speak volumes without ever saying a word. As seen in the movie *Freedom Writers,* divide your class into two groups and have them form parallel lines facing one another. As you ask a series of questions, students who wish to respond, "Yes," should step forward to a center line (i.e., a long strip of tape). Easy questions about popular culture give way to tougher questions about everything from absent parents to learning disabilities to juvenile hall. Sharing information builds community within the classroom. Your students discover commonalities where they least expect them. At the same time, new knowledge about your students' lives will enable you to craft relevant lesson plans that effectively engage them in the learning process.

## BACKSTORY FROM ROOM 203

For me, the Line Game was a turning point, dispelling stereotypes and tearing down walls, as similarities were revealed among students who saw themselves as "enemies." Momentum and spontaneity are important to the success of this risk-taking activity. I have provided a sample list of questions and recommend that you memorize them or supply yourself with a "cheat sheet" in order to keep things flowing. As mandated reporters, teachers should exercise caution: the wording "who knows someone who" protects students from disclosing direct information about sexual or physical abuse, drug use, or crimes. Because your students will have an opportunity to ask their own questions at the end of the activity, it is important to establish these ground rules early on.

## MS. G'S TIPS

To make this activity more fun and to throw the Freedom Writers off my trail, I would choose a few of our class clowns to start the Line Game off with a quirky rendition of the *Soul Train* line. As the students start to enjoy the music and humor, they also begin to relax and cohere as a group. By the end of the class, the atmosphere will probably be very emotional, because the students will realize they have opened up to one another. Don't make the mistake of packaging their experience by launching into a "here is what we did, here is why we did it" speech; instead you may want to leave time for a class discussion after the activity. Keep the atmosphere light at first, but as the questions become more serious, instruct the class that there should be absolutely no laughing or joking.

## WHAT YOU'LL NEED

- An empty area large enough to accommodate the whole class
- Something to divide the area into two equal sides (i.e., bright-colored tape, such as painter's tape)
- Music and portable stereo (optional)
- Line Game visual graphic

## PROCESS

**Step 1:** Before you begin the game, establish ground rules so that students feel more secure about revealing their vulnerabilities. Students should not talk, high-five one another, or share details about their experiences between questions. Everyone must stand, everyone must participate, and everyone must walk to the line when it is relevant.

**Step 2:** Have your students move all the chairs or desks against the wall so they have a large enough space in which to move. If you perform this activity outside of the classroom, be sure to move far away from other classes, so that your students know that no outsiders are listening.

**Step 3:** Place the tape or ribbon down the center of the area, creating two equal sides. Use a random method to separate the class into two groups. For example, have everyone count off as "one" or "two," then separate the "ones" and "twos" into two parallel lines facing one another across the center line.

**Step 4:** Familiarize students with the exercise by asking questions that are simple, silly, and obviously pertain to the majority of them. Keep the game at a brisk pace, especially as the questions get tougher, because a sense of urgency energizes participation and allows more questions to be covered. (Before getting started, consult our sample statements on the next page.)

- If the answer to a question is "yes," the student should step forward to the line until you send everyone back.
- If the answer is "no," no movement is necessary.

**Step 5:** When you are finished with your questions, invite students to ask questions. Volunteers will most likely ask questions that pertain to them (an excellent way to learn something that you may have missed) and prompt additional questions from other students. Remind them to ask their questions by saying, "Do you know someone who . . ."

**Sample Statements for the Line Game:** These statements should be adapted to fit your group of students. The questions are organized into three stages that get progressively more challenging.

## SAMPLE STATEMENTS FOR THE LINE GAME

### Set 1: Day-to-Day Activities

These statements should be easy, generally pertaining to everyday activities or pop culture.

Step on the line if:

1. You ate breakfast this morning.
2. You pressed the snooze button on your alarm clock this morning. Twice? Three times or more?
3. You like rap music.
4. You have a pet.
5. You have a boyfriend or a girlfriend.
6. You like (a particular TV show).
7. You have seen (the latest movie).
8. You watched last night's (sporting event).
9. You own a computer.
10. You like (a local sports team).

### Set 2: School, Family, and Community

Gauge your students' comfort level as you move to more specific questions. Possible topics include:

Step on the line if:

1. You have at least one brother or sister.
2. You were born in another country.
3. You take a bus to school. Two buses? Three buses?
4. Your electricity, gas, or water has ever been turned off at your home.
5. You live with only your mom or only your dad.
6. You have an adult that you trust.
7. You have ever been judged because of your ethnicity or religion.
8. You feel safe in your neighborhood.
9. You have ever been suspended from school.
10. You will be the first in your family to graduate from high school or college.

### Set 3: Personal Experiences and Sensitive Subject Matter

When you feel that the students are participating fully and truly engaged, you may start to ask more personal questions. These questions, although sensitive in nature, may be the most enlightening for you and your students. To avoid precarious situations, begin this set of questions with "Do you know someone who . . ."

Stand on the line if:

1. You have ever done something you knew was wrong just to impress your friends.
2. You or someone you know has a learning disability.
3. You know where to get (not that you would) drugs.
4. You know someone who is, or has been, homeless.
5. You know someone who has been either emotionally, physically, or mentally abused.
6. You know someone who is in a gang.
7. You know someone who has ever gone to juvenile hall.
8. You know someone who has been (or is currently) in jail or prison.
9. You have ever heard gunshots in your neighborhood.
10. You have lost someone to gang violence. Two people? Three people? Four or more?

## VISUAL GRAPHIC INSTRUCTIONS

The Line Game graphic provides an opportunity for the students to express feelings elicited by the activity through writing or drawing. On the outside of the shoes, they should write or draw how they felt during the activity. On the inside of the shoes, they can write or draw what they perceive others were thinking or feeling.

## VOCABULARY

Each of the following vocabulary words relates to the lesson plan and should be incorporated into your description of the activity and class discussion that follows:

- Acceptance
- Bias
- Prejudiced
- Relevance
- Validate

Sample sentence: I used to be <u>prejudiced</u> against people from different races, but the Line Game showed me how much we all have in common.

## ASSESSMENT

Have students use their journals to write about their reactions to the Line Game. Ask them to respond to the following questions: How did you feel standing on the line? How did you feel when there were only a few people on the line? Were you ever the only person on the line? What did you learn about yourself from participating in this activity? What did you learn about others?

### Freedom Writer Feedback

"As a shy student, this game got me to open up and share my personal experiences with a room full of strangers in a way that didn't make me feel like I was being put on the spot. Each time that I stepped on the line, I looked around and realized that I was not alone."

### *Freedom Writers Diary* Quotation

"*I was able to express my own feelings in a place where people heard my voice, and my opinions were never judged.*" —Diary #10

### Teacher Talk

"My students love the Line Game, and once we play it, they beg to play it again. They are so relieved to find people that are like them, without having to really expose themselves. This game sneaks up on them, and my favorite part is the reaction writing after the game. They always think it starts out as another goofy day in English class playing some weird game, but they walk away with new knowledge about each other and themselves, and a connection to their classmates they never thought possible. I have also used the Line Game to safely "discuss" a situation or special event. The activity brings the class together on a deep level; one day you are a group of people, the next day you are a family."

NCTE Standards: 4, 5, 9, 11, 12

## TAKING IT FURTHER

Students can use their journals to pose a question they didn't have time (or were too shy) to ask during the game and then write a response. Many students discover during the Line Game that they want to be noticed; stepping forward means they feel less alone with certain experiences. Writing in journals continues the process of stepping forward.

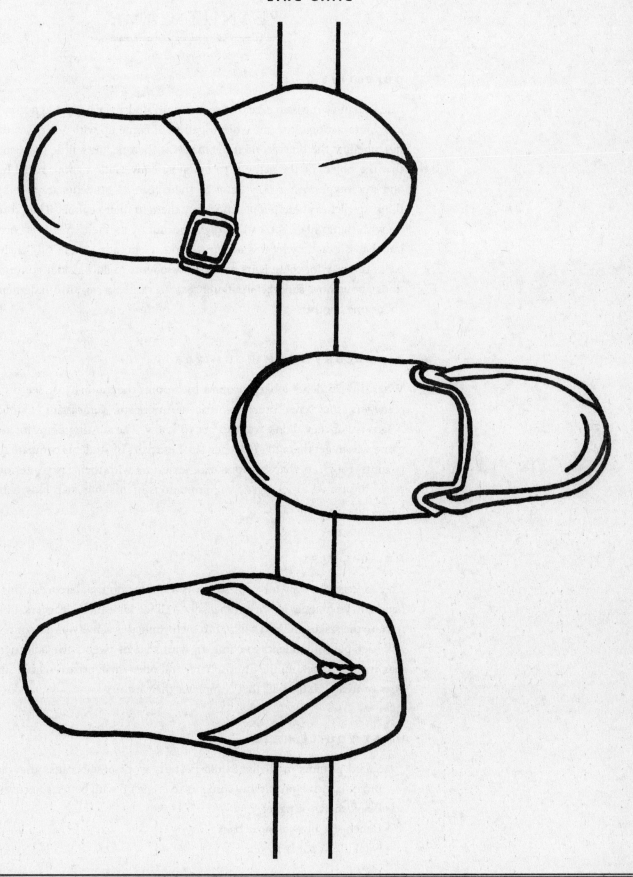

# PEANUT GAME

## OBJECTIVE

The Peanut Game is an excellent way to push students who would normally avoid interacting. Students work together to come up with adjectives that describe first the outside, then the inside of their peanuts, little suspecting that the object of the game is to initiate a conversation about racial bias and stereotypes. After they describe their peanuts, students are asked to think up clichés about people and apply them to their peanuts. They come up with things like "You can't judge a peanut by its shell." Yes, it is corny, but that is exactly why this activity works: Generating these silly clichés paves the way for these pairs of diverse students to have riskier conversations about how superficial differences can result in negative judgments about one another.

## BACKSTORY FROM ROOM 203

When my students looked around the room, they didn't just see other teenagers, they saw "others"—African Americans, Caucasians, Latinos, Asians—that they didn't want to get to know. The starting point for this game was to get them to go deeper. As these pairs of students compare the peanuts' rough, perhaps unappetizing exteriors with their tasty interiors, they are primed to recognize the limitations of making snap judgments based on appearances.

## MS. G'S TIPS

This exercise is a way for your students to learn about differences using a hands-on technique; it works especially well for kinesthetic learners. I like to raise the stakes and add a little fun by turning this activity into a contest. Ask each pair of students to come up with a list of twenty-five adjectives, play music to liven up the atmosphere, and offer small prizes (school supplies or treats) to the pair that completes their list first.

## WHAT YOU'LL NEED

- Salted peanuts in shells (Salted peanuts work best because they are more flavorful, prompting students to come up with better adjectives.)
- Blank sheets of paper
- Lunch-size brown paper bags
- Napkins or paper towels

- Peanut visual graphic
- Portable stereo (optional)
- Music (The music should add to the competitive feel, so consider using popular theme songs, or songs from game shows or movies. I used the theme music from *Mission Impossible.*)
- Many of the Freedom Writer Teachers have discovered that other food items can be used for this game. You can also use fortune cookies, edamame, M&Ms, etc. (optional)

## PROCESS

**Step 1:** This is a two-person activity, so organize the desks in groups of two before the students arrive for class. Assign each set of desks a number that corresponds to a particular pair of students. Choose partnerships based on opposites. I usually diversify based on race, gender, personality, and academic interests.

Optional: Have a student stand at the classroom door with a list of seat assignments. The anticipation will build as students are directed to their desks and discover with whom they've been partnered.

**Step 2:** Pass out the supplies. Each pair should have:
- Two pieces of blank paper
- Paper towel
- Brown paper bag
- A handful of salted peanuts
- Peanut visual graphic

**Step 3:** Ask each pair to choose one person to be the writer. Down the left side of the paper, the student should number 1 through 25.

**Step 4:** Have your students pick up a peanut and examine it closely. Ask them to think of twenty-five different adjectives to describe the outside of the peanut and write them down after you give them permission to begin. Just before you begin the activity, have the students shout out a couple of examples just to start things off. Remind them that they are not allowed to open or eat the peanuts. Reassure them that spelling will not count. The goal is for students to write down as many words as possible, as quickly as possible. To help add a sense of competition, play music that will create a sense of urgency.

**Step 5:** Ask the first pair that comes up with twenty-five adjectives to stand and read their words aloud to the class. For positive reinforcement, you can give them each a prize. This also acts as motivation for the rest of the class to work faster during the next phase of the activity. After the winners of the first round share the words from their lists, ask the other students in the class to share any additional words from their lists that have not yet been mentioned.

**Step 6:** For the second round, tell your students to switch writers. The partner who did not write in the first round should number 1 through 25 on the other sheet of paper.

**Step 7:** Have the students open the peanuts, smell them, and eat a few—tell them they are peanut connoisseurs. Next, ask them to come up with twenty-five words to describe the inside of the peanuts. Play the music again and offer a prize to the team that finishes first.
Note: For easy cleanup, have the students put their peanut shells in the brown paper bag provided.

**Step 8:** Hand out one copy of the visual graphic to each pair of students and ask them to come up with five clichés that describe how their peanuts are similar to people—for example, "Peanuts come in different shapes and sizes" or "The toughest peanuts to crack are the softest inside." Once students have come up with their five clichés, go around the room and have each pair share their favorite phrase.

## VISUAL GRAPHIC INSTRUCTIONS

Ask the students to use the area around the peanut to record their ideas for clichés. Once they have determined their favorite one, have them write it on the inside of the peanut.

## VOCABULARY WORDS

Each of the following vocabulary words relates to the lesson plan and should be incorporated into your description of the activity and class discussion that follows:

- Analogy
- Cliché
- Exterior
- Interior
- Synonymous

Sample sentence: The <u>cliché</u> "You can't judge a book by its cover" can be exchanged for "You can't judge a peanut by its shell."

## ASSESSMENT

Have each student take one of the clichés and write a journal entry about herself or himself. Ask them to try to name an external feature of theirs (a part of their own personal "peanut shell") that does *not* line up with something they feel to be true on the inside. (For example: "I may appear to be tough on the outside, but I'm actually soft on the inside.") Have them also write down if they learned anything about their partner that they were not aware of prior to the game.

## TAKING IT FURTHER

Now that you have the class thinking metaphorically, ask them what other objects they can think of that may seem uninviting on the outside but prove to be appealing on the inside (oysters with pearls, barnacle-covered seashells, old books, rocks with crystals inside, kiwis and pineapples, certain buildings, etc.). Write all their ideas down on the board. Then have your students write poems (individually or in pairs) addressed to one or more of these "misunderstood" objects.

### Freedom Writer Feedback

"The Peanut Game was one of the first activities we did with Ms. G. I didn't understand why she partnered us with people that we didn't like, and I didn't understand why we were playing with peanuts. . . . It seems silly now, but she made us realize that we didn't like each other for reasons that were beyond our control, like our ethnicity."

### Freedom Writers Diary Quotation

"My peanuts, before my very eyes, changed into human beings. Short, long, fat, thin, and otherwise odd, but nevertheless peanuts. Brown, black, white, yellow, and all in between, nevertheless human. So why is it we don't care about the contour of a peanut, but would kill over the color of a man?" —Diary #18

### Teacher Talk

"My students are taken by surprise with the Peanut Game: They come in the room, think snacking on peanuts and 'racing' to get the answers is all fun and games, and then all of a sudden they are talking about interpersonal relationships and it hits them hard. They leave my room a little bit more open-minded and thoughtful. They have done some beautiful reaction writing about the Peanut Game, and—little do they know—it is also a great introduction to discussing 'theme' and 'symbolism' in literature."

NCTE Standards: 4, 5, 6, 9, 11, 12

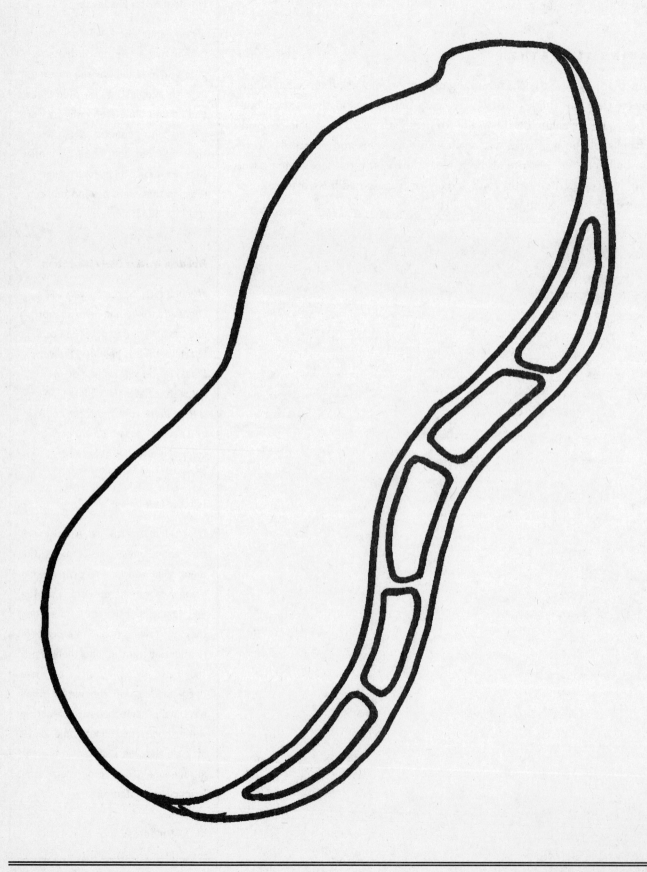

# CRAYON GAME

## OBJECTIVE

I used this activity to show the Freedom Writers the importance of working together. First, each student draws a picture (sun, clouds, grass, flowers, and house) using one crayon only; then, in groups of five, the students pool their crayons and redraw the picture using five different colors. Each group shares the same problem-solving process: Who will draw which element of the picture? Using which colors? The Crayon Game illustrates one of the Freedom Writers' core beliefs: "When diverse worlds come together, beauty is inevitable." While this activity is a great way to discover some of your students' different learning modalities, the most important objective is to have your students work together toward a common goal.

## BACKSTORY FROM ROOM 203

Often, students are annoyed by having to work with others. They feel they are perfectly capable of working by themselves. This activity creates a situation in which cooperative learning immediately improves the project. Not only are the colors multiplied, but each group is allowed to add anything they want to the picture, as long as it still contains the five original items. I have noticed that some of my best artists are either shy or English Language Learners. Showcasing their work with the class validates their individual learning modalities and allows them to take pride in their creativity. Finally, each group will share their completed drawings with the rest of the class and explain their process.

## MS. G'S TIPS

The Crayon Game is a way to take your students back to when coloring with crayons was fun and silly—and, most important, never judged as "correct" or "incorrect." All of the pictures will be unique, so make sure that each student and group is recognized for creating a work of art. By allowing the students to take artistic risks with their drawings, you will cultivate a safe space where they will feel comfortable sharing their ideas with the rest of the class. Also, the kids who like to do things differently may find kindred spirits in the room.

## WHAT YOU'LL NEED

- Crayons—each group of five should have these colors: orange, blue, brown, green, and red.

• Blank 8½" × 11" sheets of paper (one per student)
• Large pieces of butcher paper (one per group)
• Markers—each group of five should have these colors: orange, blue, brown, green, and red
• Box of crayons visual graphic

**PROCESS**

**Step 1:** Divide your students into groups of five. Make sure to diversify each group, taking into consideration gender, ethnicity, academic interests, and school affiliations, such as teams or clubs.

**Step 2:** Choose five volunteers to do the activity while standing in front of the class. Each will pass out supplies and then draw in front of the class. Each volunteer will have a different-color marker (orange, blue, brown, green, and red).

**Step 3:** Have your five volunteers give each student a blank sheet of paper and one crayon. (At this point in the game, it does not matter what color crayon the student has, as long as each group is using orange, blue, brown, green, and red crayons.)

**Step 4:** Ask students to draw the following items: a sun, clouds, grass, a house, and flowers. Have your volunteers do the same at the front of the room on the chalkboard, whiteboard, or a large piece of butcher paper. Go slowly, and have students draw each of the five items one by one while admiring one another's artwork.

**Step 5:** When your students finish, point out some of the unique elements of your five volunteers' drawings. Perhaps they put sunglasses on the sun, a chimney on the house, or shutters on the windows. Then go around the room and have other students share their drawings, showing that each is slightly different from the next.

**Step 6:** Ask your volunteers to pass out the five colored markers and one large sheet of butcher paper to each group. Next, ask each group to use all of their colors to draw the same five objects. Tell them to feel free to add anything they want, as long as their picture contains the same five objects. Generally, students will be creative and add new elements that are not part of the original picture, such as pets, people, or cars. Usually students will draw the item that corresponds with a specific color—for example, an orange sun or blue clouds—but be prepared to support the artists who have more idiosyncratic visions.

**Step 7:** Once they are done, ask each group to present their picture, making sure to mention who was in charge of drawing each element.

## VISUAL GRAPHIC INSTRUCTIONS

In the crayon box of the visual graphic, have your students write, "Our class is as colorful as a box of crayons," and then have them discuss how the metaphor pertains to their classroom. On the outside of the box, have them write, "Sometimes we need to think outside the box and color outside the lines." Discuss the meaning of these metaphors.

## VOCABULARY

Each of the following vocabulary words relates to the lesson plan and should be incorporated into your description of the activity and class discussion that follows:

- Collaborate
- Diversity
- Inclusive
- Subjective
- Tolerance

Sample sentence: The Crayon Game allowed us to <u>collaborate</u> with one another as we decided who would draw each image.

## ASSESSMENT

In their journals, have your students analyze the quote "When diverse worlds come together, beauty is inevitable." Ask them to explain what the quote means to them and how it relates to their own lives.

## TAKING IT FURTHER

Locate copies of famous artwork and ask students to respond to the following questions in their journals: Do you like the artwork? Does the piece prompt any thoughts or emotions? Why do you think the artist chose those colors? Then have students share their thoughts and reactions in their small collaborative groups. This activity demonstrates the value of multiple perspectives.

**Freedom Writer Feedback**

"When Ms. G first explained this activity, I couldn't believe that she was actually making us use crayons. Slowly, though, I let myself remember how much fun I used to have drawing with crayons as a kid. At first, this activity seemed totally simple, so it was definitely surprising to see where Ms. G was going with it—she always used the simplest things to teach us the biggest lessons."

***Freedom Writers Diary* Quotation**

"When I gave [my students] their creative license, they surpassed my expectations." —Erin Gruwell's Introduction

**Teacher Talk**

"There are so many positive outcomes of this game. My students have fun drawing with crayons and they learn that they can work together. It was useful to observe who resists using the 'wrong' color, who enjoys the spontaneity, and who emerges as a group leader. By hanging up their artwork, you have a constant reminder— a model—that when we pool talents and resources . . . and work together, amazing things can happen."

NCTE Standards: 3, 4, 5, 6, 9, 11, 12

# VOCABULARY REVIEW

The following twenty-five vocabulary words are embedded in five activities from the Engage Your Students section (Coat of Arms, Getting to Know You Bingo, the Line Game, the Peanut Game, and the Crayon Game.) We have included dictionary definitions of these words, and two activities for your students to reinforce their comprehension of these words.

| Word | Definition |
| --- | --- |
| Acceptance | favorable reception; approval |
| Affiliation | the act of becoming formally connected or joined |
| Analogy | a comparison between two similar things |
| Anonymous | having an unknown or unacknowledged name |
| Aspiration | a strong desire for high achievement |
| Bias | an unfair position or policy stemming from prejudice |
| Cliché | a trite or obvious remark |
| Collaborative | the act of working together, especially in an intellectual effort |
| Credo | a set of fundamental beliefs or a guiding principle |
| Distinct | readily distinguishable from all others |
| Diversity | variety in ethnicity, socioeconomic status, and gender in a group |
| Exterior | outer; external |
| Inclusive | including much or everything |
| Inconspicuous | not readily noticeable |
| Interior | located on the inside |
| Judgmental | inclined to make judgments, especially moral or personal ones |
| Motto | a saying that expresses a principle, goal, or ideal, often inscribed on an object |
| Personify | to think of an inanimate object as having qualities of a living thing |

| | |
|---|---|
| **Relevant** | having a connection with the matter at hand |
| **Subjective** | existing within an individual's mind rather than outside |
| **Symbolize** | to represent, express, or identify by a symbol |
| **Synonymous** | having the same or a similar meaning |
| **Tolerance** | the act of recognizing and respecting the beliefs, views, or practices of others |
| **Validate** | respectfully acknowledging a person's identity and opinions |
| **Witness** | one who can give a firsthand account of something seen, heard, or experienced |

**Directions**: Using the clues provided at the bottom of the page, complete the crossword. The word box contains all of the possible answers.

| Acceptance | Affiliation | Analogy | Anonymous | Aspiration |
| Bias | Cliché | Collaborative | Credo | Distinct |
| Diversity | Exterior | Inclusive | Inconspicuous | Interior |
| Judgmental | Motto | Personify | Relevant | Subjective |
| Symbolize | Synonymous | Tolerance | Validate | Witness |

## ACROSS

1. Inclined to make judgments, especially moral or personal ones
3. To represent, express, or identify by a symbol
9. A comparison between two similar things
14. A characteristic of reality as perceived rather than as independent of mind
16. The act of becoming formally connected or joined
18. A strong desire for high achievement
21. Variety in ethnicity, socioeconomic status, and gender in a group
22. The act of recognizing and respecting the beliefs, views, or practices of others
23. Including much or everything
24. A saying that expresses a principle, goal, or ideal, often inscribed on an object
25. One who can give a firsthand account of something seen, heard, or experienced

## DOWN

2. Having an unknown or unacknowledged name
4. Outer; external
5. To think of an inanimate object as having qualities of a living thing
6. To declare or make legally valid
7. The act of working together, especially in an intellectual effort
8. Having a connection with the matter at hand
10. Located on the inside
11. Favorable reception; approval
12. Readily distinguishable from all others
13. Not readily noticeable
15. Having the same or a similar meaning
17. An unfair position or policy stemming from prejudice
19. A trite or obvious remark
20. A set of fundamental beliefs or a guiding principle

## CROSSWORD PUZZLE KEY

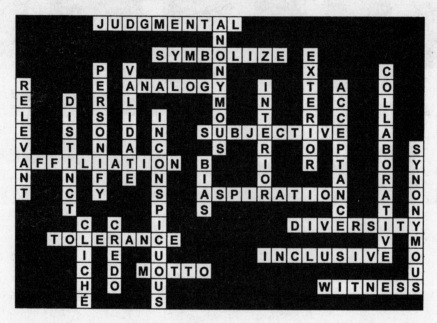

# FREEDOM WRITER BINGO

## OBJECTIVE

Freedom Writer Bingo is an opportunity for your class to review vocabulary in a fun and interactive way. For this particular activity, students will be incorporating the twenty-five words used in the Engage Your Students activities. First, students copy vocabulary words from the Engage Your Students section onto different squares on their bingo boards. Then, as you call out each word, they mark the squares with Froot Loops, hoping to be the first to get bingo. The most effective way to facilitate the bingo game is the following sequence: Start by defining the vocabulary words as you go; then use the words—or choose students to use the words—in sentences; finally, call out only the definitions, which the students will need to remember in order to mark their bingo squares. Because it incorporates different learning modalities (visual, auditory, kinesthetic), this technique tends to be much more successful than handing out lists of unfamiliar words for your students to memorize. Students will enjoy playing a game, while the repetition ensures that they have a thorough understanding of each vocabulary term.

## BACKSTORY FROM ROOM 203

Create a list of vocabulary words for your students. I usually worked with the same twenty-five words all week. The terms can be taken from the vocabulary in this guide, from SAT lists, or they can be adapted from any other texts that you are using with your class. The best thing is when you start seeing these words appear in your students' writing, and not in the awkward manner of words lifted from a thesaurus. After *The Freedom Writers Diary* was published, two of the Freedom Writers appeared with me on *The Oprah Winfrey Show*. When Oprah heard them using words like "metamorphosis" and "epiphany," she commented, "Wow, your vocabulary is amazing." Those words came directly from Freedom Writer Bingo.

## MS. G'S TIPS

I deliberately chose my toughest kids to be my Freedom Writer Bingo helpers. Before class, take some ribbon and Froot Loops and create necklaces, bracelets, and even headbands. The props add some fun to the activity, so wear them yourself and encourage your leaders to wear a Froot Loop–inspired design and the rest of the students will surely follow. I also encouraged my students to be competitive by offering them two, three, or even four bingo boards that they could play simultaneously. In their minds, the goal is to get more Froot Loops, but they are actually growing their vocabulary. If possible, offer small prizes, such as licorice, to the winners.

### WHAT YOU'LL NEED

- Freedom Writer Bingo visual graphic
- A list of vocabulary words
- Paper cupcake holders or small paper cups
- String or thin ribbon
- Prizes such as licorice or small school supplies (optional)

### PROCESS

**Step 1:** Have one of your students, preferably one of your artists, draw a large bingo board on the chalkboard for a visual reference for the class. As you play different variations of bingo (i.e., a traditional vertical or horizontal line, a diagonal line, or an X pattern), you can indicate what pattern to look for on the board. (See visual graphic.)

**Step 2:** Pick several volunteers to help you pass out supplies. Each student should receive a list of vocabulary words, a paper cupcake holder containing a handful of Froot Loops, a blank bingo board, and string or ribbon for making Froot Loop jewelry.

**Step 3:** Ask your students to use the list of vocabulary words to fill in their bingo boards. Remind them that the words should *not* be in order, or everyone will have the same bingo board.

**Step 4:** To make the game fun and a little more challenging for the students who choose to do more than one board at a time, change the way that a student can win.

Some options include a parallel pattern (two parallel lines), or an outline pattern (the four edges of the board.

**Step 5:** To start, use five minutes to call out only the words, without definitions. Then take another five minutes and move toward using the words in a sentence or asking one of your students to create a sentence. Eventually, use only the definitions so that your students can interchange the words and definitions easily. Spend a little more time using the definitions as clues, since this will help you evaluate if your students truly know the words.

### VISUAL GRAPHIC INSTRUCTIONS

Students will use the Freedom Writer Bingo board to write in their vocabulary words in the order of their choice. Once the grid is filled in with the twenty-five vocabulary words, it becomes the student's game board.

## ASSESSMENT

To test the students' mastery of their new vocabulary words, have them use each word in a sentence, or write a brief paragraph that uses at least five to ten of the words covered in the activity. Depending on what your words are, come up with an interesting topic for your students to write about.

## TAKING IT FURTHER

Pairs of students can create lists of twelve slang words or phrases and define each one. This is an opportunity for you to learn about your students' vernacular outside of the classroom. Turning the tables reinforces the point that all language has value but should be used appropriately for purpose, context, and audience.

### Freedom Writer Feedback

"Freedom Writer Bingo was my favorite activity in high school. I got lost in this game because I normally hated vocabulary word tests; because of my learning disability, I couldn't spell very well. This took off all the anxiety of learning vocabulary words because, visually, I was seeing it and learning it at the same time. So, when I was later tested on the words, I was able to visually remember how the word looked in order to spell it."

### *The Freedom Writers Diary* Quotation

"[Ms. Gruwell] plays reading and vocabulary games to help us learn, and listens to our questions. She actually cares. She talks to us on a level I can understand."
—Diary #58

### Teacher Talk

"A surefire edible technique for teaching vocabulary! It works every time. I can't think of the last time I was able to hold my students' attention while working with vocabulary for such an extended period of time. My students enjoy this activity because it helps them strengthen their vocabulary and they feel empowered learning new words and new ways to retain them."

NCTE Standards: 3, 4, 6, 12

## FREEDOM WRITER BINGO

**Directions:** Using the vocabulary below, randomly write each word in the box of your choice. The object of the game is to get a "bingo" going horizontally, vertically, or diagonally. Your instructor will call out each vocabulary word, one at a time, until someone wins.

| | | | | |
|---|---|---|---|---|
| Acceptance | Affiliation | Analogy | Anonymous | Aspiration |
| Bias | Cliché | Collaborative | Credo | Distinct |
| Diversity | Exterior | Inclusive | Inconspicuous | Interior |
| Judgmental | Motto | Personify | Relevant | Subjective |
| Symbolize | Synonymous | Tolerance | Validation | Witness |

| | | | | |
|---|---|---|---|---|
| | | | | |
| | | | | |
| | | | | |
| | | | | |
| | | | | |

# PRIMETIME LIVE

## OBJECTIVE

In the spring of 1998, ABC's *Primetime Live* aired a piece on the Freedom Writers. Since then, this clip has been used to inspire viewers across the country and provide insight into the Freedom Writers story. The video creates an emotional bridge between the Freedom Writers and the students who will soon be reading *The Freedom Writers Diary*, and can also be used as a springboard for other topics, such as gang life, making a change, the media, and achieving one's goals. Above all, this segment demonstrates the transformative power of reading and writing: students who never expected to graduate from high school make connections with literature and become inspired to tell their own stories. One such student, who experienced homelessness and lost two dozen friends to gang violence, shares his philosophy: "Just like Shakespeare said, 'To thine own self be true'— that's what I try to do."

## BACKSTORY FROM ROOM 203

When this news piece was filmed, my students learned a lot about cameras and the different ways in which stories are told. You can explain that *Primetime Live* tells the Freedom Writers' story primarily through Connie Chung's narration, and that the feature film, *Freedom Writers*, also tells a version of the story. Many teachers have told me that their students love "meeting" the students from Room 203 in the *Primetime Live* video and come away really excited about reading and discussing the book. They also get excited about telling their stories in their own journals. For students whose backgrounds differ quite a bit from those of the Freedom Writers, the video provides a context for the stories they are about to read in *The Freedom Writers Diary*.

## MS. G'S TIPS

This video has an emotional impact on its audience. I always set up the serious nature of the segment before I show it, and I put the emotional transformation the Freedom Writers go through into context to help prevent uncomfortable laughter when the students see several Freedom Writers crying. Whenever I show a video during class, I make sure to include an activity that elicits active viewing and critical thinking from the students. In this case, be sure to pass out the accompanying visual graphic as a reminder to your students that they need to pay close attention. The segment usually spurs a lively response, so allow enough time for discussion afterward. (The segment runs approximately twelve minutes.)

Explain that the students from Room 203 become intensely emotional as they will actually be graduating from high school, many of them the first in their families to do so! Occasionally students get uncomfortable when Darrius, a Freedom Writer, begins to cry. If any of your students laugh, to avoid getting emotional in front of their peers, use the laughter as a teachable moment during the class discussion.

## WHAT YOU'LL NEED

- ABC's *Primetime Live* video segment on the Freedom Writers (available for purchase at either www.freedomwritersfoundation.org or www. films.org )
- Media player (TV and VCR/DVD player)
- Filmstrip visual graphic
- Venn diagram visual graphic

## PROCESS

The *Primetime Live* segment contains emotional content. Before you begin this activity, set a serious tone during your introduction and ask your students to clear their desks of everything but the visual graphic and a pen or pencil.

Typically, students react well to the clip, but occasionally they can get uncomfortable and laugh at inappropriate times, such as when Darrius begins to cry.

Explain that the students are keenly emotional because it is hitting them that they really will be graduating from high school.

**Step 1:** Cue the video clip and set up the room so that every student gets a clear view of the television.

**Step 2:** Pass out the Filmstrip visual graphic. Explain to students that there are nine boxes (or "shots") for them to fill in with a detail from the story. Details might include information about the students, the class, the teacher, the field trips, etc.; students can also jot down questions about some aspect of the video for discussion afterward. As a way of allowing your students to explore their learning modalities, give them the option of either writing or drawing their responses to the clip.

**Step 3:** Play ABC's *Primetime Live* segment in its entirety. I recommend turning off the lights, because if students happen to cry, it will be less conspicuous to their peers.

**Step 4:** When the video is over, allow time for the students to fill in the boxes on their worksheets.

**Step 5:** Begin the discussion by asking for volunteers to share their completed Filmstrip with the rest of the class. You may discover you have some film buffs who are excited about working with visual images and the Filmstrip graphic.

## VISUAL GRAPHIC INSTRUCTIONS

The students will use the Filmstrip visual graphic to record details from the ABC *Primetime Live* video while they are watching the story. The Venn diagram visual graphic should be used by the students during the assessment component to compare and contrast themselves to the Freedom Writers featured in the segment.

## VOCABULARY WORDS

- Benefactor
- Circulated
- Confidant
- Eclectic
- Evolving
- Haphazard
- Inevitable
- Metamorphosis
- Ruthless
- Tribute

## ASSESSMENT

Have your students compare their similarities and their differences (and their classmates', if they wish) to the Freedom Writers from the *Primetime Live* video on the Venn diagram visual graphic. What are some things they have in common with the students in the video? What are some of the differences?

## TAKING IT FURTHER

Pose the following to your students: Imagine that you are a reporter working on the *Primetime Live* production and you just saw the video. Write a script for a series of questions that you would like to ask a Freedom Writer. What interesting issues or information would you like to follow up on? As a reporter, you may design questions that you would like to pose to a particular student or to the students as a group. You can also try to imagine some possible replies to your questions.

### Freedom Writer Feedback

"I remember crying the first time I saw the *Primetime Live* piece. I couldn't believe that our story had made it out of our little classroom. . . . I still find it hard to watch, but I know that every time we show it, people from all walks of life can relate to our story."

### Freedom Writers Diary Quotation

"It is ironic to see the same people in my neighborhood fight each other all the time. Yet in the classroom, we all get along. Due to our diversity, we were featured on Prime Time Live with Connie Chung." —Diary #136

### Teacher Talk

"I show the *Primetime Live* video at the beginning and end of teaching *The Freedom Writers Diary*. The students love it and it is a great introduction to the book. But the real impact comes after your kids have been reading the book, getting into the stories, and writing in their own journals. Then, when the kids see the video again, it is really amazing; they view it through a new lens because now they are part of the whole experience.

My students enjoy feeling like they have 'insider information' on the book they are about to read. One of my most challenging students told me that seeing the *Primetime Live* video gave her hope. She suddenly felt hope that she could do the same."

NCTE Standards: 1, 3, 4, 6, 9, 11, 12

Name:

Class:

**VENN DIAGRAM**

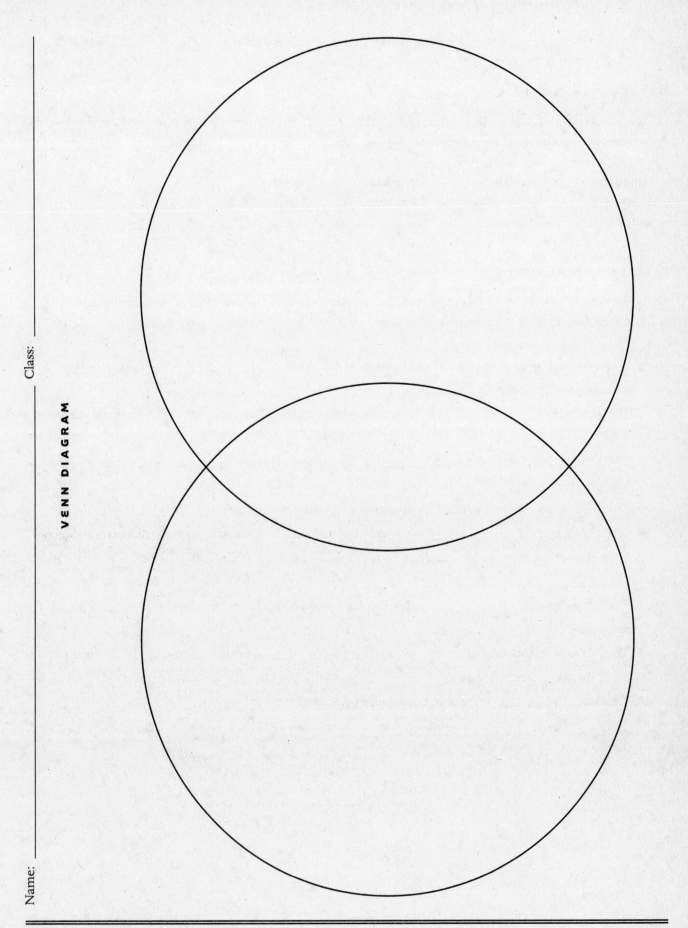

## PRIMETIME LIVE VOCABULARY

### DEFINE THE WORDS

On a separate piece of paper, use a dictionary to define each of the following words that come directly from the *Primetime Live* segment about the Freedom Writers.

| | | | |
|---|---|---|---|
| Benefactor | Circulated | Confidant | Eclectic |
| Evolving | Haphazard | Inevitable | Metamorphosis |
| Ruthless | Tribute | | |

### FILL IN THE BLANK

Using the same ten words listed above; please fill in each sentence with the word that comes directly from the *Primetime Live* segment. Since these sentences are written verbatim, be sure to listen carefully!

1. "He saw this preppy student teacher and everyday he used to do _____ things to get the class laughing, or just really to disrupt the class."

2. "It had actually _____ the room, this picture of this young man with really crude and exaggerated lips."

3. "We went to the museum as this _____, *(different word)* 4. _____ group, and when we left, we were a family."

5. "But behind this door in Room 203, anything but a typical class was _____."

6. "She even found a _____, a wealthy businessman, John Tu, who donated computers and money."

7. "The class raised money and flew Zlata from Europe to meet the students face to face. The next step was _____."

8. "For Zlata, her _____ was her diary. For some of you, your *(same word)* _____ is this computer."

9. Then on to New York City where they received a _____ they never dreamed of, the Spirit of Anne Frank Award.

10. "I had a _____ because I changed my whole way of thinking.

# TOAST FOR CHANGE

## OBJECTIVE

The Toast for Change was a pivotal moment in the Freedom Writers' journey. The goal of this activity is to acknowledge your students' past experiences, while offering them an opportunity to change the direction of their lives. Students often believe that past choices and their academic record will bias their teachers. The Toast for Change is a symbolic way of communicating to your students that what they may have done before stepping into your classroom does not matter. This activity should be considered a new start for your students, one that will help them build their road to success.

## BACKSTORY FROM ROOM 203

In the middle of the night I had this crazy idea of a ceremony that would represent a second chance for my students. The Toast for Change allowed my students to make a positive change in their lives, and each student earned the respect and support of his or her classmates. In addition to offering my students a new start, the Toast for Change provided a safe environment in which my students were able to share their emotions and form strong bonds with one another.

## MS. G'S TIPS

As your students' teacher, only you will know when the time is right to Toast for Change. For some students, the Toast is a great way to conclude the Engage activities and transition into reading *The Freedom Writers Diary* and seeing their own writing as a pathway to success. For other students, the Toast is most meaningful during the Empower activities, as a culminating activity. When you feel your students are ready, be sure to prepare everything before class so they enter a space that feels special. Be prepared for this activity to elicit intense emotional responses from your students.

## WHAT YOU'LL NEED

- Plastic champagne glasses
- Sparkling apple cider
- Paper towels
- Toast for Change visual graphic

## PROCESS

**Step 1:** Prepare one glass of sparkling cider for each student.

**Step 2:** Arrange the desks against the wall so that there is an area large enough for your students to stand in a circle.

**Step 3:** As your students arrive, ask them to leave their backpacks against the wall and form a circle in the center of the room.

**Step 4:** Ask a couple of volunteers to help you pass out the glasses. Tell your students to refrain from drinking until everyone has had a chance to share their toast.

**Step 5:** Introduce the Toast for Change. Explain to the students that the point of this activity is about making changes in their lives.

**Step 6:** Go around the circle and have each student tell the class one thing that they would like to change about their life. Share something that you, as their teacher, would like to change. Students will appreciate your willingness to be candid.

**Step 7:** Once everyone has shared their comments, have students raise their glasses and Toast for Change.

## VISUAL GRAPHIC INSTRUCTIONS

The Toast for Change visual graphic is for students to record their feelings and reactions to the Toast.

## VOCABULARY

- Epiphany

## ASSESSMENT

Discuss with your students what an "epiphany" is and have them describe how the Toast for Change could have been an epiphany for some students. After the discussion, have your students write down their epiphany and explain their Toasts for Change. (Suggestion: Meet with each student to help them create an action plan for how they intend to make their Toast for Change a reality.)

Discuss how toasts are a powerful ritual shared by many cultures and usually associated with honor, pledges, good health, good wishes, and celebration. As a way of warming up the group, your students might enjoy discussing their own cultural traditions or associations with toasts.

## TAKING IT FURTHER

Have your students create a Toast for Change for America and write about it in their journals. Another possibility is to ask the class as a whole to discuss and identify a problem in their community that they would like to change; this can become a Service Learning project for the class. Students should create an action plan to enact this change.

**Freedom Writer Feedback**

"The Toast for Change was a defining moment for me. Raising a plastic cup seems like a small step toward change, but it helped me define my goals and believe that I could reach them. The day we toasted was also the day we all started being real with each other—we shared something special, and we all bonded."

***Freedom Writers Diary* Quotation**

"*I got a second chance to change my life for the better. I thank God that he sent an angel [Ms. G] to give me that chance to change.*"
—Diary #31

**Teacher Talk**

"This is a great activity to use whenever you feel the time is right. I know it is hard to believe, but just watch as your students step up, speak out, and come away changed by the experience."

NCTE Standards: 2, 3, 4, 5, 6, 9, 10, 11, 12

# ENLIGHTEN YOUR STUDENTS

The activities in this section are designed to take your students from Engagement to Enlightenment, by reading and responding to *The Freedom Writers Diary*. To sustain a high level of interest, these activities build upon the diary entries written by the Freedom Writers in Room 203. Your students will gain confidence as writers, speakers, and critical thinkers as they complete these lessons. Enlighten Your Students is divided into five categories: Writing, Vocabulary and Grammar, Oral Communication, Culminating Activities, and the *Freedom Writers* Film Activities. Although the lesson plan format is very similar to the Engage Your Students activities, the Enlighten Your Students lesson plans do not have to be done sequentially. Some Freedom Writer Teachers report that they actually prefer to parachute into *The Freedom Writers Diary*, selecting stories and Enlighten activities that best suit their needs.

We have found that there are multiple ways to read *The Freedom Writers Diary*: Some teachers have their students read the book chronologically, while others prefer to assign specific diary entries. Some have their students read the book at home, while others designate class time. Some teachers prefer silent reading, while others prefer to read the book aloud. The approach you take may vary according to your students, classroom behaviors and challenges, and your curricular needs. Every effort was made to preserve the integrity of the stories written by the Freedom Writers. Due to the sensitive subject matter and occasional profanity, we suggest that your students have a permission slip signed by their parent or legal guardian before they begin reading.

## WRITING

*The Freedom Writers Diary*, with its diverse themes and writing styles, sets the tone for this section. Each activity shows how different writing strategies (narrative, expository, persuasive and descriptive) are needed to communicate effectively with different audiences. Students will write in their own journals as well as complete formal assignments. Writing prompts for each diary entry are listed in Appendix B and may be used to further your students' exploration of themes in *The Freedom Writers Diary*. Before beginning the writing process, we suggest that your students sign an Honor Code representing a commitment to themselves, to each other, and to the writing they do throughout this unit. The Honor Code encourages honesty, respect, and discretion, and resembles the one signed by Freedom Writers in Room 203.

## VOCABULARY AND GRAMMAR

We have included vocabulary lists and activities that are tied to each high school year represented in *The Freedom Writers Diary*. You will also find grammar assignments from freshman year through senior year that act as reviews of the text.

## ORAL COMMUNICATION

The activities in this section encourage your students to stand up and speak out about serious issues, ranging from "snitching," to murder, to book banning. Using topics that your students feel passionate about will ensure that each public speaking opportunity will be energetic and interesting to the rest of the students. Each activity is also tied with a journal writing assignment to help your students process the in-class discussions.

We have also interspersed poetry throughout the Enlighten Your Students section. Encourage your students to read the poems out loud in class. Poetry offers another way of thinking about how language and delivery affect communication. Students also have opportunities to write original poems based on the examples we've included from *The Freedom Writers Diary* and the *Freedom Writers* film.

## CULMINATING ACTIVITIES

The Culminating Activities draw on student learning and writing completed throughout the Enlighten Your Students section. We recommend that you conclude with the Magazine project and the Class Book project as a way of showcasing your students' growth in creativity, comprehension, critical thinking, and writing achievement.

## FREEDOM WRITERS FILM

An introduction to film in the classroom is followed by a series of activities that will guide you and your students through an in-depth analysis of *Freedom Writers* (2007), writer/director Richard LaGravenese's adaptation of the Freedom Writers' story. This section includes a list of film vocabulary that will strengthen students' visual literacy skills and film analysis activities that will deepen their understanding of self, culture, and community.

# LESSON PLAN FORMAT

The lesson plans for the Enlighten Your Students section of the *Teacher's Guide* are presented in a consistent format for ease of implementation. Each lesson plan contains the following components:

- **Objective:** Describes the overall goal of the activity.
- **Backstory from Room 203:** Provides context, background, and pedagogical reasoning behind the activity derived from my classroom.
- **Ms. G's Tips:** Provides anecdotal advice from my personal experience.
- **What You'll Need:** List of required materials.
- **Process:** Step-by-step explanation of how to do each activity.
- **Visual Graphics:** Brief summary of how to use our student-generated visual graphics.
- **Vocabulary:** Lists of words integral to each lesson.
- **Assessment:** Journaling topics that assess student comprehension.
- **Taking It Further:** Explores ideas that go beyond the activity for further understanding.

Each lesson in the Enlighten Your Students section also comes with a sidebar that contains comments from *The Freedom Writers Diary*, the Freedom Writers themselves, and the Freedom Writer Teachers.

- **Freedom Writer Feedback:** Comments from the Freedom Writers recalling the impact these lessons had on them.
- *The Freedom Writers Diary* **Quotation:** A passage from the book illustrating the Freedom Writers' experience.
- **Teacher Talk:** Comments from our Freedom Writer Teachers in the field who have implemented these lessons with their students.
- **National Council of Teachers of English (NCTE) Standards:** At the end of each lesson, you will find a list of the NCTE standards that each activity meets.

Note: The Film Activities were developed after the release of *Freedom Writers* in January 2007. Because this section reflects such recent work, the lesson plan format differs from the other Enlighten activities in the following ways:

- Vocabulary is listed first, separately from the individual activities.

- Substituting for "Backstory from Room 203" is a section called "Behind the Scenes."
- There is no sidebar featuring Freedom Writer Feedback, *The Freedom Writer Diary* Quotations, or Teacher Talk.

## THE FREEDOM WRITERS DIARY: PERMISSION SLIP

Dear Parent or Guardian,

On _____, your son/daughter's class will begin discussing the number-one ranked *New York Times* bestselling book *The Freedom Writers Diary: How a Teacher and 150 Teens Used Writing to Change Themselves and the World Around Them. The Freedom Writers Diary* tells the story of how 150 students from Long Beach, California, overcame the labels placed on them, such as "unteachable" and "below average," graduated from high school, and went on to college.

With heartfelt entries from the students' own diaries and a narrative text by their teacher, Erin Gruwell, *The Freedom Writers Diary* is an uplifting, unforgettable example of how hard work, courage, and the spirit of determination changed the lives of a teacher and her students. The book contains powerful, personal accounts of hope, tolerance, and second chances, presented within the context of the real issues the students faced on a daily basis, such as gang violence, peer pressure, drugs, body-image issues, suicide, and sexual abuse. Some diary entries contain profanity, which the Freedom Writers believe symbolizes the frustrations they experienced in their quest to remove the labels placed on them by others.

Due to the sensitive subject matter, which may be considered by some to be too mature for adolescents, students will not be able to participate in the activities and discussions associated with *The Freedom Writers Diary* unless a parent or legal guardian grants permission. Please respond by indicating your consent or non-consent below and return the form to _____ by _____. Students whose parents do not indicate permission and those students who do not return the parent permission form will participate in an alternate activity.

If you have any questions or would like to make an appointment to come to school and preview the book before it is used in the classroom, please call Mr. / Ms._____ at  (____) _____-_____.


Sincerely,




✂ - - - - - - - - - - - - - - - - - - - - - - - - - - - - - - - - - - - - - - - - - - - - - - - - - - - - - - - - - - - - - - - - - - - - - - - - -

Please check the appropriate box, tear off, and return.

_____ I give permission for my child, _____, to read and discuss *The Freedom Writers Diary.*


_____ I DO NOT give permission for my child, _____, to read and discuss *The Freedom Writers Diary.*


Parent / Legal Guardian Signature_____ Date_____

## FREEDOM WRITERS DIARY HONOR CODE

I, _____, agree to adhere to the following ethical code of conduct. I
          STUDENT'S NAME
understand that if I violate any of the provisions stipulated in this Honor Code, my participation in future activities
may be restricted.

1. I will be self-reliant.

2. I will always strive to be honest.

3. I will demonstrate integrity.

4. I will use words instead of weapons.

5. I will treat all members of the class with dignity and respect.

6. I will not judge based on race, ethnicity, culture, creed, sexual preference, or physical appearance.

7. I will not embellish or sensationalize my autobiographical experience.

8. Outside of the confines of this classroom, I will not discuss any other person's autobiographical history of
   which I become aware.

9. I will be a fair, conscientious, and respectful editor of other people's stories.

10. I will not stand idly by when I see or hear an injustice.

_____          _____
       STUDENT'S SIGNATURE                         TEACHER'S SIGNATURE

_____          _____
             PRINT                                     PRINT

_____          _____
             DATE                                      DATE

# MAKING A SANDWICH

**OBJECTIVE**

The goal of this activity is for reluctant writers to connect with something unfamiliar, the writing process, by comparing it with something very familiar, a sandwich. After observing how the addition of extra ingredients can have delicious results—in sandwiches and in stories—students will read Diary #22 from *The Freedom Writers Diary*. Through literary response and analysis, students will identify the key components of a successful story, including an introduction and conclusion, a theme, vivid details, and a crisp writing style.

**BACKSTORY FROM ROOM 203**

The more ingredients in a sandwich, the better it tastes; the more elements included in a piece of writing, the better it will be—provided, of course, that the ingredients or elements are thoughtfully selected! Make sure your students understand that the idea isn't to randomly pile on more: Combining, say, ham, peanut butter, and hot peppers isn't going to please many palates.

**MS. G'S TIPS**

Bring actual sandwiches into the classroom to ensure that students participate in an activity that is both sensory and kinesthetic. In order to make the contrast between two sandwiches more dramatic, conceal each one under a napkin until it is time to begin the "taste test."

**WHAT YOU'LL NEED**

- Sandwich #1 containing a minimum of: two slices of bread, meat, cheese, lettuce, tomato
- Sandwich #2 containing only: two slices of bread and meat, and absolutely no other ingredients
- Sandwich visual graphic
- *The Freedom Writers Diary* (Diary #22)
- Overhead transparency of sandwich visual graphic (optional)
- Additional materials that one would use at a picnic: plates, napkins, candles, tablecloth (optional)

**PROCESS**

**Step 1:** Choose two volunteers to come to your picnic and sample the sandwiches. The hammier the students (pun intended), the more entertaining this experiment will be; also, the more props you use, the better. Add candles (they don't need to be lit) and checkered napkins for ambience, and select students who enjoy role playing.

**Step 2:** Serve the first student Sandwich #1 and the second student Sandwich #2. (The "showier" the better.)

**Step 3:** Have each student take a bite of his or her sandwich and describe the contents to the class in vivid, sensory language (emphasizing sight, touch, taste, and smell). Then initiate a class discussion about which sandwich they think tastes better and why.

**Step 4:** Explain that each sandwich serves as an analogy for the contents of a student's written work. On the Sandwich visual graphic transparency, label each writing component: the bread represents the introduction and the conclusion; the meat is the body (characters and events); the cheese enriches the writing with a motif and/or theme; the tomatoes are the juicy details; and the lettuce represents a fresh, crisp writing style.

**Step 5:** Choose six students (one for each paragraph) to read Diary #22 aloud to the class.

**Step 6:** Put your students in groups of four and on their own Sandwich visual graphics, have students work together to identify the components of the story.

**Step 7:** After your students complete their visual graphics, fill in the transparency as a class:
- Bread: introduction and conclusion
- Meat: John Tu as a father figure
- Cheese: Cinderella motif
- Tomatoes: specific details, such as the fancy hotel bathroom
- Lettuce: fresh, crisp writing style

**VISUAL GRAPHIC INSTRUCTIONS**

Have students fill in their Sandwich graphics, identifying each ingredient (component) of Diary #22. (Refer to Step 7.)

**ASSESSMENT**

Repetition is a successful and often much-needed technique for struggling students and/or English Language Learners. Have students work in collaborative groups or as partners, and read a second diary entry and complete another Sandwich visual graphic. (A suggestion is the "Dear Zlata" letter on pages 78–79 of *The Freedom Writers Diary*.)

## TAKING IT FURTHER

Apply the Sandwich visual graphic to a piece of student writing or a literary work read for class. Have students identify the main ingredients. What makes these texts so good?

### Freedom Writer Feedback

"This activity was so much fun! I always felt that I was a really bad writer, but comparing the writing process to a sandwich showed me that the more 'ingredients' my story has, the more 'appetizing' it will be. There is a risk of overloading a sandwich with too many ingredients, which is also true of a story, but achieving that perfect story is easier if I imagine that it's a sandwich."

### *Freedom Writers Diary* Quotation

*"I didn't realize writing was so hard. It's very tedious and overwhelming, but satisfying at the same time. The writing assignments I do for Ms. G's class require draft after draft until everything is perfect." —Diary #108*

### Teacher Talk

"My students really responded to the concreteness of the sandwich/ writing comparison, so I had them come up with more analogies: creating an ice cream sundae? designing a house? Each group sketched their idea and presented it to the class, after which the class voted for the winning idea."

NCTE Standards: 1, 2, 3, 4, 5, 6, 7, 11, 12

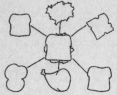

SANDWICH

# ONCE UPON A TIME: JOURNAL WRITING

### OBJECTIVE

In the preceding activity, students learned that a piece of writing benefits from a variety of carefully selected ingredients. By reading Diary #22 in *The Freedom Writers Diary*, the students also saw how a literary device—the fairy-tale motif—was used to express a writer's personal experience. This activity builds on those lessons. Students will select a significant moment (an event or experience) from their lives and write a story about it, using a fairy-tale motif to convey the significance of that moment. This writing activity combines literary analysis, personal narrative, editing, peer editing, and rewriting.

### BACKSTORY FROM ROOM 203

Most young people come to us with some prior knowledge of fairy tales, whether from books, television, or Disney movies. Fairy tales are powerful vehicles for exploring human journeys, such as the loss of a parent or fantasies of magical transformation (both themes appear in Diary #22). By using their journals to write about their own journeys, students gain insight and self-awareness, and improve the odds that their choices will be the right ones.

### MS. G'S TIPS

Explain to your students that they can use the fairy-tale elements however they wish. For example, a student may wish to use a fairy tale sarcastically: Beauty went to a prom with the Beast, but the Beast never transformed into a handsome prince.

### WHAT YOU'LL NEED

- Journal
- Pen or pencil
- Journal visual graphic
- Computers for revising stories (optional)
- Sample story for peer editing (optional)
- Art supplies for illustrations

### PROCESS

In Steps 1–3, students write stories in their journals and present what they did to the class. It is possible to end this activity here. For Steps 4–7, students copy their stories onto separate pieces of paper (using computers, if possible) and focus on editing and rewriting. Be sure to let your students know if this stage will conclude with finished work turned in for a grade.

**Step 1:** In the Journal visual graphic, students should write "Once upon a time" and briefly describe a significant moment (an event or experience) from their lives; on the outside of the journal, students should put the title of their fairy tale, and details from the story that are similar to their own story. Possible pairings include: losing or gaining a parent/guardian (Cinderella); taking risks (Jack and the Beanstalk); cleverly getting out of a tough spot (Hansel and Gretel); getting caught in a lie (The Emperor's New Clothes); or the triumph of brains over brawn (David and Goliath).

**Step 2:** Students write their stories in their journals. Remind the class that they should allow their creativity to flow, without worrying about spelling or grammar at this stage.

**Step 3:** Ask for volunteers to present what they wrote about to the class. Some may feel comfortable reading their pieces aloud. (Teachers: You can complete this activity here.)

**Step 4:** Students will now copy their stories onto separate paper (preferably typing them on computers) for peer editing and revising.

**Step 5:** Pair your students and have them give each other help and feedback on each other's stories: Does each story hook the reader's attention from the start? Are the characters and events vivid? Has the writer used specific details and sensory language? Is the fairy-tale motif clear? Does the story have a theme?

**Step 6:** Build in a rewrite session at this point or skip ahead to peer editing. Editors should eliminate irrelevant material, improve organization so that paragraphs flow logically, improve sentence style by removing extra words, and correct grammar and spelling. If possible, model this process with a sample story.

**Step 7:** After peer editing, have students write a final draft of their stories. (Suggestion: Students may wish to include their stories in the Class Book project at the end of the Enlighten Your Students section or the Magazine Project from the Empower Your Students section.)

### VISUAL GRAPHIC INSTRUCTIONS

In the Journal graphic, students should write "Once upon a time" and briefly describe a significant moment (event or experience) from their lives; on the outside of the journal, students should put the title of their fairy tale. (Refer to Step 1.)

## TERMINOLOGY FOR WRITING PROCESS

- Brainstorm
- Draft
- Edit
- Peer editing
- Revision

## ASSESSMENT

Students will turn their journal activity into a story using the steps of the writing process. (Refer to Steps 4–7.) After the final draft of the story is complete, students share their stories aloud to the class.

## TAKING IT FURTHER

This activity will equip your students with a solid foundation for writing in their journals. After they have written several entries, try the following experiment that a Freedom Writer Teacher does with his own students: After obtaining permission, type up several student entries and fit them inside a copy of *The Freedom Writers Diary*. Read these anonymous entries aloud, with passion, as if you were reading directly from the text. When you are done, explain that the entries you just read were from your class. Talk to them about how impressed you have been with the writing in the journals. Your students will be impressed that the author was not from Room 203, but is actually from their own classroom! Your students will be inspired, and this will show up in the quality of their writing.

### Freedom Writer Feedback

"Writing in my diary often times allowed me to imagine a new reality. When the pressures at home became too intense, journaling gave me a safe place in which to escape."

### *Freedom Writers Diary* Quotation

"*I did not find out how much other teenagers go through until we started writing and editing our stories. The more I read, the more I found out about my peers' personal problems. . . . I believe that the person behind our stories will speak as loud as the words in it.*"
—*Diary #79*

### Teacher Talk

"Part of what makes fairy tales fun are the illustrations. Have your class illustrate their stories. Provide them with plenty of art supplies. To reassure your less artistic students, point out that there are many possible styles they can opt for, from stick figures to comic-book style. You might also bring in magazines, scissors, and glue for those who would prefer to make collage illustrations."

NCTE Standards: 2, 3, 4, 5, 9, 10, 11, 12

# DEAR FREEDOM WRITER:
## ADVICE COLUMN

### OBJECTIVE

This activity asks students to get into the head of a Freedom Writer and analyze the problem he or she faces. Following the format of an advice column, students will select an entry from *The Freedom Writers Diary* and write two letters, the first seeking help for the problem described in the entry, the second offering advice about the problem. As students work together brainstorming possible solutions, they bond over their shared concern for another teenager's problems. This activity will broaden your students' humanistic and cultural perspective through literary response, while also forging a natural link between reading and writing.

### BACKSTORY FROM ROOM 203

Students respond well to models. Bring in examples of advice column letters for your students to evaluate from a newspaper (like "Dear Abby") or a magazine. Such letters tend to be written in a simple style, making them accessible models for teaching students how to write clearly and concisely. Refer back to the Sandwich lesson and point out that this genre does not allow for all the extra ingredients (juicy details) of a full journal story.

### MS. G'S TIPS

This activity works best if you begin by reading Diary #24 so that your students become emotionally invested. The entry has fourteen paragraphs: Have different students read each one aloud, or read the whole piece yourself. The letters your students write for this activity could make a great addition to the culminating Magazine project; the promise of publication always motivates better writing.

### WHAT YOU'LL NEED

- *The Freedom Writers Diary* (make sure everyone has their book)
- Examples of advice columns from magazines and/or newspapers
- Suitcase visual graphic
- Transparency of Suitcase visual graphic (optional)
- Overhead projector (optional)
- Pen or pencil
- Paper

• Butcher paper
• Markers

## PROCESS

**Step 1:** Show students several examples of advice columns. Read one or two and discuss the format, style, and content.

**Step 2:** Read Diary #24 aloud.

**Step 3:** Get the class brainstorming about the teenager's problems. Using the Suitcase graphic transparency, "pack up the troubles" of this Freedom Writer by listing them inside the Suitcase. Now ask the class to brainstorm possible solutions to those problems, writing the results around the outside of the Suitcase.

**Step 4:** Share with your class the sample letters we have supplied. Call attention to the details of the editing process: what stays, what goes, and why.

**Step 5:** Divide students into groups. Direct each group to read another diary entry and work collaboratively on this project.

**Step 6:** On their visual graphics, students should first "pack" the Suitcase with problems faced by the Freedom Writer, and then surround the Suitcase with possible solutions.

**Step 7:** Next, each group will use butcher paper to draft and edit a letter from the Freedom Writer asking for help, then draft and edit a response. Individual group members should copy the final versions of these letters onto separate pieces of paper to be turned in at the end of class.

**Step 8:** When the letter writing has been completed, go around the room and have each group present their letters to the rest of the class.

## VISUAL GRAPHIC INSTRUCTIONS

Students will use the empty space inside the Suitcase to "pack up the troubles" facing the Freedom Writer. Then they will brainstorm possible solutions to those problems and write them outside of the Suitcase.

## ASSESSMENT

Teachers can move among the groups as the students are working and see how each student is doing; group work can be assessed when you collect their letters at the end of class. To see how well individual students have absorbed this lesson, assign them independent work on another entry of their choice from *The Freedom Writers Diary*. Provide each student with a clean copy of the visual graphic for the "Taking it Further" assignment listed below.

## TAKING IT FURTHER

Have your students write anonymous letters asking for help with problems. Ideally, they or you should type these short letters. Students will then work in pairs to write responses to the letters. After sharing these letters and responses with the class, ask which responses they found most helpful and why.

© *The Freedom Writers Diary Teacher's Guide, 2007.*

---

**Freedom Writer Feedback**

"Writing an advice column gave us the opportunity to give helpful advice to our friends in an anonymous way."

**Freedom Writers Diary Quotation**

"Ms. Gruwell and the Freedom Writers want to help me get through my difficult time. . . . Now I need to make a choice to open up and not push people away."
— Diary #113

**Teacher Talk**

"For the 'Taking It Further' activity, one of my students wrote a great letter giving advice to another student struggling with a family dilemma. The 'advisor' also happened to be going through the same situation at home. Students learn so much when they are asked to help another person."

NCTE Standards: 1, 2, 3, 4, 5, 6, 7, 9, 11, 12

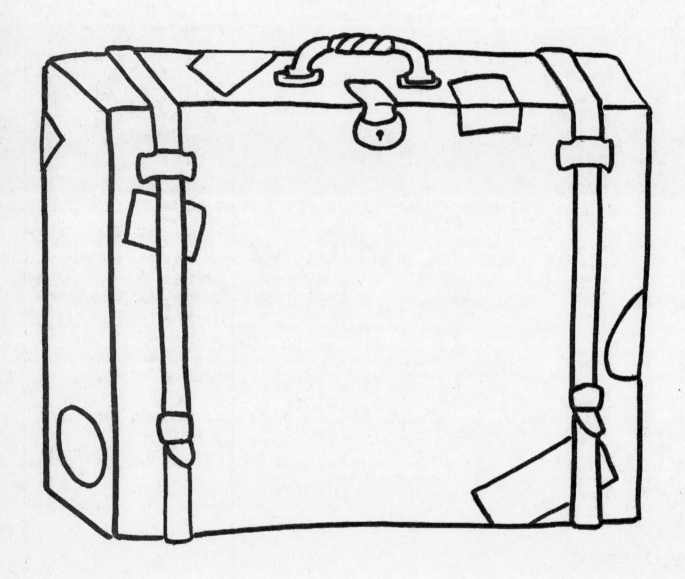

## DEAR FREEDOM WRITER: SAMPLE LETTERS

Dear Freedom Writer,

It is the night before the first day of school and I feel like throwing up. I should be laying out new clothes and filling a backpack with new school supplies. But I don't have any of that stuff. I don't even have a home. During the summer, my mom and I were evicted by a sheriff. My mom cried and pleaded for more time. She didn't know what to do. Now we are temporarily at a stranger's house. I know I will get laughed at the minute I step off the bus. Why even bother going to school? What if my friends find out I am homeless? I feel like it's hopeless to try to feel good and make good grades. What's the point? What should I do?

Sincerely,
Scared and Homeless

---

Dear Scared and Homeless,

I know this must be a very difficult time for you. You can't control what happens with your mom or your home, and that is scary. But you can control what happens at school. Try to do your best and that will make you feel stronger. Come to school early or stay late to do homework. Use Room 203 as your home away from home. What you need to remember is that you are not alone. Remember the friends you made last year in Ms. G's class? They are your second family, and they don't care about what you wear or where you live. I know it is hard, but try to hang on to hope. That will help you and your mom.

Sincerely,
A Freedom Writer

Name: _____    Class: _____

## AN INNOCENT FREEDOM WRITER

*A young black boy filled with innocence and care,*
*Looking for someone, but no one is there.*
*His first day of school, the father's not around,*
*To comfort his son when he's sad and down.*
*Looks up to his brother who knows money and power,*
*Watching his back at every single hour.*
*An innocent boy is now twelve years of age,*
*And finds himself locked up in a human-sized cage.*
*An innocent young man is now a criminal mind,*
*Having nightmares of murders every single time.*
*But this time you'll think this fool will see the light,*
*But he's jumped in a gang and they nickname him "Snipe."*
*Kicked out the house and left in the cold,*
*Have you ever been through this at eleven years old?*
*He says to himself, "no one cares for me,"*
*Then makes his bed in an old park tree.*
*The next time a park bench, how long can it last?*
*Will he forget this dreadful, dreadful past?*
*He goes to Wilson High with a messed up trail,*
*And meets a guardian angel named Erin Gruwell.*
*He learns about the Holocaust, Anne Frank and the Jews.*
*Now comes the time that he should choose.*
*He meets Anna, Terri, Tommy, and others.*
*These are the innocent boy's new sisters and brothers.*
*A 0.5 now a 2.8—*
*Change is good for those who wait.*
*He's back to innocence, but still has fear,*
*That death is upon him, drawing near.*

—Freedom Writer, Diary #78

The lines below are the shell of a poem waiting to be filled by your life and your expectations. The Freedom Writer of Diary #78 uses the poem *An Innocent Freedom Writer* to share the experience and emotions of life. Use this shell to share the experiences and emotions of your life. You are free to be as creative as possible. (Using a rhyme scheme is optional.)

*For Example:*

A young <u>soldier</u>,
Looking for <u>someone to see who I am</u>.
On my first day of school <u>I get the cold shoulder</u>.
To comfort me <u>a friend who does all he can</u>.

### AN INNOCENT

_____

A young _____.
Looking for _____.
On my first day of school _____.
To comfort me _____.

An innocent _____.
I find myself _____.
An innocent _____.
Will I forget _____?

I go to _____.
And meet _____.
I learn about _____.
Now comes the time _____.

**Extended Assignment:** Use your words and experiences to break out of the shell of this poem. Create your own poem using your own form to explain an issue or struggle in your life.

# INTERVIEW

## OBJECTIVE

Conducting and writing an interview provides an unusual way for your students to acquire new knowledge. Students will interview someone in their class from a different background to get an alternative perspective on anything from family roles and food to popular culture. Even if the classroom demographics are fairly homogeneous, challenge your students to ask probing questions to uncover interesting information. As students explore another person's story, they move from an autobiographical to a biographical focus.

## BACKSTORY FROM ROOM 203

Bring in sample magazines that have a traditional Q & A interviewing format, and assign pairs of students to read them aloud, playing interviewer and interviewee. As these samples should illustrate, successful interviewers come up with focused and thought-provoking questions in advance. At the same time, students should also be willing to branch off in a new direction if something intriguing emerges in the conversation.

## MS. G'S TIPS

Before you have your students begin, model the interview process by asking one of your students a sample question and have the rest of the class take notes on his or her responses. Ideally, get your student's permission to tape-record the question and answer. Play back the results and point out that when we answer questions orally, we use lots of extra words, slang or informal language, and we don't necessarily speak in full sentences. Explain to your students that when writing up their interviews they will need to edit away some of the extra words while still protecting the truth and integrity of their subject's responses.

## WHAT YOU'LL NEED

- Paper
- Pens or pencils
- Samples of interviews from magazines
- 5" × 7" index cards for interview questions
- Open Head visual graphic
- Butcher paper and colored markers

### Freedom Writer Feedback

"You think you've got somebody all figured out, but when they begin telling their story, you see things about them that weren't visible. The person I interviewed seemed like my exact opposite, but I was wrong. I wonder if Ms. G did that on purpose."

### *Freedom Writers Diary* Quotation

"Ms. G made us do an assignment dealing with other cultures where we had to interview fellow Freedom Writers about their family heritage."
—Diary #110

### Teacher Talk

"In my community, we have dozens of teenagers murdered each year but the media pays almost no attention to the situation. Many of my students have lost friends, so my students interview the parents and grandparents of murder victims to try and answer the question 'What is lost when a child is killed?' My aim is to sensitize my students to the true pain and cost of killing each other, in hopes of creating some peacemakers in our city."

NCTE Standards: 1, 2, 3, 4, 5, 6, 7, 8, 9, 10, 11, 12

• Tape recorder (optional)
• Journals

## PROCESS

**Step 1:** After you tell your students who their pre-assigned interview subjects are, give them time to write five to ten questions on a 5" × 7" index card. You might want to brainstorm possible topics (family roles, food, religion, clothing, health, holidays, popular culture, even pets). (As with the Peanut Game, it's a good idea to make an effort to arrange pairings of students who are likely to know the least about each other.)

**Step 2:** Have students conduct interviews with one another and take notes inside the Open Head graphic. The image represents a lack of knowledge at the start of the process, to be filled in through the conversation. (If possible, have your students turn their desks so that they are facing one another.)

**Step 3:** When they are done with their interviews, the students will design a magazine cover, using butcher paper and markers, that reflects something interesting or important about the information they generated.

**Step 4:** Each pair of students will present their magazine cover to the class as they tell the rest of the class about their interview subject.

## VISUAL GRAPHIC INSTRUCTIONS

Students take notes on their interview subjects inside the Open Head graphic. On the inside, they write about internal issues, like thoughts, feelings, likes, and dislikes. On the outside, they write about external issues like environment, family, etc.

## ASSESSMENT

Students will use the information they gleaned from their in-class interviews to write about one another in their journals. They can choose to write a summary of the interview, put their information into a Q & A format, or use the information to write a story.

## TAKING IT FURTHER

Have students choose an interview subject from their school, family, or community. If your students have access to tape recorders and get permission from their interview subjects, have them record the interview. They should then transcribe the most interesting parts of the conversation into a Q & A format, editing in a way that preserves the integrity of the interviewee.

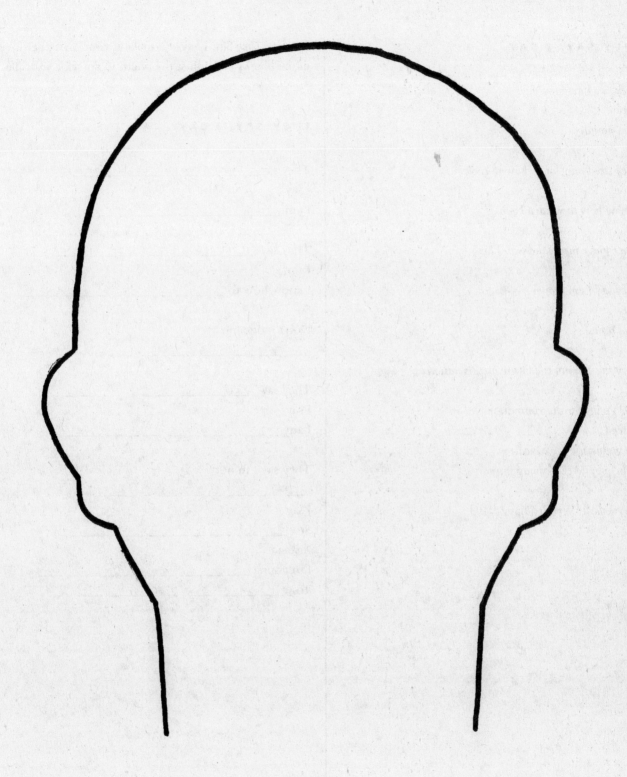

Name: _____ Class: _____

### THEY SAY, I SAY

*They say I am brown*
*I say*
*I am proud.*

*They say I only know how to cook*
*I say*
*I know how to write a book*
*So*
*Don't judge me by the way I look*

*They say I am brown*
*I say*
*I am proud.*

*They say I'm not the future of this nation*
*I say*
*Stop giving me discrimination*
*Instead*
*I'm gonna use my education*
*To help build the human nation.*

—Freedom Writer Diary #103

Rewrite *They Say, I Say* and make it your own poem. Fill in the blanks and adjust the poem to describe your life.

### THEY SAY, I SAY

They say _____

I say

I am _____

They say _____

I say

I know how to _____

So

Don't judge me by

_____

They say _____

I say

I am _____

They say I'm not

_____

I say

Stop _____

Instead

I'm gonna _____

To _____

# LETTER WRITING

## OBJECTIVE

When my students wrote letters to Miep Gies or Zlata Filipovic, they felt that their writing had a purpose. For this activity, your students will write a letter about a problem, injustice, or inequality they see in their school or community, and offer their ideas for change. Before they write their letters, students should decide the proper venue for their concerns and choose an appropriate recipient. This letter offers an opportunity to speak out while learning the genre of persuasive writing. By initiating a communication that can lead to positive change, students will gain a deeper knowledge of writing as empowering.

## BACKSTORY FROM ROOM 203

I found that when writing projects bridge the gap between the classroom and the real world, students recognize that "academic" things such as content, tone, word choice, and sentence style really do matter and will directly affect how their messages are read and responded to by the recipient. My students were amazed at the power of writing when Zlata actually responded to their heartfelt letters. Possible venues for these letters include the editor of a community newspaper, a City Council member, the mayor, or the C.E.O. of a business. Once the notion of audience is made concrete, students experience a new sense of accountability for their work.

## MS. G'S TIPS

Rather than writing a "boring book report" on Anne Frank's *The Diary of a Young Girl,* I had my students write letters to Miep Gies, the woman who hid her for two years. Their letters described the impact Anne's diary had on them. We sent the letters to Amsterdam, like a message in a bottle, and were amazed that Miep washed up on our shores to bring Anne's words to life.

## WHAT YOU'LL NEED

- Paper
- Pen or pencil
- Computer (optional)
- Envelopes
- Postage

• Lightbulb visual graphic
• Transparency of graphic and overhead projector (optional)
• Journals

## PROCESS

**Step 1:** Show examples of well-written letters to give students ideas for how to craft their own letters. Discuss how these letters illuminate an issue (how they turn on a light!). Demonstrate proper format for date, address, salutation, and closing. (Refer to the letters written by Miep in *The Freedom Writers Diary* on page 149 or the letter written to Zlata by a student on page 78.)

**Step 2:** Ask the class to brainstorm about the qualities of a well-written letter (concise, lucid, well-organized, persuasive use of examples and specific details, etc.). (Teachers can list ideas on a transparency or at the board.)

**Step 3:** Now invite students to brainstorm about problems, injustices, or inequalities they see in their school or community. Working independently, students should pick an idea and write it down inside the Lightbulb, along with their thoughts about the problem and ideas for change.

**Step 4:** Students draft their letters.

**Step 5:** When students finish their drafts, arrange them into partners (or small groups) to work on peer editing of each other's letters. Each partner should pretend to be the person who will receive the letter in the mail and then point out confusing or disorganized parts, as well as any basic errors they find.

**Step 6:** Since these letters will actually be mailed, they should be revised to reflect any editing changes and rewritten in the student's best handwriting or typed on a computer. Before mailing the letter, make a photocopy to include in each student's portfolio.

**Step 7:** Address, stamp, and mail letters.

## VISUAL GRAPHIC INSTRUCTIONS

Inside their Lightbulb, students write down the problem their letters will address, along with ideas for how to effect change. Outside the Lightbulb, students can brainstorm on what elements may stand in the way of their "good ideas" from effecting real change.

## TERMINOLOGY FOR LETTER WRITING

• Salutation
• Sincerely

- Recipient
- Correspondence
- Testimonial

## ASSESSMENT

In their journals, have students write another letter in order to make change happen. Whom would the letter be addressed to? What would it say?

## TAKING IT FURTHER

Link this letter-writing assignment to the Guest Speaker activity in the Empower Your Students section. You can also have your students set up correspondences with pen pals (using regular mail or e-mail).

**Freedom Writer Feedback**

"Writing letters to Zlata took writing to another level. I didn't just write an essay, or a personal entry in my journal—I poured my heart out in the hopes that a stranger on the other side of the world would be able to read my letter and understand how I felt."

**The Freedom Writers Diary Quotation**

"I can't believe that Zlata Filipovic is coming! Our letters actually paid off. . . . Not only did she personally write back to us, but she also mentioned that she would be more than happy to meet us." —Diary #44

**Teacher Talk**

"My students have been writing letters to students in classes taught by other Freedom Writer Teachers and they love it. Although the demographics and geography may be different, the students realize that they have a surprising amount in common."

NCTE Standards: 1, 2, 3, 4, 5, 6, 9, 11, 12

# SPEAKING OUT: FEATURE STORY

## OBJECTIVE

Although feature stories may be inspired by news headlines, they take a "human interest" approach to their subjects and seek to illuminate something about people's lives in contemporary society. For this writing assignment, your students will choose a topic based on their favorite entries from *The Freedom Writers Diary*. The students' feature stories can include quotations from the text, background research on their topics, and evidence from interviews with their classmates and peers. By drawing connections between *The Freedom Writers Diary* and their own concerns, students develop an appreciation for how reading can increase knowledge of themselves and the human experience.

## BACKSTORY FROM ROOM 203

I quickly learned from my students that in order to become motivated, they needed to know why reading and writing assignments mattered. As they work on their feature stories, students will think critically about issues they care about while practicing the basics of effective essay writing: an attention-grabbing introduction, a series of paragraphs that support and develop the main idea, and a conclusion.

## MS. G'S TIPS

These days, there are many opportunities for teens to publish their writing on the Internet, such as teenink.com. Print out some sample nonfiction articles from Teen Ink and get your students excited about submitting their own completed feature stories.

## WHAT YOU'LL NEED

- *The Freedom Writers Diary*
- Paper and pens
- Computers (if possible)
- Copy of Anna Quindlen's article, "Write for Your Life"
- Megaphone visual graphic
- Journals

## PROCESS

**Step 1:** Have students review their favorite entries from *The Freedom Writers Diary* and choose a topic for their feature stories. Possibilities include drugs, body-image issues, dysfunctional families, gangs, peer pressure, and discrimination.

**Step 2:** Students should carefully read and analyze the relevant diary entries, then consult other sources, including Internet and library research, as well as interviews with their classmates.

**Step 3:** Now it is time to outline the stories. Explain to the class that the megaphone represents speaking out and sharing ideas with lots of people. On the body of the Megaphone visual graphic: Students identify their topic and what they want to say about it. On the first line: Indicate Diary entry by number and include a sample quotation. On the remaining lines: List evidence and ideas.

**Step 4:** Have students exchange their Megaphone outlines in groups of two or three and give one another feedback. Is the writer making a forceful point about the topic? Does the evidence develop and support the writer's main point (thesis)?

**Step 5:** As an example of a feature story, distribute Anna Quindlen's article about *Freedom Writers*. Quindlen's topic: Writing is an invaluable way of making sense of our selves and our lives. She develops her ideas by interweaving evidence from the film, history, contemporary life, and literature.

**Step 6:** Ask students to write rough drafts, setting a page limit appropriate for your class. If possible, have your students type their drafts on the computer.

**Step 7:** When the rough drafts are completed, make several copies and distribute to the original small groups for peer editing. Ask writers/editors to make sure the feature story makes an interesting point, and that there is evidence to support and develop that point. Writers/editors should also eliminate material not relevant to the piece, improve organization so that each paragraph flows logically to the next, improve sentence style by eliminating extra words, and correct grammar and spelling.

**Step 8:** Students revise their feature stories and then submit final drafts.

## ASSESSMENT

Preserve a clean copy of each essay and return it to the writer for a self-critique and final revision. Explain that this is part of the writing process, a stepping-stone toward publication in a class magazine or an online teen journal. Have your students present their finished work to the rest of the class as if they were journalists or talk-show hosts.

## TAKING IT FURTHER

Invite a journalist or editor from your local newspaper to come to your class to discuss their industry. They may even be inspired to write a story about your students.

**Freedom Writer Feedback**

"Meeting a journalist like Nancy Wride, who wrote an article about us for the *Los Angeles Times*, made me realize how writing can come to life. After watching her scribble in her notebook for weeks, interviewing Freedom Writers, and sharing multiple drafts of her story, I realized that writing really is a process . . . not just a homework assignment."

**Freedom Writers Diary Quotation**

*"I have a friend who was . . . killed in cold blood. It's been a year since he died and like Miep not a day goes by that I don't think about him. I think to myself 'Was his death in vain?' No. I have to do something about it so others will know his death was not in vain!" —Diary #71*

**Teacher Talk**

"As a teacher, it was so exciting to have an article about writing that I am having my students prepare published on the front page of our local paper. My students were so thrilled. I read it out loud to my students. It was amazing for our students to be on the front page without it being about theft, gangs, fights, or drugs. Let this be the start of a new direction for us in the media!"

NCTE Standards: 1, 2, 3, 4, 5, 6, 7, 8, 9, 11, 12.

# Write for Your Life

PHOTOGRAPH BY CHARLES OMMANNEY FOR NEWSWEEK

THE NEW MOVIE "FREEDOM WRITERS" ISN'T entirely about the themes the trailers suggest. It isn't only about gang warfare and racial tensions and tolerance. It isn't only about the difference one good teacher can make in the life of one messed-up kid. "Freedom Writers" is about the power of writing in the lives of ordinary people. That's a lesson everyone needs. The movie, and the book from which it was taken, track the education of a young teacher named Erin Gruwell, who shows up shiny-new to face a class of what are called, in pedagogical jargon, "at risk" students. It's a mixed bag of Latino, Asian and black teenagers with one feckless white kid thrown in. They ignore, belittle and dismiss her as she proffers lesson plans and reading materials seriously out of step with the homelessness, drug use and violence that are the stuff of their precarious existences.

And then one day, she gives them all marbled composition books and the assignment to write their lives, ungraded, unjudged, and the world breaks open.

"My probation officer thinks he's slick; he swears he's an expert on gangs."

"Sorry, diary, I was going to try not to do it tonight, but the little baggy of white powder is calling my name."

"If you pull up my shirtsleeves and look at my arms, you will see black and blue marks."

"The words 'Eviction Notice' stopped me dead in my tracks."

"When I was younger, they would lock me up in the closet because they wanted to get high and beat up on each other."

Ms. G, as the kids called her, embraced a concept that has been lost in modern life: writing can make pain tolerable, confusion clearer and the self stronger.

How is it, at a time when clarity and strength go begging, that we have moved so far from everyday prose? Social critics might trace this back to the demise of letter writing. The details of housekeeping and child rearing, the rigors of war and work, advice to friends and family: none was slated for publication. They were communications that gave shape to life by describing it for others.

But as the letter fell out of favor and education became professionalized, with its goal less the expansion of the mind than the acquisition of a job, writing began to be seen largely as the purview of writers. Writing at work also became so stylistically removed from the story of our lives that the two seemed to have nothing in common. Corporate prose conformed to an equation: information x polysyllabic words + tortured syntax = aren't you impressed?

And in the age of the telephone most communication became evanescent, gone into thin air no matter how important

---

## Wouldn't all of us love to have a journal, a memoir, a letter, from those we have loved and lost? Shouldn't all of us leave a bit of that behind?

---

or heartfelt. Think of all those people inside the World Trade Center saying goodbye by phone. If only, in the blizzard of paper that followed the collapse of the buildings, a letter had fallen from the sky for every family member and friend, something to hold on to, something to read and reread. Something real. Words on paper confer a kind of immortality. Wouldn't all of us love to have a journal, a memoir, a letter, from those we have loved and lost? Shouldn't all of us leave a bit of that behind?

The age of technology has both revived the use of writing and provided ever more reasons for its spiritual solace. E-mails are letters, after all, more lasting than phone calls, even if many of them r 2 cursory 4 u. And the physical isolation they and other arms-length cyber-advances create makes talking to yourself more important than ever. That's also what writing is: not just a legacy, but therapy. As the novelist Don DeLillo once said, "Writing is a form of personal freedom. It frees us from the mass identity we see in the making all around us. In the end, writers will write not to be outlaw heroes of some underculture but mainly to save themselves, to survive as individuals."

That's exactly what Gruwell was after when she got the kids in her class writing, in a program that's since been duplicated at other schools. Salvation and survival for teenagers whose chances of either seemed negligible. "Growing up, I always assumed I would either drop out of school or get pregnant," one student wrote. "So when Ms. G started talking about college, it was like a foreign language to me." Maybe that's the moment when that Latina girl began to speak that foreign language, when she wrote those words down. Today she has a college degree.

One of the texts Erin Gruwell assigned was "The Diary of a Young Girl" by Anne Frank. A student who balked at reading a book about someone so different, so remote, went on to write: "At the end of the book, I was so mad that Anne died, because as she was dying, a part of me was dying with her." Of course Anne never dreamed her diary would be published, much less read by millions of people after her death at the hands of the Nazis. She wrote it for the same reason the kids who called themselves Freedom Writers wrote in those composition books: to make sense of themselves. That's not just for writers. That's for people.

---

MEGAPHONE

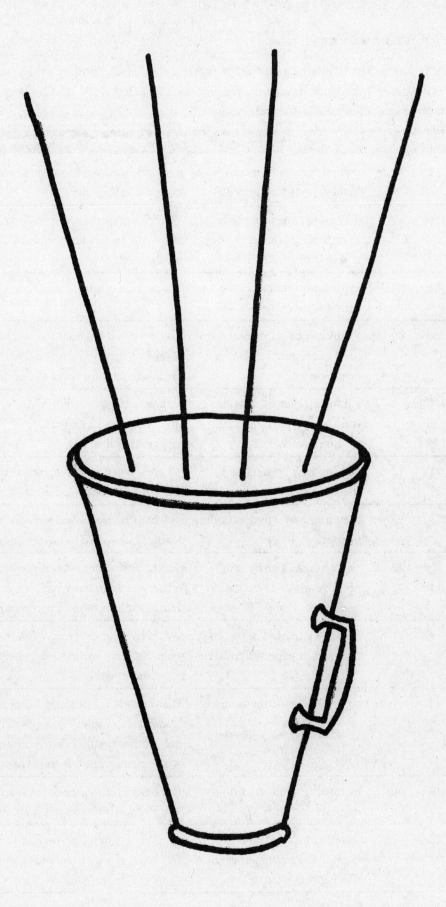

## FRESHMAN YEAR VOCABULARY

The following twenty-five vocabulary words from the freshman year section of *The Freedom Writers Diary* are embedded in activities from the Enlighten Your Students section. We have included dictionary definitions of these words and activities for your students to reinforce their comprehension.

| Word | Diary | Page | Definition | Sentence From The Freedom Writers Diary |
|---|---|---|---|---|
| **Absurdity** | 18 | 39 | something that is irrational, incongruous, or illogical | It sounds strange, somewhat on the line between irony and **absurdity**. . . . |
| **Accumulating** | 17 | 37 | gathering something together or collecting something over a period of time | The feeling of their spit striking me, running down my neck, and their germs **accumulating** on my face, felt disgusting. |
| **Alibis** | 22 | 44 | explanations offered to justify something | There were more courses than O.J. has **alibis**. |
| **Barrack** | 20 | 40 | a building or set of buildings used as lodging for soldiers or prisoners | Mas lived in a **barrack** that was close to the author of that book, Jeanne Wakatsuki Houston, so he was able to answer all our questions about it. |
| **Caricature** | Ms. G, #1 | 2 | a drawing that exaggerates somebody's physical features for humorous effect | A classmate got tired of Sharaud's antics and drew a racial **caricature** of him with huge, exaggerated lips. |
| **Confines** | Ms. G, #1 | 2 | the limits or borders of a space or area | There's every race, religion, and culture within the **confines** of the quad. |
| **Contour** | 18 | 38 | the outline of a figure, body, or mass | So why is it we don't care about the **contour** of a peanut, but would kill over the color of a man? |
| **Demographics** | Ms. G, #1 | 2 | characteristics of human populations and population segments | Due to busing and an outbreak in gang activity, Wilson's traditional white, upper-class **demographics** have changed radically. |
| **Dependable** | 9 | 21 | able to be trusted in the way required or expected; reliable | My teachers always said, "I'm here to help," but when the time came to start helping they were never **dependable**. |
| **Depiction** | Ms. G, #1 | 1 | a portrayal of something | Thanks to MTV dubbing Long Beach as the "gangsta-rap capital" with its **depiction** of guns and graffiti, my friends have a warped perception of the city, or LBC, as the rappers refer to it. |
| **Derogatory** | 19 | 40 | expressing a low opinion or negative criticism | The ticking often begins with a **derogatory** comment, which can spark an explosion. |
| **Expectation** | Ms. G, #1 | 4 | a confident belief or strong hope that a particular event will happen | After all, if a film does well, you make a sequel— if a class surpasses everyone's **expectations**, you . . . |

| Word | Diary | Page | Definition | Sentence From The Freedom Writers Diary |
|---|---|---|---|---|
| **Hypocrisy** | 20 | 40 | the false claim to or pretense of having admirable principles, beliefs, or feelings | The movie was about **hypocrisy** in our society and people's prejudice. |
| **Integral** | Ms. G, #1 | 6 | being an essential part of something or any of the parts that make up a whole | Each teenager played an **integral** role in developing the diary entries—reading, editing, and encouraging one another. |
| **Internment** | 20 | 40 | imprisonment; the confinement of somebody in a prison, concentration camp, or other place, especially during a war | His family came to America to follow the American Dream, but when the Japanese bombed Pearl Harbor, they were forced into **internment** camps. |
| **Intimidate** | 14 | 29 | to threaten, frighten, bully | I didn't talk to him much because he was a bully and he **intimidated** me. |
| **Irony** | 18 | 39 | form of speech in which the real meaning is concealed or contradicted by the words used | It sounds strange, somewhat on the line between **irony** and absurdity, to think that people would rather label and judge something as significant as each other but completely bypass a peanut. |
| **Meticulous(ly)** | Ms. G, #1 | 3 | extremely careful and precise | I immediately decided to throw out my **meticulously** planned lessons. |
| **Perish** | 6 | 16 | to die; to come to an end or cease to exist | A war has left family and friends crying for loved ones who have **perished**. |
| **Potential** | 23 | 46 | the capacity or ability for future development | So one day when Ms. Gruwell pointed out my 0.5 GPA, but said that I had **potential**, I felt guilty. |
| **Propaganda** | Ms. G, #1 | 2 | deceptive or distorted information that is systematically spread | When I got ahold of the picture, I went ballistic. "That is the type of **propaganda** that the Nazis used during the Holocaust," I yelled. |
| **Restitution** | 12 | 26 | compensation for a loss, damage, or injury | I also had to pay the **restitution** of $1,500 to the boy I had beaten up. |
| **Stereotype** | Ms. G, #2 | 30 | an oversimplified standardized image or idea held by one person or group of another; to categorize individuals | The system separates them and they're **stereotyped** as "basic," but in reality, they're anything but basic. |
| **Stigma** | Ms. G, #2 | 30 | the shame attached to something regarded as socially unacceptable | So to avoid the **stigma**, one kid even turns in his homework wadded in a ball because he'd get beat up for carrying a folder. |
| **Tradition** | 15 | 34 | a long-established custom or belief | All this rivalry is more of a **tradition**. |

Name: _____ Class: _____

## THE FREEDOM WRITERS DIARY: WORD SEARCH

**Directions:** The following vocabulary words have been taken from the freshman diary entries in *The Freedom Writers Diary*. The words can be hidden forward, backward, upward, downward, or diagonally. Circle each word as you find it.

```
A  W  E  R  H  A  B  S  U  R  D  I  L  T  G  B  D  P  D  I
H  D  E  P  E  N  T  U  O  N  O  C  K  W  E  G  O  E  T  N
K  I  Y  R  E  S  T  I  T  U  T  I  O  N  Y  T  P  U  A  T
O  O  P  L  K  J  T  Y  C  I  P  E  D  U  E  E  C  H  I  E
T  S  O  O  R  Y  P  E  R  I  S  H  K  U  N  P  Q  G  N  R
G  G  T  U  C  D  E  P  I  B  Y  T  E  D  I  X  I  F  O  N
H  H  M  I  Q  R  I  N  T  I  M  I  A  K  J  F  N  V  S  L
C  R  T  Y  G  B  I  N  M  K  I  B  T  C  O  N  T  O  U  R
T  A  G  D  D  M  D  S  G  T  L  J  G  A  O  S  E  D  T  P
I  V  R  R  L  O  A  T  Y  E  A  D  G  R  Y  T  G  E  T  I
N  B  T  I  P  O  T  E  N  T  I  A  L  R  P  E  R  P  U  T
T  H  F  O  C  D  E  P  E  N  F  T  R  A  R  R  A  I  Y  E
E  J  U  R  O  A  Y  T  I  D  R  U  S  B  A  E  L  S  A  N
R  U  I  D  E  Y  T  H  Y  P  E  V  G  J  H  O  A  U  L  T
N  O  P  Y  N  Z  X  U  I  N  T  P  K  U  J  T  E  O  I  Y
M  L  M  O  J  U  I  C  R  R  F  G  I  Z  U  Y  I  L  B  U
E  W  R  I  N  T  R  H  Y  E  J  K  L  C  A  P  C  U  I  A
N  I  A  C  C  U  M  U  L  A  T  I  N  G  T  E  T  C  S  D
T  P  R  O  P  I  G  B  T  Y  R  Y  B  I  R  E  P  I  J  N
R  E  X  P  E  C  T  A  T  I  O  N  S  G  I  O  L  T  N  A
F  T  R  A  D  I  T  I  O  N  S  T  I  G  M  H  J  E  M  G
H  J  U  I  D  E  P  I  C  C  O  N  F  I  N  E  S  M  A  A
D  E  M  O  G  R  A  P  H  I  C  S  U  T  I  T  S  E  R  P
I  H  F  R  D  E  R  O  G  A  T  O  R  Y  A  Z  X  C  G  O
Y  J  I  M  E  T  I  V  Y  T  R  E  F  G  H  N  Y  B  O  R
Y  W  K  L  T  G  G  I  N  T  I  M  I  D  A  T  E  D  J  P
```

| | | | | |
|---|---|---|---|---|
| Absurdity | Accumulating | Alibis | Barrack | Caricature |
| Confines | Contour | Demographics | Dependable | Depict |
| Derogatory | Expectations | Hypocrisy | Integral | Internment |
| Intimidated | Irony | Meticulous | Perish | Potential |
| Propaganda | Restitution | Stereotype | Stigma | Tradition |

# THE FREEDOM WRITERS DIARY: WORD SEARCH KEY

```
                                                                    D
H                                                                   E
   Y     R E S T I T U T I O N           P
      P                                        E
      S     O           P E R I S H           N
      T        C                       D                I
         I        R                   A K              I N
C                    I           B         C O N T O U R
      A              M     S           L       A     S E
I                       A     Y E         R       T     G
N        I  P O T E N T I A L     R       E R
T           C                         A       R A
E                 A Y T I D R U S B A E L S A
R                   Y T           E               O     U L
N           N           U             P       T       O I
M        O               R           I       Y       L B
E     R                     E           C     P     U I A
N I A C C U M U L A T I N G T E       C S D
T                                           I     N
   E X P E C T A T I O N S               T     A
   T R A D I T I O N S                   E     G
               C O N F I N E S M       A
D E M O G R A P H I C S                         P
      D E R O G A T O R Y                     O
                                              R
         I N T I M I D A T E D       P
```

## SOPHOMORE YEAR VOCABULARY

The following twenty-five vocabulary words are embedded in activities from the sophomore year section of *The Freedom Writers Diary*. We have included dictionary definitions of these words, and activities for your students to reinforce their comprehension of these words.

| Word | Diary | Page | Definition | Sentence from The Freedom Writers Diary |
|---|---|---|---|---|
| Accelerated | 28 | 57 | completed in less time than usual | Ever since elementary school I've always been in **accelerated** classes. |
| Amendment | 27 | 56 | a revision or alteration to a document or procedure | His lawyer came and advised him to plead the fifth **amendment**—no statement, no conviction. |
| Belittle | 28 | 58 | cause a person to seem little or less | It's wonderful to feel like a real person and not just someone for my teachers to **belittle**. |
| Blatant | 29 | 60 | obvious offensive manner | Even though the teacher eventually apologized to me for this **blatant** discrimination, I forgave him but didn't forget. |
| Circumstances | 41 | 84 | factors that lead up to a situation or event | They lost their innocence due to uncontrollable **circumstances**. |
| Contemplated | Ms. G, #3 | 48 | debated or considered | I **contemplated** leaving Wilson after a teacher printed and then dispersed a letter I'd written to Spielberg's secretary thanking her for helping with my spring field trip to the Museum of Tolerance. |
| Deliberately | 34 | 68 | done on purpose or by intention | The story that sticks with me the most is how the Nazis **deliberately** hurt innocent people like Anne Frank. . . . |
| Discrimination | 47 | 93 | unfair treatment of one person or group | Were these the same adults that preached how wrong racism and **discrimination** are? |
| Empathize | Ms. G, #4 | 83 | to understand or be sensitive to a person or situation | Not only will the students be able to **empathize** with Gerda's feelings of persecution and loss, but I hope they'll be able to understand how Anne Frank must have felt. |
| Entourage | Ms. G, #4 | 81 | friends or associates | Would we have to bring her parents, a translator, an **entourage**? |
| Façade | 41 | 85 | false, superficial, or artificial | Since I feel out of place, I often put on a **façade** so that I fit in. |
| Fatigued | 34 | 68 | to be extremely tired or weak | Everyone thought it was because I was feeling **fatigued**, but I knew it was because I was drunk. |
| Ghastly | 48 | 94 | terrifying; horrible | I thought of my three-year-old brother, and pictured him standing in Tony's place, telling his **ghastly** story. |

| Word | Diary | Page | Definition | Sentence from The Freedom Writers Diary |
|---|---|---|---|---|
| **Harassed** | 39 | 75 | persistently approached to the point of hostility | How about that man standing in the back? Had he ever **harassed** a little girl? |
| **Hereditary** | 34 | 67 | passed or received from family member | It has got to be **hereditary,** because not only do I have this problem, but my grandfather, my dad, and his mom had this problem also. |
| **Humane** | Zlata | 103 | having consideration for humans or animals | But, I also want to thank you for doing what you are doing today for my country, for children and young people who truly need people like your-selves, who will unselfishly and in a 100% **humane** way to do something for them. |
| **Overwhelm** | Ms. G, #3 | 47 | to overcome by strong emotions | If only she knew how nervous and **overwhelmed** I really was as a first-year teacher. |
| **Perpetuating** | Ms. G, #3 | 49 | a continuation; everlasting | So I decided to stay at Wilson and devote my energy to teaching literature, rather than **per-petuating** petty rivalries. |
| **Persecute** | 47 | 92 | punish or harassed to the point of suffering | This would be our first encounter with people who had been **persecuted** in Bosnia. |
| **Prophecy** | Ms. G, #4 | 80 | prediction of something to come | Some of them truly believed that if they wrote to her, she would come, as if it were a self-fulfilling **prophecy.** |
| **Prosecution** | 27 | 56 | to bring legal action against a person | It seemed just when the **prosecution** began to present a strong case against him, his dream team displayed something else to weaken their evidence, and softened the hearts of the jury. |
| **Regulate** | 53 | 107 | to control or rule over people | If not, I'll have to **regulate,** because as far as I'm concerned, they're the ones on probation in my "Ghetto Class!" |
| **Reiterate** | Ms. G, #3 | 48 | to repeat or explain again | Holocaust survivor Renee Firestone **reiterated** my point by telling my students, "Don't let actions of a few determine the way you feel about an entire group." |
| **Solicit** | Ms. G, #4 | 82 | to request or obtain favors | I got quotes on airline tickets, **solicited** local restaurants to donate gift certificates . . . |
| **Unorthodox** | Ms. G, #3 | 47 | not conventional; untraditional | According to them, I was too enthusiastic, too preppy, and my teaching technique was too **unorthodox.** |

Name: _____    Class: _____

## THE FREEDOM WRITERS DIARY: FILL IN THE BLANKS

**Directions:** The following vocabulary words have been taken from the sophomore year diary entries in *The Freedom Writers Diary*. In each section there are five vocabulary words. Fill in the blank with the word that best completes the sentence.

| I. | fatigued | hereditary | harassed | deliberately | prophecy |
|---|---|---|---|---|---|

1. It has got to be _____, because not only do I have this problem, but my grandfather, my dad, and his mom had this problem also.

2. Everyone thought it was because I was feeling _____, but I knew it was because I was drunk.

3. The story that sticks with me the most is how the Nazis _____ hurt innocent people like Anne Frank, and in my case, I'm the only one who's hurting myself.

4. How about that man standing in the back? Had he ever _____ a little girl?

5. Some of them truly believed that if they wrote to her, she would come, as if it were a self-fulfilling _____ .

| II. | overwhelmed | unorthodox | contemplated | perpetuating | reiterated |
|---|---|---|---|---|---|

6. According to them, I was too enthusiastic, too preppy, and my teaching technique was too _____.

7. If only she knew how nervous and _____ I really was as a first-year teacher.

8. I _____ leaving Wilson after a teacher printed and distributed a letter I'd written to Spielberg's secretary thanking her for helping with my spring field trip to the Museum of Tolerance.

9. Holocaust survivor Renee Firestone _____ my point by telling my students, "Don't let actions of a few determine the way you feel about an entire group."

10. So I decided to stay at Wilson and devote my energy to teaching literature, rather than _____ petty rivalries.

| III. | blatant | belittle | prosecution | amendment | accelerated |
|---|---|---|---|---|---|

11. It seemed just when the _____ began to present a strong case against him, his dream team displayed something else to weaken their evidence, and softened the hearts of the jury.

12. His lawyer came and advised him to plead the fifth _____ —no statement, no conviction.

13. Ever since elementary school I've been in _____ classes.

14. It's wonderful to feel like a real person and not just someone for my teachers to _____.

15. Even though the teacher eventually apologized to me for this _____ discrimination, I forgave him but didn't forget.

| IV. | solicited | entourage | empathize | circumstances | façade |
|---|---|---|---|---|---|

16. Would we have to bring her parents, a translator, or a/an _____?

17. I got quotes on airline tickets, _____ local restaurants to donate gift certificates, and my hotel even offered two rooms if she accepted our invitation.

18. Not only will the students be able to _____ with Gerda's feelings of persecution and loss, but I hope they'll be able to understand how Anne Frank must have felt.

19. They've lost their innocence due to uncontrollable _____.

20. Since I feel out of place, I often put on a _____ so that I fit in.

| V. | regulate | persecuted | discrimination | ghastly | humane |
|---|---|---|---|---|---|

21. This would be our first encounter with people who had been _____ in Bosnia.

22. Were these the same adults that preached how wrong racism and _____ are?

23. I thought of my three-year-old brother and pictured him standing in Tony's place, telling his _____ story.

24. But, I also want to thank you for doing what you are doing today for my country, for children and young people who truly need people like yourselves, who will unselfishly and in a 100% _____ way do something for them.

25. If not, I'll have to _____, because as far as I'm concerned, they're the ones on probation in my "Ghetto Class"!

## ANSWER KEY: FILL IN THE BLANKS

**I.**
hereditary
fatigued
deliberately
harassed
prophesy

**II.**
unorthodox
overwhelmed
contemplated
reiterated
perpetuating

**III.**
prosecution
amendment
accelerated
belittle
blatant

**IV.**
entourage
solicited
empathize
circumstances
façade

**V.**
persecuted
discrimination
ghastly
humane
regulate

## JUNIOR YEAR VOCABULARY

The following twenty-five vocabulary words are embedded in diary entries from the junior year section of *The Freedom Writers Diary*. We have included dictionary definitions of these words and activities for your students to reinforce their comprehension of these words.

| Word | Diary | Page | Definition | Sentence from The Freedom Writers Diary |
|---|---|---|---|---|
| Accolades | Ms. G, #5 | 109 | praise and public recognition of somebody's achievements | Despite all the **accolades** she received, she doesn't think her actions were heroic. |
| Alienate(d) | 69 | 145 | to make somebody feel that he or she does not belong to or share in something | For the first time I am feeling **alienated** from the rest of the class. |
| Alleged(ly) | 55 | 115 | claimed to have taken place | **Allegedly** my father had poured kerosene on her and lit the kitchen stove. She caught on fire immediately. |
| Animosity | Ms. G, #5 | 110 | a feeling or spirit of hostility and resentment | There is still a lot of **animosity** and racial tension. |
| Audacity | 65 | 134 | lack of respect in somebody's behavior toward another | When my mother comes home, she has the **audacity** to take the money and go buy beer and drugs, more specifically cocaine. |
| Camaraderie | 79 | 161 | a feeling of close friendship and trust among a particular group of people | Our **camaraderie** has more than just two sides, and I feel really fortunate to be a part of this new movement that's not just black and white. |
| Conventional | Ms. G, #5 | 108 | conforming to socially accepted behavior or style that lacks imagination | I didn't really have summer break in the **conventional** sense because I started teaching at a university. |
| Delusional | 66 | 138 | having a false or mistaken belief or idea about something | Was he sane or **delusional**? |
| Embellish(es) | Ms. G, #6 | 140 | to make an account or description more interesting by exaggerating details | To ensure that no one **embellishes** or sensationalizes their stories, I'm going to ask them to sign an honor code. |
| Humility | Ms. G, #5 | 109 | the quality of being modest or respectful | What impresses me most was her **humility**. |
| Intrigue(d) | 55 | 115 | to make somebody interested or curious | Our class is really **intrigued** by Emerson because Ms. Gruwell is encouraging us to be independent thinkers and to question authority. |
| Loitering | Ms. G, #6 | 140 | to stand around without any obvious purpose | I've never had to worry about drug dealers **loitering** on street corners or helicopters patrolling from above. |

| Word | Diary | Page | Definition | Sentence from The Freedom Writers Diary |
|---|---|---|---|---|
| **Mayhem** | Ms. G, #6 | 139 | absolute chaos or severe disruption | Room 203 is a place where they can seek refuge from all the **mayhem**. |
| **Misogyny** | 61 | 125 | the hatred of women | Ms. G introduced the word called "**misogyny**" and everyone in the class was like "What?" |
| **Muse** | Ms. G, #6 | 139 | think about something in a deep and serious or dreamy and abstracted way | Using her as our **muse,** the students will begin compiling the diaries they've been keeping into a collaborative book. |
| **Nonchalant** | 54 | 113 | unconcerned about things | I tried to tell her in a **nonchalant**, offhand sort of way. |
| **Permeating** | Ms. G, #6 | 139 | entering something and spreading throughout it, so that every part of it is affected | Even though they're not held captive in an attic or dodging bombs in a basement, the violence **permeating** the streets is just as frightening— and just as real. |
| **Plight** | 54 | 114 | a difficult or dangerous situation, especially a sad or desperate predicament | Well, actually it's a tale of how one woman, with a blind eye to stereotypes, had the eraser that took "National Spokesperson for the **Plight** of Black People" off my forehead. |
| **Poignant** | 54 | 112 | particularly penetrating and effective or relevant | Up until that point it had always been: "So Joyce, how do black people feel about Affirmative Action?" **Poignant** looks follow. |
| **Reminisce** | Ms. G, #5 | 108 | to talk or write about events remembered from the past | With a twelve-hour flight ahead of me, I have plenty of time to **reminisce** about the summer. |
| **Segregate** | 79 | 161 | to separate one person or group from the rest; keep things separate | Freedom Riders stood out among the crowd, trying to bring an end to **segregation** between whites and blacks by traveling from Washington, D.C., to New Orleans. |
| **Spontaneous** | 82 | 165 | arising from natural impulse or inclination | I knew Ms. G was up to something, because she's always trying to do something **spontaneous** that has some kind of symbolism in it. |
| **Stipulate** | Ms. G, #6 | 141 | to make a specific demand for something, usually as a condition in an agreement | John and I came up with a contract **stipulating** that once the computers arrived, the 35 students with the highest grade point average would win a computer when they graduated. |
| **Strewn** | Ms. G, #6 | 140 | scattered, especially carelessly or untidily | The parks aren't **strewn** with hypodermic needles or broken glass. |
| **Suffice(d)** | 54 | 113 | to be enough for somebody or something | Whoa there, slow down lady, a simple "It's inappropriate" would have **sufficed**. |

Name: _____ Class: _____

## THE FREEDOM WRITERS DIARY: WORD MATCH

**Directions:** Each of the following vocabulary words has been taken from the junior year diary entries in *The Freedom Writers Diary*. In each of the five sections below, there are five vocabulary words and five definitions. Write the letter of the definition next to the corresponding vocabulary word.

**I.**

_____ 1. **Accolades**

_____ 2. **Alienate**

_____ 3. **Alleged**

_____ 4. **Animosity**

_____ 5. **Audacity**

a. a feeling or spirit of hostility and resentment
b. praise and public recognition of somebody's achievements
c. lack of respect in somebody's behavior toward another
d. claimed to have taken place
e. to make somebody feel that he or she does not belong to or share in something

**II.**

_____ 1. **Camaraderie**

_____ 2. **Conventional**

_____ 3. **Delusional**

_____ 4. **Embellishes**

_____ 5. **Humility**

a. to have a false or mistaken belief or idea about something
b. a feeling of close friendship and trust among a particular group of people
c. the quality of being modest or respectful
d. to make an account or description more interesting by exaggerating details
e. conforming to socially accepted behavior or style that lacks imagination

**III.**

_____ 1. **Intrigue**

_____ 2. **Loiter**

_____ 3. **Mayhem**

_____ 4. **Misogyny**

_____ 5. **Muse**

a. absolute chaos or severe disruption
b. to make somebody greatly interested or curious
c. to stand around without any obvious purpose
d. to think about something in a deep and serious or dreamy and abstracted way
e. the hatred of women

**IV.**

_____ 1. **Nonchalant**

_____ 2. **Permeating**

_____ 3. **Plight**

_____ 4. **Poignant**

_____ 5. **Reminisce**

a. to talk or write about events remembered from the past
b. entering something and spreading throughout it, so that every part of it is affected
c. calm and unconcerned about things
d. particularly penetrating and effective or relevant
e. a difficult or dangerous situation, especially a sad or desperate predicament

**V.**

_____ 1. **Segregation**

_____ 2. **Spontaneous**

_____ 3. **Stipulate**

_____ 4. **Strewn**

_____ 5. **Suffice**

a. scattered, especially carelessly or untidily
b. to separate one person or group from the rest; keep things separate
c. to make a specific demand for something, usually as a condition in an agreement
d. to be enough for somebody or something
e. arising from natural impulse or inclination

## SENIOR YEAR VOCABULARY

The following twenty-five vocabulary words are from the diary entries from the senior year section of *The Freedom Writers Diary*. We have included dictionary definitions of these words, and activities for your students to reinforce their comprehension of these words.

| Word | Diary | Page | Definition | Sentence from The Freedom Writers Diary |
|---|---|---|---|---|
| **Advocate** | 106 | 206 | somebody who acts or intercedes on behalf of another | Ms. Gruwell is an **advocate** of the team method. |
| **Apprehensive** | 135 | 257 | worried that something bad will happen | I told James my decision and though he was obviously **apprehensive**, he was willing to go along with what I wanted to do. |
| **Assumption** | 142 | 270 | something that is believed to be true without proof | It was a second chance to prove everyone's **assumptions** wrong. |
| **Commiserate** | 142 | 271 | to express sympathy or sorrow | Our lives were shaped in this room and now it will never again be the place of people crying, hugging, **commiserating,** or tolerating, but who knows? |
| **Destiny** | 130 | 251 | the inner purpose of a life that can be discovered and realized | At this point in my life, I feel like a dry leaf dropping from a branch of a tree, uncertain of its **destiny**. |
| **Deteriorate** | 141 | 267 | to become or make something worse in quality, value, or strength | Knowing that my health was **deteriorating** every day took its toll on my mother. |
| **Disingenuous** | Ms. G, #8 | 222 | not straightforward or candid; insincere or calculating | If I feel they have ulterior motives or are the slightest bit **disingenuous**, I try to shelter the kids from them. |
| **Doctrine** | 128 | 246 | a rule or principle that forms the basis of a belief, theory, or policy; a body of ideas | Young boys were taken away from their families to be brainwashed in a communist **doctrine** and trained for war. |
| **Emulate** | 137 | 261 | to try hard to equal or surpass somebody or something | I had no one to look up to or to **emulate** until I met John. |
| **Engulf** | 135 | 257 | to surround, cover over, and swallow up somebody or something | It took almost three years to recover from the depression that **engulfed** me after the abortion of my first child. |
| **Eradicate** | 137 | 261 | to destroy or get rid of something completely | I want to **eradicate** the violence that is going on in my neighborhood . . . |
| **Exhilarate** | 135 | 258 | to cause to feel happily refreshed and energetic | No longer was I choked with fear. Instead, I breathed deep, **exhilarating** breaths. |

| Word | Diary | Page | Definition | Sentence from The Freedom Writers Diary |
|------|-------|------|------------|------------------------------------------|
| **Frantic** | 138 | 261 | in a state in which it is impossible to keep feelings or behavior under control, usually through fear or worry | Then I **frantically** searched through my covers and looked under the bed. |
| **Heritage** | 128 | 247 | something such as a way of life or traditional culture that passes from one generation to the next in a social group | I never knew about my **heritage**, or the positions that my parents had in the government, until we started talking about my culture in Ms. Gruwell's class. |
| **Inhibited** | 135 | 258 | unable to behave spontaneously or express feelings openly | As I breathed, truly released from the grasp of all that **inhibited** me, I began to see how blessed I was. |
| **Mediocre** | 137 | 260 | adequate but not very good | I raised my attendance from **mediocre** to perfect. |
| **Predominantly** | 133 | 254 | mainly; in the greatest number or amount | My AP Government class is **predominantly** white. |
| **Prestigious** | 130 | 249 | having a distinguished reputation | I was accepted into a **prestigious** technical school. |
| **Regime** | 128 | 245 | a particular government or managing group, especially one that is considered to be oppressive | I was born in Nicaragua, a country where a communist **regime** was implanted, after Somoza lost his presidency. |
| **Remorse** | 138 | 263 | a strong feeling of guilt and regret | Unfortunately, there are people who are like my parents, who shamelessly take from others with no **remorse**, but I will break that cycle and be a giver. |
| **Seniority** | Ms. G, #7 | 192 | a state of being older than others or higher in rank than another | Since I have no **seniority** to speak of, teaching seniors sort of rocked the boat. |
| **Surreal** | 113 | 222 | having an oddly dreamlike quality | It was very **surreal**, since we've lived in virtual anonymity for three years and in one weekend we suddenly had the opportunity to win an award—and now perhaps to appear on a TV show. |
| **Tedious** | 108 | 210 | boring because of being long, monotonous | Writing is very **tedious** and overwhelming, but satisfying at the same time. |
| **Transformation** | 131 | 251 | a complete change, usually into something with an improved appearance or usefulness | This **transformation** took two years before full-on addiction. |
| **Treacherous** | 118 | 231 | marked by betrayal of fidelity, confidence, or trust | One weekend when my siblings and I were visiting my father, he flew into a **treacherous** rage. |

Name: _____   Class: _____

## THE FREEDOM WRITERS DIARY: UNSCRAMBLE THE WORDS

**Directions:** Unscramble the vocabulary words below. They have all been taken from the diary entries from the senior year section of *The Freedom Writers Diary*.

1. _____ RENIDRGTEIOAT — to become or make something worse in quality, value, or strength

2. _____ CODIRENT — a rule or principle that forms the basis of a belief, theory, or policy; a body of ideas, particularly in religion, taught to people as truthful or correct

3. _____ TIHGNILAREXA — to cause to feel happily refreshed and energetic

4. _____ LAIYNTARFCL — in a state in which it is impossible to keep feelings or behavior under control, usually through fear, worry, or frustration

5. _____ YETORLNADNMPI — mainly; in the greatest number or amount

6. _____ NGEDLFEU — to overwhelm somebody or something with a great amount or number of something; to surround, cover over, and swallow up somebody or something

7. _____ URAROCTEHES — marked by betrayal of fidelity, confidence, or trust

8. _____ GREEMI — a particular government or managing group, especially one that is considered to be oppressive

9. _____ GHAITEER — something, such as a way of life or traditional culture, that passes from one generation to the next in a social group

10. _____ MFOOTRRISTANNA — a complete change, usually into something with an improved appearance or usefulness

11. _____ VTCAEADO — to support or speak in favor of something; somebody who acts or intercedes on behalf of another

12. _____ VESNIPRHEAEP — worried that something bad will happen

13. _____ SITEYDN — the inner purpose of a life that can be discovered and realized

14. _____ IITDHNBIE — unable to behave spontaneously or express feelings openly

15. _____ TALEMUE — to try hard to equal or surpass somebody or something, especially by imitation

16. _____ RITDCAAEE — to destroy or get rid of something completely, so that it can never recur or return

17. _____ SUTIDEO — boring because of being long, monotonous, or repetitive

18. _____ SOMRREE — a strong feeling of guilt and regret

19. _____ RLSAREU — having an oddly dreamlike quality

20. _____ USEOGRTPSII — having a distinguished reputation

21. _____ RTIYESNIO — to be older than others or higher in rank than another

22. _____ TASMSUOISPN — something that is believed to be true without proof

23. _____ GASOIMIRTNMEC — to express sympathy or sorrow

24. _____ SNGEUODISINU — not straightforward or candid; insincere or calculating

25. _____ RDIOEEMC — adequate but not very good

## UNSCRAMBLE THE WORDS KEY

1. DETERIORATING — to become or make something worse in quality, value, or strength

2. DOCTRINE — a rule or principle that forms the basis of a belief, theory, or policy; a body of ideas, particularly in religion, taught to people as truthful or correct

3. EXHILARATING — to cause to feel happily refreshed and energetic

4. FRANTICALLY — in a state in which it is impossible to keep feelings or behavior under control, usually through fear, worry, or frustration

5. PREDOMINANTLY — mainly; in the greatest number or amount

6. ENGULFED — to overwhelm somebody or something with a great amount or number of something; to surround, cover over, and swallow up somebody or something

7. TREACHEROUS — marked by betrayal of fidelity, confidence, or trust

8. REGIME — a particular government or managing group, especially one that is considered to be oppressive

9. HERITAGE — something, such as a way of life or traditional culture, that passes from one generation to the next in a social group

10. TRANSFORMATION — a complete change, usually into something with an improved appearance or usefulness

11. ADVOCATE — to support or speak in favor of something; somebody who acts or intercedes on behalf of another

12. APPREHENSIVE — worried that something bad will happen

13. DESTINY — the inner purpose of a life that can be discovered and realized

14. INHIBITED — unable to behave spontaneously or express feelings openly

15. EMULATE — to try hard to equal or surpass somebody or something, especially by imitation

16. ERADICATE — to destroy or get rid of something completely, so that it can never recur or return

17. TEDIOUS — to be boring because of being long, monotonous, or repetitive

18. REMORSE — a strong feeling of guilt and regret

19. SURREAL — having an oddly dreamlike quality

20. PRESTIGIOUS — having a distinguished reputation

21. SENIORITY — a state of being older than others or higher in rank than another

22. ASSUMPTIONS — something that is believed to be true without proof

23. COMMISERATING — to express sympathy or sorrow

24. DISINGENUOUS — not straightforward or candid; insincere or calculating

25. MEDIOCRE — adequate but not very good

### SLANG GRAMMAR

**Directions:** When they first met Ms. G, the Freedom Writers hadn't seen or known much of the world beyond their neighborhoods. The language they used held power in those neighborhoods. As they grew and learned more about the world outside of their neighborhoods, they learned that using standard English could bring them greater power in their expanding world.

I. The words below are slang or "vernacular" words used early in *The Freedom Writers Diary*. Think of how you would describe your life to someone who doesn't know you. On a separate sheet of paper, write at least one paragraph explaining your life using as many slang words as you can.

**Freedom Writers Slang**

| | | | | | |
|---|---|---|---|---|---|
| Homie | Beef | Mad Dog | Down | Baller | Banging |
| Kickin' it | Trip | Chilling | Bust a cap | Hood | 411 |
| Slick | Strapped | Roll out | Pad | Freak | 24/7 |

II. When you have completed your story, rewrite it using standard English, eliminating all use of slang.

### REFLECTION QUESTIONS

1. Who would get the most out of reading the first piece of writing? Who would get the most out of reading the second?
2. At what times when you are writing would it be helpful to use slang?
3. When would slang work against you?
4. Which of the two versions was the more difficult to compose? Why do you think that was?

Name: _____ Class: _____

## THE FREEDOM WRITERS DIARY: MISSPELLED WORDS AND PUNCTUATION

**Directions:** The sentences below have been taken from *The Freedom Writers Diary*. Yet for this activity, they contain misspelled words and punctuation errors. On the lines provided, rewrite the sentences and correct all of the mistakes.

1. by meeting these people it made the book's weve bin reading more meaningfull it also made me reilize that any thing is possible!

   _____

   _____

   _____

   _____

2. and for the first time in my life the image of my mother made me belive that I could change the way things were becuase at that moment i locked eyes with paco and said paco did it paco shot the guy

   _____

   _____

   _____

   _____

3. color is the last thang that coms to mind when we hang out to gether we have more importent things to be concearned about

   _____

   _____

   _____

   _____

4. a truly self relient person finds his week link and strengthenes it i want to be a self reliant person now and fore ever

   _____

   _____

   _____

   _____

5. their are many tragedies that could be stoped if only we spoke up more offen from this point on I will not be silant.

   _____

   _____

   _____

   _____

6. when I finnished reading the story i dont feel so alone some body in my class share's my seceret i actualy wrote her an anonimous note and simply said i feel your pain—you are not alone

_____

_____

_____

_____

7. luckiley ms g and the freedom writers dont see being poor and latino as an obstacal to becoming a filmmaker they belive i can acheive my dream and with their support i know i can

_____

_____

_____

_____

8. he could not face his own sun like a reel man from this expierence i don't want to try to meat him agin learning form my fathers misstakes i no i am not gonna bee a cowerd like him

_____

_____

_____

_____

9. its good to no i dont need to change for others but to search for people who will take me as i be with out any strings atached

_____

_____

_____

_____

10. he has given sew much to me and 'cause of his actions i want to give to others and hopefuly someone will follow after me and the cicle of hope will continue

_____

_____

_____

_____

## MISSPELLED WORDS AND PUNCTUATION KEY

Below are the correct sentences from *The Freedom Writers Diary*.

1. By meeting these people, it made the books we've been reading more meaningful. It also made me realize that anything is possible! (Diary #21, page 43)

2. And for the first time in my life, the image of my mother made me believe that I could change the way things were. Because at that moment I locked eyes with Paco and said, "Paco did it. Paco shot the guy!" (Diary #33, page 66)

3. Color is the last thing that comes to mind when we hang out together. We have more important things to be concerned about. (Diary #46, page 92)

4. A truly self-reliant person finds his weak link and strengthens it. I want to be a self-reliant person, now and forever. (Diary #57, page 120)

5. There are many tragedies that could be stopped if only we spoke up more often. From this point on, I will not be silent. (Diary #67, page 143)

6. When I finished reading the story, I didn't feel so alone. Somebody in my class shares my secret. I actually wrote her an anonymous note and simply said, "I feel your pain—you are not alone!" (Diary #74, page 152)

7. Luckily, Ms. G and the Freedom Writers don't see being poor and Latino as an obstacle to becoming a filmmaker. They believe I can achieve my dream. And with their support, I know I can. (Diary #104, pages 204–205)

8. He could not face his own son like a real man. From this experience, I don't want to try to meet him again. Learning from my father's mistakes, I know I am not going to be a coward like him. (Diary #110, pp. 212–214)

9. It's good to know I don't need to change for others but to search for people who will take me as I am—without any strings attached! (Diary #126, pp. 242–243)

10. He has given so much to me, and because of his actions I want to give to others, and hopefully someone will follow after me and the cycle of hope will continue.(Diary #137, pp. 260–261)

Name: _____ Class: _____

## THE FREEDOM WRITERS DIARY: HOMONYMS AND SYNONYMS

### A. HOMONYMS

**Directions:** A homonym is a word that sounds like another word but has a different definition. Circle the word that best fits the sentence. Each of these sentences has been taken from *The Freedom Writers Diary*.

1. It was just like in the movie, (**accept, except**) in this movie when the characters bleed, the blood is real.
2. (**They're, There, Their**) are many tragedies that could be stopped if only we spoke up more often. From this point on, I will not be silent.
3. Now when I (**write, right**), I'll remember Jim's work and what he risked his life for. Like him, I am willing to step forward, unafraid of who or what lies ahead. After all, history tells me that I am not alone.
4. I (**know, no**) that my decision to go to college will (**effect, affect**) my sisters' decisions, and they will not be as afraid as I was of traveling this road.
5. We gave them hugs and words of encouragement to hold on to their dreams and goals and to always (**sore, soar**) high.
6. Reading the list would mean finding out (**weather, whether**) my dream had come true, or (**weather, whether**) it would just be another triumph for those who had no faith in me.
7. We hope this book will inspire you to be the (**forth, fourth**) leg of the race by encouraging you (**too, to, two**) pick up a pen and be a catalyst for change.

### B. SYNONYMS

**Directions:** A synonym is a word that means the same thing as another word. Using the bold words in the parentheses at the end of each sentence, circle the choice that can be interchanged with the underlined word. If you need to, use a dictionary to get definitions for the words.

1. Students come in from every corner of the city: Rich kids from the shore sit next to poor kids from the projects . . . there's every race, religion, and culture within the <u>confines</u> of the quad. (**reticence, restrictions, placation**)
2. My teachers always said, "I'm here to help," but when the time came to start helping they were never <u>dependable</u>, so what I do at school is what I do out in the streets. (**improvident, steadfast, tranquil**)
3. The ticking often begins with a <u>derogatory</u> comment, which can spark an explosion. (**deprecating, serendipitous, zealous**)
4. Room 203 is a place where they can seek refuge from all the <u>mayhem</u>. (**foible, bedlam, penitence**)
5. Even though they're not held captive in an attic or dodging bombs in a basement, the violence <u>permeating</u> the streets is just as frightening—and just as real. (**ceasing, pontificating, pervading**)
6. No longer was I choked with fear. Instead, I breathed deep, <u>exhilarating</u> breaths. (**egregious, invigorating, restricting**)
7. This <u>transformation</u> took two years before full-on addiction. (**compulsion, askance, metamorphosis**)

Name: _____   Class: _____

## THE FREEDOM WRITERS DIARY: CORRECT THE MISTAKES

**Directions:** Below is a summary about *The Freedom Writers Diary*. This passage contains grammatical mistakes, misspelled words, and run-on sentences. Find all the mistakes and rewrite the text on the lines provided below. (If you need more room to write, use the back of this page or attach a separate sheet of paper.)

the freedom riders diary is an amaizng true story of strenth, curage, and acheivement in the face of adversity. in the Fall of 1994, in Room 203 at Woodrow wilson high school in long beach california, an ideialistic 24 year old teecher named Erin Gruwell faced her 1st groop of studints, dubbed by them administrations as "unteachable, at-risk" teenagers. that class were a diverse mix of african-american latino cambodian vietnamese and caucasian studints, many of who had grew up in ruff 'hoods in long beach. in the first few weeks of class they students made it clear that them were not interested in what they're teacher got to say, and made bets about how long she would last in there class room

then a pivital moment changed theyre lifes forever? when a racial charicature of one of the african-american students curculated the classroom Erin angrly entercepted the drawling and compared it to the Nazi caricature's of jews during the holocaust. to her amiazement, them students responded with puzled lookes. erin was appauled to discover that she students had been never hearing of no holocaust. when she asked how many be shot at, however almost all they raised they hands, and began liftin' there shirt's to show there scars! this inishiated a battle-scar show-and-telll that left erin Grumwell shoked and enspired to take advantidge of that powerfull energy she had done sparked

## REWRITE THE PASSAGE CORRECTLY

_____

_____

_____

_____

_____

_____

_____

_____

_____

_____

_____

_____

_____

## CORRECT THE MISTAKES KEY

Below is the correct summary of *The Freedom Writers Diary*.

*The Freedom Writers Diary* is an amazing true story of strength, courage, and achievement in the face of adversity. In the fall of 1994, in Room 203 at Woodrow Wilson High School in Long Beach, California, an idealistic twenty-four-year-old teacher named Erin Gruwell faced her first group of students, dubbed by the administration as "unteachable, at-risk" teenagers. The class was a diverse mix of African-American, Latino, Cambodian, Vietnamese, and Caucasian students, many of whom had grown up in rough neighborhoods in Long Beach. In the first few weeks of class, the students made it clear that they were not interested in what their teacher had to say, and made bets about how long she would last in their classroom.

Then a pivotal moment changed their lives forever. When a racial caricature of one of the African-American students circulated the classroom, Erin angrily intercepted the drawing and compared it to the Nazi caricatures of Jews during the Holocaust. To her amazement, the students responded with puzzled looks. Erin was appalled to discover that her students had never heard of the Holocaust. When she asked how many had been shot at, however, almost all of them raised their hands, and began lifting their shirts to show their scars! This initiated a battle-scar show-and-tell that left Erin Gruwell shocked and inspired to take advantage of the powerful energy she had sparked.

# TALK SHOW

## OBJECTIVE

This activity creates an interactive way for your students to discuss *The Freedom Writers Diary* while tapping into their interest in the media. Reference a popular talk show, such as *Oprah*, and set up a makeshift television show complete with a host, audience, guests, and a full list of characters from a diary entry in the book. Making use of the talk-show format creates an opportunity for students to engage in interesting dialogue concerning issues such as equality, justice, injustice, cycles of violence, and family loyalty. Whether they play the part of characters or audience members, students will explore the text in deeper ways as they pose questions and create dialogue from "inside" the story world, thereby adopting and articulating a variety of cultural and social perspectives.

## BACKSTORY FROM ROOM 203

You can use this format to discuss literature in a new way, as your students play the roles of characters in texts from *The Odyssey* to *The Color Purple*. (Some of my students with learning disabilities hit their stride with this activity because they could express their critical thinking about the text through role playing instead of writing.) We use Diary #33 in this activity because there is no simple solution to the problem faced by the Freedom Writer.

## MS. G'S TIPS

Teachers play the role of the host in order to control and direct the activity. Assign the largest parts to your most enthusiastic students, since their active participation will be essential. As students begin to improvise (especially those playing gang members), it is very possible they will lapse into slang and even profanity. If they are truly in character and "feeling it," I recommend that you go with the flow and allow for this authenticity. At the same time, you need to maintain order in the classroom. That's why I prefer to model Oprah instead of, say, Jerry Springer . . . no physical acting out is permitted.

## WHAT YOU'LL NEED

- *The Freedom Writers Diary*
- 5" × 7" index cards
- Talk Show visual graphic

• Name tags for the following characters:
  Judge
  Public defender (for the falsely accused boy)
  Freedom Writer witness/author of Diary #33
  Freedom Writer's mother
  Freedom Writer's father
  Freedom Writer's younger brother
  Freedom Writer's younger sister
  Paco
  Young man accused of murder
  Accused man's mother
  Accused man's girlfriend (and mother of the accused man's baby)

## PROCESS

**Step 1:** Select one student per paragraph to read Diary #33 aloud to the class.

**Step 2:** Pick which students will be your twelve "guests" on the talk show and pass out the name tags associated with their characters. Try to choose students who are likely to have some insight into their assigned character's thoughts and feelings.

**Step 3:** Give each student an index card and explain that everyone will participate, even the "audience." The "guests" should write down dialogue (comments their characters would be likely to contribute). As the Talk Show action takes place, students in the "audience" should write down questions for the characters on their index cards.

**Step 4:** Move twelve chairs to the front of the class and form a semicircle that faces the rest of the class. The "guests" will create a panel facing the "audience," which will be in a semicircle.

**Step 5:** Ask the students playing characters on the panel to sit next to characters with whom they are associated. In full host character, introduce the characters to the audience.

**Step 6:** Take an assertive position as host, and stand between the audience and the panel. Set boundaries to ensure that panel members do not leave their seats or break character. Make sure to moderate the dialogue so that everyone gets a chance to speak. Use questions to keep your students on task and make sure that the discussion does not lose its relevance to the text. Refer to the following character list and sample questions below for further guidance.

## CAST OF CHARACTERS AND POSSIBLE QUESTIONS

**Judge:** The judge wants justice, but he's seen it all before. He is dealing with a public defender as well as the teenagers involved in the trial and their families.

**Questions:** You see cases of teenagers committing murders all the time. How did you feel when these people walked into your courtroom? What do you expect from today's trial?

**Public Defender:** Due to lack of money, the African-American boy falsely accused of murder has been appointed a public defender. This public defender is overwhelmed and, like many public defenders, gets cases five minutes before the trial begins.
**Questions:** How do you feel about the kids you defend going through the system like a "conveyor belt"? Are you cynical or do you think you can make a difference? How are you affected by today's testimony?

**Freedom Writer's Father:** The Freedom Writer's father, joining the panel via satellite, is incarcerated in San Quentin State Prison for a crime he didn't commit. In the past, he has preached family, ethnic, and gang solidarity.
**Questions:** Thank you for joining us from San Quentin. How does it feel to witness a case where an innocent person could end up incarcerated like you? Do you want your daughter to lie to keep Paco out of jail? What went through your mind when she said, "Paco did it"? If you could, would you change any of your past actions or choices?

**Freedom Writer's Mother:** This is the mother of the Freedom Writer who wrote Diary #33. She's going to talk about what it feels like to have a daughter on the stand facing this ethical dilemma, a daughter who will be in danger whatever she chooses to do. The Freedom Writer's mother, who works three jobs, also has two younger children who will be affected by today's testimony.
**Questions:** What did you want your daughter to do before you all came into court today? Do you support her decision? How do you feel about your husband's involvement in a gang? Do you fear your children will end up in prison instead of college?

**Freedom Writer's Little Brother:** The Freedom Writer's little brother looks up to his sister but also identifies with the men of his family, especially his father.
**Questions:** You know the rules of the street. One of those rules is "You can't rat on a homeboy." Do you agree with what your sister did on the stand? With your father in jail, do you feel responsible for the family?

**Freedom Writer's Little Sister:** Because her mother is away at work so much, the Freedom Writer's little sister looks up to her older sibling and feels very dependent on her.
**Questions:** What did you want your sister to do on the stand? Are you afraid for her future and for your own future? Who do you look up to? How do your sister's choices affect your own choices?

**Paco:** In the story, Paco sits in the front row of the courtroom with a smug expression on his face, but now he is on the stage confronting the consequences of the shooting and the many people affected.

**Questions:** What did you expect coming into court today? What are the unwritten codes you and your friends live by? How do you feel about your girlfriend—and fellow gang member—breaking the code and pointing you out in court? Do you feel remorse about killing an innocent bystander?

**Young Man Accused of Murder:** He is a member of the gang that beat up the Freedom Writer a few weeks ago, but today he is falsely accused of murder. His fate lies in the hands of a rival gang member.

**Questions:** How did it feel to be falsely accused of murder and face the prospect of spending the rest of your life in prison? Did you worry about not getting a fair trial because of your race? Do you live by the same street rules Paco was describing? A rival gang member saved your life today. How did her testimony affect you? Will you make a change in your life?

**Accused Man's Mother:** This woman's son, her only child, is accused of murder.

**Questions:** How does it feel to have your son on trial for murder? He is innocent, but he is also a gang member. Could you have done anything differently as a parent to prevent these circumstances?

**Accused Man's Girlfriend:** She and her boyfriend have a young daughter whom she is now caring for by herself.

**Questions:** How do you feel about your boyfriend being accused of murder? What would have happened to you and your daughter if he had been locked behind bars for murder? Your boyfriend will be released today, but do you have doubts that he can be there for you and for your daughter?

**Freedom Writer:** This is the Freedom Writer who walked into the courtroom, testified, and wrote Diary #33.

**Questions:** What is going through your mind as you hear from all the people affected by the shooting and by your testimony? Do you fear for your physical safety? Will your relationships with your family members change after today? What about your relationship with yourself?

## VISUAL GRAPHIC INSTRUCTIONS

At the end of the Talk Show, have students use the space inside the Talk Show visual graphic to write down the names of the characters whose point of view they feel they now understand better. Below the graphic, students should explain briefly what new insights they have gained about these characters and/or their story.

## ASSESSMENT

Have your students write about the character they most identified with during the Talk Show activity. Similarly, have your students write about the character they least identified with and why. This writing exercise should prompt a lively discussion.

Choose any character besides the Freedom Writer who wrote Diary #33, and rewrite the courtroom story from that other character's point of view. Include details about your character's past in order to help us understand their thoughts and feelings about the Freedom Writer's testimony.

This activity can be adapted for a research project on any famous courtroom trial, past or present. Students will research the issues and parties involved, and then create dialogue to bring the trial to life.

## TAKING IT FURTHER

Have your students take the activity further by discussing the controversial "codes of the street" such as not snitching, and how those messages have even made their way into pop culture, such as in the song, "Stop Snitchin, Stop Lyin" by The Game.

### Freedom Writer Feedback

"I think this was one of the trickiest assignments Ms. G ever gave us. I remember being really excited about not having to write an essay about *The Color Purple*, not realizing that I was actually writing all these pages of dialogue!"

### The Freedom Writers Diary Quotation

"As I sat in the chair, I felt as if I was exposed to different eyes. Those eyes, in some strange way, were touching a part of me that was deep inside. Everyone was waiting for my reaction." —Diary #33

### Teacher Talk

"I love this exercise because everybody participates. Although a diary entry may only have two or three characters, you can adapt it to fit as many characters as you need for your classroom by adding friends or family members. Watch what happens when you assign a major character to more than one student: suddenly, two students are 'competing' over whose interpretation of the character is more accurate and persuasive. This sends everyone back to the text looking for evidence."

NCTE Standards: 1, 2, 3, 4, 5, 6, 7, 9, 11, 12

# TAKE A STAND

## OBJECTIVE

This activity allows students to share their opinions without requiring an explanation. In response to a question, students simply walk to the "Agree" or "Disagree" side of the classroom. In this way, Take a Stand resembles the Line Game as students demonstrate kinesthetically their connection with an experience and one another. However, this activity also incorporates a great opportunity for students to defend their views verbally and persuade others to join them on the side they have chosen.

## BACKSTORY FROM ROOM 203

Take a Stand can be adapted to discuss a myriad of topics, but for this particular exercise we focus on issues raised in *The Freedom Writers Diary*. Students may have intense feelings about such topics as sororities or interracial dating. However, they will learn that the most effective way of changing the minds of their classmates is through sharpening their oral communication skills and rhetorical strategies, not shouting or browbeating.

## MS. G'S TIPS

While you should encourage students to provide explanations and try to persuade their peers to change sides, always keep control of the class. To maintain order, use a prop to indicate who can talk. As in *Lord of the Flies*, students can only speak if they are holding on to your symbolic equivalent of the conch. Remind students that they are not allowed to talk unless they are holding the prop. (I used signs stating Agree or Disagree.)

## WHAT YOU'LL NEED

- A large sign that reads "Agree"
- A large sign that reads "Disagree"
- A prop for students to hold while they talk (i.e., a gavel, a microphone, or even a stuffed animal with significance, such as your school mascot)
- Take a Stand visual graphic
- Journals

## PROCESS

**Step 1:** Create a large, open area by asking your students to help you move all of the desks to one side of the room.

**Step 2:** Hang the "Agree" and "Disagree" signs on opposite walls in your classroom. There should be a wide, empty space to move around in.

**Step 3:** Explain the rules to your students:

1. This is a physical game, so they must walk to "take a stand" on either side of the room.

2. After you read or say a statement out loud, they should walk to the side of the room that corresponds to "Agree" or "Disagree."

3. After the students have settled into their positions, they will have the chance to explain why they agreed or disagreed. Encourage them to try to get other students to change their minds and join their side of the classroom.

4. Students are allowed to talk only if they are holding the prop you have chosen for this exercise.

5. Students are allowed to change their answers and walk to the opposing side of the room at any time.

6. Before beginning the activity, everyone must "agree to disagree." Remind your students that they will not always be able to change the minds of their peers, and that this is okay.

**Step 4:** Start off the exercise by asking your students to agree or disagree with a couple of simple statements to warm up and check that the rules are well understood. ("Eating breakfast will help you do better in school"; "Dogs make better pets than cats.")

**Step 5:** Now move into more serious territory. Agree or disagree:

• Sororities and fraternities are like gangs.
• This school is as segregated as the city.
• Students with learning disabilities should be separated from other students.
• You should turn in your friends if you know they have committed a crime.

## VISUAL GRAPHIC INSTRUCTIONS

Above the picture of the gavel, have students write down a statement they want to use for the next Take a Stand activity. Below the gavel, students should jot down a few arguments that either support or undermine the statement.

## ASSESSMENT

In their journals, have students tell a story about a time when they were persuaded against their better judgment to do something that challenged their personal beliefs. How did they feel before that decision? How did they feel after?

## TAKING IT FURTHER

Have your students write about the last time they took a stand on an issue, even when it was unpopular. Did they win anyone over to their side? Why or why not?

**Freedom Writer Feedback**

"I liked the Take a Stand activity, because it allows students that are a little shy to communicate by using their bodies, not their words. Sometimes, I was shocked to see where some of my friends decided to stand. Trying to convince people to switch sides was challenging, but also exciting."

***The Freedom Writers Diary* Quotation**

*"There are many tragedies that could be stopped if only we spoke up more often. From this point on, I will not be silent." —Diary #67*

**Teacher Talk**

"My students routinely ask me, 'When can we play the Take a Stand game again?' They seem to enjoy being mobile, silently claiming their opinions, and occasionally engaging in this structured debate. Take a Stand is also an incredible door to journaling topics after the activity is over."

NCTE Standards: 4, 5, 11, 12

## STAND

Stay Black—
        Stay Proud
Stay White—
        Stay Proud
Stay Brown—
        Stay Proud
Stay Yellow—
        Stay Proud

Don't be afraid of what you are,
'cause all you can be, is you!
You'll never be anything else but you,
So be the best you, you can be.
Keep it real—
        By all means.
                At all times.
Whether a lawyer, a doctor, a football player,
A toilet cleaner, a garbage handler, a panhandler—
Keep it real
        And still—
                Be the best you can be.

Have pride, have dignity, stand!
Stand proud, talk proud, be proud!

Don't lay down,
Back down,
Bow down, run away,
Sell out yourself,
Sell into criticism.
Be real and realize that the ones who criticize,
Best recognize that you are you—
Take it or leave it.

"MMM HMM!"
I knew you'd get it.
Get what?
The stuff—
The stuff called pride, that attitude, that aura,
Your identity, your self, your pride, piece of mind,
Worry free.
See, I can't be you, but I'm a damn good ME!
Righteous.

—Freedom Writer (Diary 88, page 174)

## SLAM POETRY

Slam poetry, the "sport of spoken word," is a poetry competition. It is very inclusive and intense.

Poets can talk about anything they want as long as they feel passionate enough about it to get up in front of a roaring crowd.

The rules of slam are simple:

1. Poets have three minutes on stage, starting when they say their first word.
2. No music, no props.
3. A different, original poem is required in every round.
4. The judges are always selected from the audience.

A slam usually lasts three rounds. At the end of the competition a winner is declared.

Winners sometimes receive prizes, but sometimes the prize is simply the satisfaction of knowing you are the best poet in the room, the exhilaration of being on stage, or just simply sharing your words.

## ASSESSMENT

Find a song or a poem that pertains to someone who lost his or her innocence and present it to the class in a slam fashion.

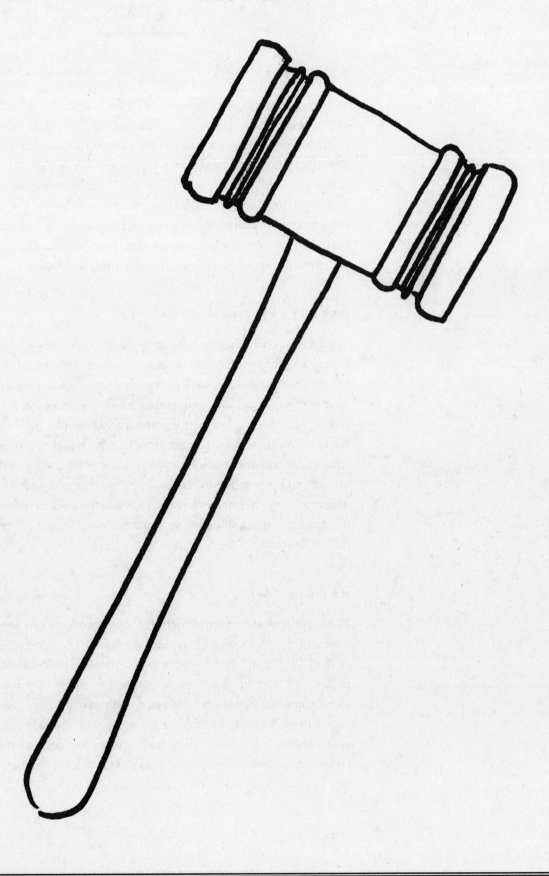

# DEBATE

## OBJECTIVE

Reading literature opens up new worlds for your students, but bridging the gap between old and new can be challenging. Debate situations push students to connect with a text emotionally and intellectually because students like to argue . . . and to win arguments. For this activity, students are assigned to be either "for" or "against" the following statement: "*The Freedom Writers Diary* should be banned in schools because of its controversial content." Students will use critical thinking skills and textual evaluation strategies (comprehension, interpretation, appreciation) to communicate their opinions and feelings as persuasively as possible.

## BACKSTORY FROM ROOM 203

The Debate activity uses a polarizing claim to elicit strong reactions from students. I chose this topic because it ties in with actual controversies. In Michigan in 2007, a "values" organization accused a local high school teacher of violating child pornography laws by assigning *The Freedom Writers Diary*. (Also on the list were "pornographic" books by Toni Morrison, Richard Wright, and Kurt Vonnegut.) This is a wonderful opportunity for your students to discuss the educational value of a book focused on improving lives and promoting tolerance. The pro-censorship side in this student debate will find themselves forced to misread the book in order to interpret (for example) an anguished story about molestation as if it were written to titillate the reader.

## MS. G'S TIPS

There are two ways to approach this topic: Students can argue as themselves, or you can assign characters, such as "PTA [Parent Teacher Association] President," "School Principal," "Parent," or "Student." Allowing students to take on aliases when they debate adds to the fun and allows more points of view to be addressed. This activity often becomes quite entertaining, as students who do not agree with the side they have been appointed to begin using irony and sarcasm to "defend" their opinion. Debates require no major preparation and provide the teacher with a great way to assess student reactions to a book.

## WHAT YOU'LL NEED

- A prop for students to hold while they talk (i.e. a gavel, a microphone, or even a stuffed animal with significance, such as your school mascot)
- Scales of Justice visual graphic
- Journals

## PROCESS

**Step 1:** Before setting up the debate, have the class brainstorm about content that could be considered controversial in *The Freedom Writers Diary*. Two topics likely to draw the most attention: sexuality and rough language. Explain that in order to be legally defined as pornography, a book must be found to appeal to readers' prurient interest in sex, while lacking literary or educational value. In the case of language, students will need to consider context: Is a diary entry's use of a profanity or a racial epithet wholly destructive and gratuitous, or is its use in keeping with the writer's purpose and meaning? How does a word change meaning, depending on who uses the word and for what audience?

**Step 2:** Use a random method to divide your students into two groups.

**Step 3:** Ask the students to rearrange the desks, forming two parallel rows, with each group's row facing the other. There should be at least five to ten feet in between each row of desks, depending on the size of the room.

**Step 4:** Pass out the Scales of Justice visual graphic and ask the students to write this statement in the center of the page: *"The Freedom Writers Diary* should be banned." Give each group time to jot down a few arguments on one side of their Scales.

**Step 5:** A student on one side will take a turn presenting one argument, then toss the prop across the room to someone on the other team. Remind students that they are allowed to speak only when holding the prop.

**Step 6:** Pay close attention to the debate, and bring it to a close when both sides run out of arguments.

## VISUAL GRAPHIC INSTRUCTIONS

In the center of the Scales of Justice, students will write the statement *"The Freedom Writers Diary* should be banned," and then on one side of the scales jot down several ideas supporting one side of the debate. After the debate is finished but still fresh in their minds, have students use both sides of the scales to list arguments on each side of the debate.

### Freedom Writer Feedback

"Debates are pretty common in school, but Ms. G's debate was the only one that made me feel like my opinion was valid. The topics that we discussed in class were always relevant, which kept me interested even when I disagreed with the stance I had to take."

### *The Freedom Writers Diary* Quotation

*"Ms. Gruwell structured a debate called 'Misogyny or Mayhem?' She started by having us analyze the cover of Snoop Doggy Dog's album with cartoon characters representing a male and female dog. [ . . . ] If you were looking for someone to give you an example of misogyny, my family would be the prime illustration." —Diary #61*

### Teacher Talk

"Today I did the debate activity with my students and after a few minutes, our discussion about racial epithets moved to the climate on campus and race issues, both real and perceived. . . . We sat and shared our opinions in a nonthreatening way. . . . When the class was over, I had several students come over and ask when we could do that again."

NCTE Standards: 2, 3, 4, 5, 6, 7, 9, 10, 11, 12

## ASSESSMENT

Using the notes on their visual graphics, students should summarize in their journals as many of the arguments made by each side as they can remember. Ask them to assess which were the weakest and strongest, and to explain why. In order to motivate your students to listen carefully during the debate, let them know ahead of time that this will be their assessment.

## TAKING IT FURTHER

Today's debate has prepared the ground for your students to research and write newspaper stories about book-banning controversies associated with *The Freedom Writers Diary* (or another text of your choice). To help students organize their research, you can photocopy and distribute the 5 W's and How and K-W-L worksheets from the next activity, Parallel Lives from the Past.

# PARALLEL LIVES FROM THE PAST

**OBJECTIVE**

Most of the books that I chose for the Freedom Writers were written by, about, and for young people who lived through war—because I had a roomful of students who knew what it was like to grow up in a "war zone." By reading about war, terror, and civil strife, my students discovered parallel worlds and their own ability to empathize with strangers. The purpose of this assignment is to give your students a better understanding of the historical tragedies touched upon in *The Freedom Writers Diary*: the Holocaust, the Cambodian genocide, the Bosnian civil war, Japanese internment camps, and U.S. racism. In order to research how others faced fear and found courage, students can draw on *The Freedom Writers Diary* as well as consult library books, Internet Web sites, and audiovisual materials. Along the way, the class will develop important language arts and social science skills in research, collaborative problem-solving, and oral presentation.

**BACKSTORY FROM ROOM 203**

"You can take history and relate it to something that's going on in the present, and that's the beauty of it." These words are uttered (in the *Primetime Live* segment) by the student who was the target of a racist caricature in my class, the student whose pain prompted me to teach about the Holocaust. Hearing this statement, I was reminded of how critical it is to infuse history into our lesson plans. For the oral presentation, encourage students to design an activity that truly expresses their interests and strengths. These could include timelines or charts; a song or poem; a poster or compilation of film clips; a PowerPoint presentation; a map; a dramatic monologue.

**MS. G'S TIPS**

This project can be time-consuming, so I recommend that you read through the steps in advance and determine how to arrange your timetable. Ideally, teachers should model what the stages of a completed student presentation should look like, using for your example another historical event that comes up in *The Freedom Writers Diary*, such as the Oklahoma City Bombing.

## WHAT YOU'LL NEED

- K-W-L and 5W's and How worksheets
- Venn diagram (optional)
- Computer access
- Library resources
- Butcher or chart paper
- Blank sheets of white paper
- Markers
- Binders for group portfolios
- TV and DVD player (optional)
- Stereo (optional)

## PROCESS

**Step 1:** Explain to students that this project is developed through several small "stepping-stone" assignments that can be done individually or in pairs. The assignments are then synthesized in an oral presentation. Student work for all activities will be collected in a group portfolio.

**Step 2:** Put your students into groups of five or six, making an effort to bring together students with different learning styles and skills. It is probably simplest to randomly assign each group their topic.

### Topics

- The Holocaust
- The Bosnian civil war
- Cambodian genocide
- Japanese internment
- U.S. Civil Rights Movement

**Step 3:** Assign one student to record their group's conversations and another to serve as project manager, whose job will be to make sure that all group members participate in the project activities. Have students fill in their K-W-L handouts as a starting point for what sort of research to pursue (either individually or in pairs).

**Step 4:** Using the 5W's and How worksheet, students will now research some aspect of the group's historical event much as a journalist might do. To keep these projects interesting, advise the students to find a specific focus for their research (a particular conflict, a specific individual).

**Step 5:** After completing their individual 5W's and How worksheets, group members will come back together to share their results. If possible, collect student worksheets before class and make enough copies for the group. This is an excellent opportunity for students, having taught themselves, to teach one another what they have learned. If you wish, provide each group with a Venn diagram to organize their data.

© *The Freedom Writers Diary Teacher's Guide*, 2007.

© *The Freedom Writers Diary Teacher's Guide,* 2007.

**Freedom Writer Feedback**

"This project helped us make connections to the struggles of young people like ourselves throughout history. You never learn anything as well as when you are responsible for teaching it to others."

**Freedom Writer Diary Quotation**

*"Zlata and I seem to have a lot in common because while Zlata was living through a war in Sarajevo, I was living through a different kind of war—the L.A. riots. Ironically, Zlata and I were both eleven years old when our city was under siege. I can understand how afraid and scared she was to see her city go up in flames, because my city was on fire, too." —Diary #38*

**Teacher Talk**

"Learning about the inhumanity and suffering inherent in certain historical events tugs at my students' hearts, regardless of their background or current level of oppression. When exploring these difficult topics in a safe classroom environment, my students become empowered to fight their own struggles in positive ways and be more compassionate to each other and people they don't even know in the process. Some of my students took their learning further by creating petition letters."

NCTE Standards: 1, 2, 3, 4, 5, 6, 7, 8, 9, 10, 11, 12

**Step 6:** After pooling their research, the groups will work collaboratively to decide how to present what they have learned to the rest of their classmates through a variety of activities:

• Write a poem or short story about your historical event or figure.
• Compile statistics relevant to your historical topic. Create charts or tables to express your findings.
• Create a comic book (or graphic novel) version of a historical scene.
• Create a timeline of important dates and figures pertaining to your topic.
• Create or find a song, provide the lyrics, and present an interpretation of the meaning behind the song in relation to your historical event.
• Find or create pictures, posters, or film clips about your historical topic.
• Design a map reflecting locations of conflict and zones of resistance.
• Act out a scene or dialogue, or create a dance or performance concerning your historical topic.
• Create a PowerPoint presentation on your historical topic.

**Step 7:** Group oral presentations will be the culminating activity for the Parallel Lives project. Each group member will present his or her activity to the rest of the class. In addition, all student work should be collected in the group portfolios.

**ASSESSMENT**

This project offers multiple opportunities for assessing student work. Students may be assessed individually on their work samples for each activity (collected in the group portfolio). In addition, students may be assessed on their contributions to the group oral presentation.

**TAKING IT FURTHER**

Make additional copies of the 5 W's and How worksheet and have students research other topics that relate to the theme of Facing Fear, Finding Courage, whether from *The Freedom Writers Diary*—the Oklahoma City bombings, civil war in Latin America—or tragedies beyond the text, such as the impact of Hurricane Katrina, genocide in Darfur or Rwanda, or the devastation of malnutrition, malaria, or AIDS in Africa.

Name: _____ Class: _____

## K-W-L WORKSHEET

| -K-<br>What I know . . . | -W-<br>What I want to know . . . | -L-<br>What I learned . . . |
|---|---|---|
|  |  |  |

Name: _____    Class: _____

## FIVE W'S AND HOW

| WHO? | |
|---|---|
| WHAT? | |
| WHERE? | |
| WHEN? | |
| WHY? | |
| HOW? | |

## JOURNEY THROUGH THE FREEDOM WRITERS DIARY

On the Timeline visual graphic, students will select their favorite journal entry from each semester of *The Freedom Writers Diary*. The visual graphic contains eight journals, and in the space provided, have your students write down the diary number, the page, and any relevant facts that pertain to each entry. By choosing eight different entries in the book, students will review their journey through the entire text.

Next, in their journals, have students describe how each of these entries affected them. What about the story did they find especially moving or meaningful? In addition, students should be prepared to discuss one of the eight entries they selected with the rest of the class. The discussion will serve as an opportunity to share reading experiences and interpretations, thus enriching the class review of *The Freedom Writers Diary*.

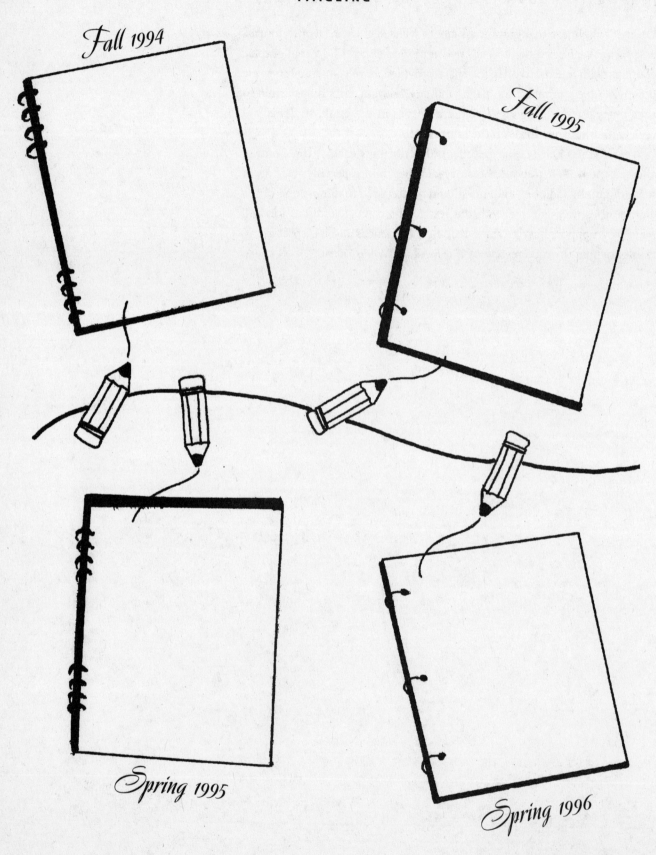

Fall 1994

Fall 1995

Spring 1995

Spring 1996

Fall 1996

Fall 1997

Spring 1997

Spring 1998

# MAGAZINE

## OBJECTIVE

The Magazine project is a culminating assignment that bridges the Engage and Enlighten activities. In groups, students will integrate past work with new work and then "publish" these compilations as magazines, making copies for the rest of the students in the class. Students may also wish to circulate the magazines to their families and to the other students in their grade. The required pieces of writing include genres taught in the Enlighten section of the unit: Personal Narrative (Diary Entries and Interviews), Responses to Literature (Advice Column), Persuasive Writing (Letter Writing), and Expository Writing (Feature Stories).

## BACKSTORY FROM ROOM 203

This assignment encourages collaborative groups, promotes inclusion, showcases students' creativity, taps into their artistic ability, and serves as an authentic way to assess their knowledge and comprehension of *The Freedom Writers Diary*. As they work on this activity, students will review—and be impressed by—all the writing they have completed for this unit.

## MS. G'S TIPS

At this stage, your students are likely to be familiar with one another's strengths as writers, peer editors, organizers, artists, techies, and so on, which results in a more efficient distribution of tasks among group members. This is a good moment to think back to those early Engage Your Students exercises and feel good about establishing trust and community in your classroom.

## WHAT YOU'LL NEED

- Magazine Checklist worksheets
- Sample magazines
- Pens, pencils, and paper
- Student writing portfolios
- Computer

## PROCESS

**Step 1:** Create groups of five to six students, seeking a balanced combination so that there will not be major discrepancies in the work each group produces.

**Step 2:** Provide the groups with several sample magazines and the Checklist worksheets. Students will work together brainstorming ideas of what they will include in their magazines. The Checklist worksheets can be used for taking notes.

**Step 3:** Students will also go over their writing portfolios together and use their Checklists to keep track of writing requirements and which pieces they decide to include. Groups may choose from work created earlier in the unit and/or write new pieces for their magazines. Some students may opt to combine ideas or elements from one another's previously written assignments and rewrite them into a single piece.

**Step 4:** Leave time for peer editing within and among groups.

**Step 5:** The final product should be word processed into a magazine format that can be shared with other classmates. Students will need to make decisions about their magazine's page layouts, color schemes, and overall appearance.

**Step 6:** Groups will present their magazines to the rest of the class and talk about where else they'd like to circulate their work.

## WORKSHEET INSTRUCTIONS

Students will use their Checklists to brainstorm about ideas for their magazines, and to keep track of writing requirements and which pieces they decide to include.

## ASSESSMENT

The magazine project reflects an array of assignments and activities completed by students throughout the Engage and Enlighten sections of the *Teacher's Guide*. The contributions of students who made a serious commitment to the unit will really stand out at this stage.

## TAKING IT FURTHER

The magazines can be used as a starting point for Empower activities, which focus on building bridges with the larger community. For example, for additional articles, students can interview possible guest speakers or report on organizations in need of volunteers. When completed, the magazines can be shared with these interview subjects as well as with potential mentors or sponsors for the class.

### Freedom Writer Feedback

"What I learned from Ms. G's class is that my tendency to procrastinate can be kept on a short leash as long as I am allowed to speak my mind and write from my heart."

### *The Freedom Writers Diary* Quotation

"*Peter Maass's article about Bosnia that we read today in Vanity Fair was like a gun that triggered the lost memory in my mind. . . . The mere fact that the story revived the lost memory within my mind gave me goose bumps.*" —Diary #39

### Teacher Talk

"It was late in the school year when we did our magazines and I let my students get really creative (go crazy?) with their imaginations. I was amazed at how much new writing my students were willing to do at this point in the term, but the truth is they appreciated that I trusted them to work independently."

NCTE Standards: 1, 2, 3, 4, 5, 6, 7, 8, 9, 10, 11, 12

## MAGAZINE CHECKLIST

**Required**

\_\_\_\_ Cover

\_\_\_\_ About the authors/contributors/editors

\_\_\_\_ Table of contents

\_\_\_\_ Letter to the editor

\_\_\_\_ Advice column

\_\_\_\_ Interview (possibly with potential guest speaker)

\_\_\_\_ Feature story (possibly about a local organization in need of volunteers)

**Optional**

Book review

Movie review

Food or travel review (possibly based on a diary entry)

Poem or song

Q & A interview (with someone significant in the community)

Crossword puzzle

# CLASS BOOK

## OBJECTIVE

Following in the footsteps of *The Freedom Writers Diary*, students will create a Class Book that contains their own journal entries. Once their stories have been submitted, the class will edit each other's work. When the editing has been completed to everyone's satisfaction, the stories will be bound into a book. Teenagers tend to feel so alone with their problems. The collaborative editing process fosters trust and tolerance as students discover some of their own struggles reflected in the lives of their peers.

## BACKSTORY FROM ROOM 203

Putting together a Class Book was the highlight of the Freedom Writers' experience. It is an exciting activity that truly unites the class in a common goal, cultivating community both on the page and in the classroom. Students will want their stories to be as polished as possible, so try to build in plenty of time for the editing process (Step 4). I find that student accountability is much higher when they realize that everyone's participation is crucial. This purpose-driven assignment helps motivate reluctant writers and turn them into published authors.

## MS. G'S TIPS

There is a hurdle here: If your students do not have access to computers, you may need to do the work of typing each story into a computer yourself to help protect their anonymity. Then you will be able to print out the stories and circulate them among the students for editing. Depending on the comfort level, the Class Book can contain either named or anonymous (numbered) diary entries.

## WHAT YOU'LL NEED

- Journals
- Pens or colored pencils with erasers
- Computers
- Fishbowl visual graphic

## PROCESS

**Step 1:** Establish guidelines for the Class Book. Decide whether each entry will be named or anonymous (numbered). You may use the honor code included in the Honor Code (see p. 72) that will establish the rules for this project.

**Step 2:** Have students choose a favorite piece of their own writing for the project. They should type their stories (double-spaced) and submit them to the teacher. If the class has chosen anonymous entries, erase the students' names and number each story before making photocopies for the editing session.

**Step 3:** Make copies of typed stories and distribute to the class randomly, making sure not to give students their own work. Keep clean copies of the original for the student's portfolio.

**Step 4:** Brainstorm with students about the qualities of excellent writing and list the elements on the board:

- "Hook" readers with the first sentence
- Use active verbs and sensory descriptions
- Use "showing-not-telling" sentences
- Develop a main idea or theme
- Organize paragraphs in a logical sequence
- Eliminate wordiness
- Check for proper grammar, spelling, and punctuation

**Step 5:** Using the list on the board as a guideline, students will now edit one another's work (new pens or brightly colored pencils make it more fun). Some students feel more confident making changes when working in pairs. If editors don't understand some aspect of the piece, they may also write questions in the margins. But be sure to emphasize that all feedback should be positive and constructive.

**Step 6:** After peer editing, return stories to the authors (continuing to protect anonymity). Authors should then revise their work and resubmit papers to the teacher. If possible, organize at least one more round of revisions, assigning new editors to papers.

**Step 7:** Photocopy final drafts of each piece and organize a class reading aloud. Decide who should read the stories (some teachers prefer to do all the reading themselves).

**Step 8:** Student must next decide how to organize their collective work (by topic? chronologically?) and come up with a title, a title page, and a table of contents. They should also explore options for binding their book (local copy center? desktop publishing?).

**Step 9:** Bind the book and make copies for the entire class.

## VISUAL GRAPHIC INSTRUCTIONS

Once the writing process is over and the piece has been made public, authors no longer control their words. The finished product hangs there, like a fish in a bowl, to be looked at, interpreted, and one hopes admired by readers. Explain this analogy to your students. Inside their fishbowls, students should jot down any uncomfortable thoughts or feelings they have about their story being exposed to the eyes of other people. (Sketches are also okay.) Now, outside the bowl, have your students write down the positive comments and reactions their stories deserve.

## ASSESSMENT

The Class Book is an achievement in authentic assessment: The end product reflects a series of writing and editing tasks in which every student has participated.

## TAKING IT FURTHER

As "self-published" authors, your students may wish to host a book reading at a local bookstore or library to share their text with their family and community. Invite the local paper to this literary celebration!

**Freedom Writer Feedback**

"I remember when Ms. G gave us the assignment to create a class book. As we got deeper into creating it, the more excited I grew knowing that I was following in the footsteps of Anne and Zlata."

**The Freedom Writers Diary Quotation**

"*For our book to work, we have to work as a team. There can't be one star athlete and 149 benchwarmers. Ms. G can coach us, but she can't play for us. Just like the saying, 'You can lead a horse to water, but you can't make it drink.'" —Diary #122*

**Teacher Talk**

"After reading the book aloud in class, I walked down our hall and kids ran up to me and handed me papers, saying, 'Here—I wrote this for our book.' Students who had never engaged in class suddenly had a story to share. They began to spend lunch and free time in the computer lab writing new diary entries. They worked on their writing and grammar skills, asking my favorite question: 'How do I make it sound better?' Some of them even ended up in conversations with their parents, sparked by their journal entries, in which parents got some much-needed insight to their child's feelings and life."

NCTE Standards: 1, 2, 3, 4, 5, 6, 9, 11, 12

Name: _____ Class: _____

## CHANGE POEM

**Directions:** Fill in the blanks below to complete this original poem. Think about all the students you came to know through reading *The Freedom Writers Diary*. Keep in mind all of the unique things you have learned about yourself. Share your poem with the class in your own way, with your own style.

### CHANGE

I was _____.
                                 (a description of who you were)

I remember _____.
                                 (describe a sad memory from your past)

I heard _____.
                                 (something you wish you had not heard)

I saw _____.
                                 (something you wish you had not seen)

I worried _____.
                                 (something that troubled you)

I thought _____.
                                 (a description of where your life was headed)

But, I want to change.

I am _____.
                                 (an accurate characteristic of who you are)

I think _____.
                                 (how you perceive the world)

I need _____.
                                 (a goal you wish to fulfill)

I try _____.
                                 (something that will help you improve yourself)

I feel _____.
                                 (describe an emotion)

I forgive _____.
                                 (someone or something that caused you pain)

Now I can change.

I will _____.
                                 (a positive prediction of who you will be)

I choose _____.
                                 (something you want to do differently)

I dream _____.
                                 (something you dare to dream about)

I hope _____.
                                 (something positive you strive for)

I predict _____.
                                 (how you see yourself in the future)

I know _____.
                                 (a description of your future self)

I will change.

# FREEDOM WRITERS
# FILM ACTIVITIES

## TEACHING FILM IN THE CLASSROOM

*Freedom Writers,* written and directed by Richard LaGravenese, provides a wonderful opportunity for supplementing your students' study of *The Freedom Writers Diary.* By incorporating the film into your lesson plans, you will also fulfill the NCTE standard that students should read "nonprint texts" in order to develop a deeper understanding of culture, society, humanity, and themselves. The question is, why learn to read a nonprint text, such as a film?

Students today are immersed in images, from Internet Web sites like YouTube and MySpace, to computer games, television, movies, and music videos. All of the activities in this section will help students evolve from passive watchers of entertainment into active and empowered readers of visual culture.

In some respects, reading a film isn't all that different from reading novels or plays. Students need to understand plot and character, identify and interpret themes, and think critically about the story's cultural perspective on society and humanity. The key difference is that, instead of studying words on the page, students analyze how a film's visual techniques—its visual "language"—work to create plot, character, theme, and cultural meanings.

You will find that it is a big leap for your students to think about a film as constructing a story with images and sound, not simply showing us a story (as if through a window). We recommend the following approach: First, show a scene normally, then show it again without volume while counting the shots, and finally show the scene yet again, freezing (pausing) on each shot. This will allow your students time to become aware of the visual elements a shot contains and how these elements contribute to the meaning of the scene.

Finally, the activities in this part of the *Teacher's Guide* were developed after the release of the Paramount Pictures film in January 2007, in consultation with Dr. Sabrina Barton, a professor of English and Film, and in workshops with the Freedom Writer Teachers. Thus, the lesson plan format differs from the other Enlighten activities in the following ways:

- Vocabulary is listed first, instead of within the individual activities.
- Substituting for "Backstory from Room 203" is a section called "Behind the Scenes."
- There is no sidebar featuring Freedom Writer Feedback, *The Freedom Writer Diary* Quotations, or Teacher Talk.

## FILM VOCABULARY

The following terms will help you identify film techniques when you analyze scenes from *Freedom Writers*. We have included definitions of these words and an activity to reinforce comprehension. The vocabulary below has been organized into five main categories: Cinematography, Editing, Narrative, Visual Content, and Sound.

### Cinematography

Refers to everything the camera does as it films the story. When you analyze a shot, try to figure out where the camera is in relation to what it is filming. Important terms associated with cinematography include:

- **Camera distance:** How close or far the camera is from the subject matter or action it is filming.
- **Close-up shot:** The camera shows only a small part of the subject, such as a person's head or hand.
- **Medium shot:** The camera shows a larger portion of its subject, such as a human figure from the waist up.
- **Long shot:** The camera moves back to show a subject and its surrounding setting.
- **Camera angle:** The position from which the camera shoots the subject matter or action.
- **High-angle shot:** The camera is located above the subject or action, filming at a downward slant.
- **Level shot:** The camera is looking straight ahead at the subject.
- **Low-angle shot:** The camera is located below the action, filming at an upward slant.
- **Point-of-view shot:** The camera films from the perspective of a character looking at the action, creating the illusion that we are looking through the character's eyes.

### Editing

Refers to how the shots of a film are arranged in a particular order, usually to tell a story and create an artistic effect. Important terms associated with editing include:

- **Shot:** An unbroken stretch of film with no edits; shots can last anywhere from a fraction of a second to many minutes.
- **Cut:** The instantaneous "break" (or edit) that separates one shot from the next.
- **Dissolve:** One shot overlaps (or is superimposed with) the next, indicating that some time has passed.
- **Fade:** The screen darkens to black between shots, indicating that quite a bit of time has passed.

- **Reaction Shot:** The camera cuts to a character reacting to something that has just happened onscreen.

### Narrative

Refers to the film's story and how it is presented to the audience. Usually directors try to present the film's narrative as clearly as possible, but sometimes narratives will be presented out of order or even backward. Important terms associated with narrative include:

- **Scene:** A part of the plot that happens in a single time and place, usually with the same characters.
- **Screenplay:** An original film script, which includes the narrative, setting, characters, dialogue, and some camera directions.
- **Adapted screenplay:** A script based on a previous work, such as a novel or story.
- **Flashback:** When the narrative jumps back in time to show us an earlier scene, often indicated by an editing technique such as a dissolve.
- **Foreshadowing:** When a narrative hints about a plot development that will come later in the film.

### Visual Content

Refers to all the elements that fill the space of a shot, including actors, costumes, setting, and props. Important terms associated with visual content include:

- **Frame:** The four edges of a shot (like the edges of a picture frame) that contain the visual elements.
- **Lighting:** Where the lights are placed, their brightness or softness, and the use of shadows.

### Sound

Refers to the film's use of music, dialogue, noises, and sound effects. Some important terms associated with sound:

- **Voice-over:** The voice of an unseen narrator or character, or the voice of a character who is onscreen but not seen speaking.
- **Film score:** Music written to accompany a film's story and images, often used to heighten emotion; a soundtrack may also include popular songs.

Name: _____ Class: _____

**FILM VOCABULARY**

**Directions:** Pretend that you are a director making the *Freedom Writers* movie. There are thirty terms total, which are broken into three sections. Within each screened box, match the appropriate film term with the statement that best expresses its meaning.

| I. | Camera angle | Close-up shot | Film score | Lighting | Frame |
|---|---|---|---|---|---|
| | Point-of-view shot | High-angle shot | Dissolve | Narrative | Cut |

1. I want the audience to feel like they are looking through the eyes of the Freedom Writers when they enter Wilson High School on the first day of school.

   _____

2. I want the camera high up and looking at a downward slant on the quad at Wilson High School.

   _____

3. I want the shot to contain the students of Room 203 on all four sides, like a painting.

   _____

4. I want to go instantly from the shot of Ms. G standing at the chalkboard, to the shot of her students sitting in the back row of the classroom.

   _____

5. I want to tell the story of this gritty book, *The Freedom Writers Diary,* as realistically as possible.

   _____

6. During the last scene of the movie, I want to use music that will make the audience cry and feel inspired.

   _____

7. I want the camera to shift from a downward slant, to an upward slant as Ms. G grabs the racial caricature from her student.

   _____

8. As the Freedom Writers approach the Washington Monument in Washington, D.C., I want to alternate between bright scenes and shadowy scenes to build suspense.

   _____

9. I will overlap one shot with the next to show time passing when the Freedom Writers move from their freshman year to their sophomore year.

   _____

10. Up on the screen, the audience will see Ms. G reading a student's journal.

    _____

| II. | Fade | Screenplay | Medium shot | Cinematography | Sound |
|---|---|---|---|---|---|
| | Shot | Voice-over | Foreshadowing | Adapted screenplay | Camera distance |

11. I want to give the audience subtle clues that the Freedom Writers will graduate from high school.

    _____

12. The Freedom Writer will sit on the witness stand silently as we hear her inner thoughts about ratting on her homeboy.

    _____

13. I am going to figure out everything the camera should shoot during the riot scene that broke out on the quad.

14. I want to write a script about the lives of teenagers in high school.

_____

15. I can't decide if the camera should be near or far when the Freedom Writers receive their high school diplomas.

_____

16. After the screen fades to black, the Freedom Writer will see the eviction notice on his door.

_____

17. I'm going to write a script based on a powerful book, *The Freedom Writers Diary*.

_____

18. I am going to film the entire Toast for Change in one unbroken stretch of film.

_____

19. I'm going to frame Miep Gies from the waist up during her speech about heroes.

_____

20. I want to hear a burst of cheers, clapping, and music when the Freedom Writers win the Spirit of Anne Frank Award.

_____

| III. | Level shot | Flashback | Low-angle shot | Editing | Reaction shot |
| | Long shot | Director | Visual content | Setting | Scene |

21. When the Freedom Writer attends the funeral of his friend who died in "an undeclared war," the shot should be full of dark elements, such as the setting, clothing, and lighting.

_____

22. After someone spots a swastika in Washington, D.C., I want to cut to the faces of each Freedom Writer.

_____

23. During this segment of the film, I want to capture the Freedom Writers' field trip to the Museum of Tolerance.

_____

24. I want to put the camera near the ground and film at an upward slant the hotel where the Freedom Writers stayed in Times Square.

_____

25. On the studio lot, I want to build a replica of Room 203, which served as a safe haven for Ms. G's students.

_____

26. After Renee Firestone, a Holocaust survivor, cries telling her story, the film will cut back to scenes from her experience in Auschwitz.

_____

27. I am in charge of everything from shot design to coaching the actors who will bring the Freedom Writers story to life.

_____

28. I want the camera looking straight at Ms. G's face while she tells her students that Zlata Filipovic is coming to visit.

_____

29. I will sequence the shots in a way that builds excitement as the audience sees John Tu help the Freedom Writers from year to year.

_____

30. I want this shot to show all the students and their classroom exchanging meaningful glances at one another as they play the Line Game.

_____

## FILM VOCABULARY KEY

1. Point-of-view shot
2. High-angle shot
3. Frame
4. Cut
5. Narrative
6. Film score
7. Camera angle
8. Lighting
9. Dissolve
10. Close-up shot

11. Foreshadowing
12. Voice-over
13. Cinematography
14. Screenplay
15. Camera distance
16. Fade
17. Adapted screenplay
18. Shot
19. Medium shot
20. Sound

21. Visual content
22. Reaction shot
23. Scene
24. Low-angle shot
25. Setting
26. Flashback
27. Director
28. Level Shot
29. Editing
30. Long shot

# VIEWING FREEDOM WRITERS

## OBJECTIVE

This activity will give your students an opportunity to voice their opinions and express their feelings about the Freedom Writers film before going in-depth with specific scenes.

## BEHIND THE SCENES

Whenever I show a video, I make sure to include an activity that elicits active viewing and critical thinking from the students. The first time the Freedom Writers and I saw the film, it was a surreal experience for us.

## MS. G'S TIPS

Distribute the Filmstrip visual graphic before the screening as a reminder to your students to pay close attention while viewing *Freedom Writers*.

## WHAT YOU'LL NEED

- DVD of *Freedom Writers*
- TV and DVD player
- Filmstrip visual graphic (see p. 60)

## PROCESS

**Step 1:** Pass out the Filmstrip visual graphic. Explain to students that there are nine boxes (or "shots") for them to fill in with details from the story. Details might include information about the students, the class, the teacher, the field trips; students can also jot down questions about some aspect of the film for discussion afterward.

**Step 2:** For the best viewing experience, screen *Freedom Writers* in its entirety (if possible). When the video is over, allow time for the students to fill in the boxes on their visual graphics.

**Step 3:** Begin the discussion with something simple, such as "Who liked this movie? What did you like about it?" With their visual graphics in front of them, all your students will have something to contribute to the conversation.

## ASSESSMENT

Ask your students to write in their journals about the experience of watching *Freedom Writers* after reading *The Freedom Writers Diary*. What did they like about the movie? What would they have done differently? What are the biggest challenges in turning a book into a movie?

## TAKING IT FURTHER

Have the class brainstorm examples of other books that have been turned into movies, such as the "Harry Potter" series. Discuss what choices the writer and the director made in order to adapt the printed page into a visual medium.

## VISUAL GRAPHIC INSTRUCTIONS

Students will fill in the nine boxes (or "shots") of their filmstrip visual graphics with story details from their viewing of *Freedom Writers*.

NCTE Standards: 1, 2, 3, 4, 6, 11, 12

# WHO AM I? CHARACTER ANALYSIS

## OBJECTIVE

*Freedom Writers* begins with "live" footage of the Los Angeles riots, establishing a real-world context of racial conflict and social-economic injustice for the story to follow. The next scene introduces the audience to Eva, one of the film's primary characters. After a shot of Eva's journal, the following fifteen shots show us her story (in a flashback). When she was a little girl, Eva's father brought her to a toy store where, instead of a Barbie, he bought her a pair of shiny red boxing gloves. For this activity, students analyze what the toy store scene reveals about Eva's character, especially Eva's self-image as a fighter for her people. Students will learn to identify and interpret film techniques while they develop familiarity with a central theme in *Freedom Writers:* the consequences of living in a world that teaches us to define one another—and ourselves—by the color of our skin.

## BEHIND THE SCENES

Although the "boxing gloves" episode does not appear in *The Freedom Writers Diary,* the story comes directly from the real life of the young woman on whom Eva's character is based.

## MS. G'S TIPS

The best way to teach your students—and yourself—how to identify and interpret film techniques is to plunge right into the scene and begin. We have provided you with a list of shot details for this scene to help you become familiar with the film techniques in the toy store scene. (Before class begins, cue the clip to make sure everything is working.) I also recommend that you copy the words of Eva's voice-over onto the board for students to refer to as they look at individual shots. You may be surprised by how much your students have to say about these shots, so be sure to leave plenty of time for discussion.

## WHAT YOU'LL NEED

- DVD of *Freedom Writers*
- TV and DVD player (with remote control, if possible)
- Paper and pens or pencils
- Film Vocabulary handout (refer to pp. 155–57)
- Filmstrip visual graphic (refer to p. 60)

---

- Who Am I? visual graphic (refer to p. 169)
- Journals

## PROCESS

**Step 1:** Explain to students that their job is to analyze how the film introduces Eva's character. What does this scene express about who Eva is and how she sees herself? How does this scene foreshadow the conflicts Eva will face when she is an adolescent?

**Step 2:** Show your students the scene of Eva and her father in the toy store, from the shot of Eva's journal (shot 1) to the shot of her father smiling and proudly holding Eva's gloved hands (shot 16). The first time, show the scene with sound and make sure everyone understands the plot. Explain to your students that the shot of Eva's journal introduces a flashback, a scene that takes the story back to an earlier time. Eva is therefore the narrator of the scene: Her point of view is communicated by the voice-over and through what we see on the screen.

**Step 3:** Now show the same scene with the volume turned off. Ask students what the difference was. They will probably report that, when not pulled into the story by the voice-over and dialogue, they were better able to notice visual details. Run the scene without the volume once more, and this time have your students count the number of shots out loud (they should count sixteen).

**Step 4:** Explain to your students that now you will show the scene one shot at a time, freeze-framing (pausing) on each one, as the students fill out their Filmstrip visual graphic. For each shot, students should jot notes or sketch visual elements that help to introduce Eva's character. Stop after six shots and discuss what your students have come up with so far. There should be some lively discussion about the contrast between the Barbie doll and the Aztec Princess doll.

**Step 5:** Now have your students complete their Filmstrip graphics and resume discussion. Or continue as a group and discuss the rest of the shots together. Topics of discussion might include: the influence of parental love and expectations, and the symbolism of the boxing gloves.

**Step 6:** When your class has finished their analysis of the toy store scene, show them the remainder of the flashback, which takes place in three short scenes: Eva witnesses her cousin getting shot; Eva witnesses her father's arrest; Eva gets jumped into the gang (for this last scene, point out how shadowy lighting, rapid camera movements, and quick cuts capture the chaos and violence). These three scenes summarize Eva's character when we meet her in the next (present day) scene as she walks to school, saying in voice-over: "In Long Beach, it all comes down to what you look like. If you're Latino, Asian, or Black, you could get blasted anytime you walk out your door."

**Step 7:** Complete this activity by having students fill out their Who Am I? visual graphics. Ask them to think about what lessons Eva learns about her Mexican heritage, her specific family heritage, and her identity as a young girl in Long Beach, California. In what ways do these lessons teach Eva how to be strong? How do these lessons create difficulties for her later on?

## VISUAL GRAPHIC INSTRUCTIONS

For the Filmstrip graphic, students should fill each blank "shot" with notes about and/or sketches of visual elements that help to introduce Eva's character to the audience. For the Who Am I? graphic, students should write the character's name in the middle and fill in the other images with the relevant information.

## ASSESSMENT

In order to assess how well your students understand the concept of character development, have them complete an autobiographical Who Am I? visual graphic. Then have students write in their journals about a moment when, as young children, they learned who they were "supposed" to be. Ask them to consider: Who or what taught you this lesson? How has claiming that identity helped or hindered you? What expectations did you feel—and do you feel—you must live up to?

## TAKING IT FURTHER

Compare Eva's relationship with her father to Erin Gruwell's relationship with her father. How are they similar? How do they differ? You may wish to have your students fill out a Who Am I? graphic on Ms. G or other characters in the movie. Another option is to choose a popular song, book, movie, or television show (or even go to a toy store!) and analyze what "lessons" are taught to boys and girls about who they are expected to become in our society.

NCTE Standards: 1, 2, 3, 4, 5, 6, 9, 11, 12

**LIST OF SHOTS FOR WHO AM I?**

**Shot 1**    **Camera Distance:** Close-up on journal.

**Lighting:** Bright light emphasizes blank page ("tabula rasa") of self.

**Visual Content:** Eva's hand represents power to write her story (thanks to Ms. G).

**Sound:** Voice-over represents Eva's power to tell her story.

**Shot 2**    **Editing:** Dissolve (superimposition) between first and second shots signals a flashback.

**Camera Distance:** Close-up on two Barbie dolls.

**Lighting:** Bright light emphasizes blondness, paleness of complexion.

**Visual Content:** Pink color of boxes, bow, and lips emphasizes "packaged" (plastic) femininity of mainstream culture.

**Shot 3**    **Editing:** Cut (remainder of shots also joined by cuts).

**Camera Distance:** Close-up on Eva's face emphasizes contrast with Barbie dolls (Eva's darker eyes, complexion, hair appealingly real).

**Lighting:** Light on Eva, background shadowed . . . Eva lost in her own fantasy world.

**Visual Content:** Contrast between bland plastic Barbie and vitality of this young girl.

**Shot 4**    **Camera Distance:** Close-up on Barbie.

**Camera Angle:** Low-angle camera looking up from Eva's point of view (POV) emphasizes that Barbie is an elevated, out-of-reach dream.

**Visual Content:** Cool blue / white colors and nonsmiling Barbie evoke aloofness; jewels and fur reinforce idea of money and status.

**Shot 5**    **Camera Distance:** Close-up on Eva's face shows a partial smile, dreamy quality.

**Lighting:** Beam of light on Eva represents innocence, not glamour.

**Visual Content:** Contrast of Eva's simple clothes with fancy Barbie. Eva lowers eyes.

**Shot 6**    **Camera Movement:** Follows direction of Eva's eyes, lowers level (to Eva's POV).

**Camera Angle:** Level camera emphasizes accessibility of "Aztec Princess" doll.

**Camera Distance:** Close-up shows darker brown complexion of this doll.

**Visual Content:** Brightly-colored yarn vs. pastels of ethereal Barbie. Big round eyes emphasize seeing, rather than being looked at as beautiful object.

Shot 7   **Sound:** Eva's voice-over says "chosen for blood," as father calls "Eva!"

**Camera Distance:** Close-up shows Eva turning her head, as if answering call of destiny voiced by father ("chosen").

Shot 8   **Camera Movement:** Camera moves closer to Papi.

**Visual Content:** Father crouching and holding red boxing gloves, choosing Eva's path. Store setting and woman in background evoke ordinary, humble scene (contrast with the Barbie fantasy of status/wealth).

Shot 9   **Camera Distance:** Medium shot of Eva (i.e., more of her included in shot).

**Camera Angle:** Low-angle camera from father's POV. (Perhaps implies that Eva as narrator knows how her father once saw her.)

**Visual Content:** Eva reaches arm to have glove put on: signals obedience to father's wishes. Tea/cooking sets in background represent girl culture Eva was called away from.

Shot 10   **Camera Distance:** Medium close-up of Papi.

**Lighting:** Light on his face emphasizes paternal "glow" of love, hopes, expectations for daughter.

**Visual Content:** Eva now has hands of fighter, enclosed in boxing gloves; bright red color of gloves catches eye.

Shot 11   **Camera Distance:** Medium shot of Eva.

**Camera Angle:** Low-angle camera from Papi's POV.

**Visual Content:** Eva listens to father: reveals her obedience to his wishes.

Shot 12   **Camera Distance:** Medium close-up of Papi.

**Visual Content:** Father outfitting his daughter for her destiny; puts up his hands to train her.

Shot 13   **Camera Distance:** Medium shot of Eva.

**Camera Angle:** Low-angle camera from Papi's POV.

**Camera Movement:** Still camera adds impact to motion and action of Eva punching.

**Visual Content:** Eva's facial expression determined; contrast with dreamy expression as she looked at dolls.

Shot 14   **Camera Distance:** Medium shot of Papi.
**Visual Content:** Papi with hands up; emphasizes his strength and power as teacher and trainer. But image also foreshadows father/daughter conflict when Eva "fights back" against her destiny as a gang member.

Shot 15   **Camera Distance:** Medium shot of Eva.
**Visual Content:** Eva laughing: indicates joy and vitality. Papi gives Eva the strength she will need to fight for herself. At same time, the playful innocence of boxing scene sets up contrast with loss of innocence when Eva sees her cousin shot.

Shot 16   **Visual Content:** Papi holds Eva's hands/gloves: emphasizes power of his vision of daughter as a fighter.
**Lighting:** Hazy white light throughout these shots of the store . . . possibly evoking flashback?
**Editing:** Fade (screen goes dark).

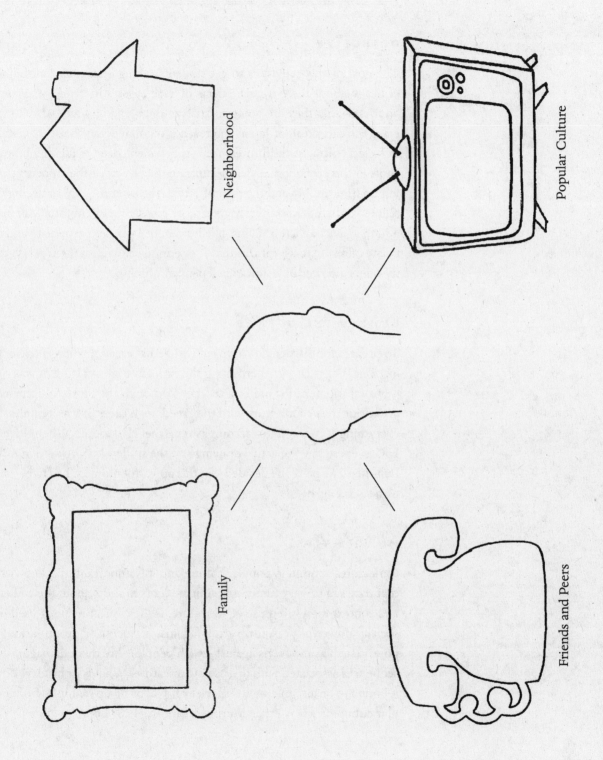

Neighborhood

Popular Culture

Family

Friends and Peers

# "DO YOU THINK THIS IS FUNNY?"

**OBJECTIVE**

The goal of this activity is to get students asking questions and thinking critically about the potential effects of race-based caricatures. Explain to your class that they are going to analyze the scene in which Ms. G intercepts the caricature of Jamal and teaches them a lesson about the damaging effects of racist caricatures. Your students will need to identify how the shots in this scene visually communicate the power of the students ganging up (the "mob") and the pain of Jamal (the "victim"). By analyzing this scene, your students will recognize how rapidly racist "humor" can unite a mob against a victim. Films, like human beings, can perpetuate and circulate offensive racist caricatures . . . or critique and reject them. This activity offers a powerful lesson in independent thinking.

**BEHIND THE SCENES**

To prepare for this activity, have your students reread my first entry in *The Freedom Writers Diary*. Intercepting the caricature of my student was such a pivotal moment for me as a teacher. Although the incident occurred a year prior to my four years with the Freedom Writers, it was a catalyst for everything I wanted to accomplish in the classroom. When Richard LaGravenese saw the actual drawing and the student it portrayed in ABC's *Primetime Live* piece, he decided that this powerful moment had to be a part of his screenplay.

**MS. G'S TIPS**

Caricatures abound in popular culture and it is important to acknowledge that they can be very funny. Ask your students to think about the audience and context for a given use of caricature: Is the caricature being used by a socially powerful person or group against a person or group lacking in power (such as the Nazis against Jewish people)? Are there damaging consequences associated with this use of caricature? What is its history? There is bound to be disagreement, especially if you bring up examples from popular culture (such as Eddie Murphy's caricatures or Borat).

**WHAT YOU'LL NEED**

- DVD of *Freedom Writers*
- TV and DVD player

• Film Vocabulary handout (refer to pp. 155–57)
• Mob vs. Victim visual graphic
• Filmstrip visual graphic, optional (refer to p. 60)
• Journal

## PROCESS

**Step 1:** First, go over the following two definitions and discuss how a caricature erases a human being's individuality.

**Individual** — The qualities, abilities, traits, or features that distinguish a specific person.

**Caricature** — A drawing or verbal description that distorts and exaggerates someone's physical/behavioral features (sometimes grotesquely so) for humorous effect, often with the intent to ridicule.

Explain to your students the difference between a caricature and a stereotype (although, of course, they are related): A stereotype means having a fixed, preconceived image of a person or persons; instead of seeing an individual, one sees a type. A caricature functions by purposeful distortion and exaggeration.

**Step 2:** Show students the caricature scene, beginning with Ms. G copying ungrammatical sentences about Odysseus onto the blackboard, and ending with Tito's comment ("But it ain't.").

**Step 3:** Now split the class into two groups: One group will analyze how the film conveys the power of the Mob, while the other analyzes how the film conveys the pain of the Victim:

1. The Power of the Mob: Why do the class members of Room 203—who normally do not agree on anything or help one another out—become complicit in passing the note with the caricature?

2. The Pain of the Victim: How does the film elicit empathy from the audience in what it feels like for Jamal to be bullied?

**Step 4:** Show the scene several times without volume. Using their Mob vs. Victim visual graphic, students in each group should keep track of visual elements related to their topic. For example, the repeated shots of hands emphasize the growing power of the bullying group; in some cases, hands aggressively recruit the next member of the mob. Shots of Jamal laughing serve to emphasize his exclusion from—and therefore vulnerability to—the shared joke.

**Step 5:** If you have time, go shot by shot (freeze-framing on each) through the last sixteen shots of the scene, starting with the student handing the note to Jamal and ending with the shot of Tito. First, though, have the two groups trade their "mob" or "victim" focus, so that the students have a chance to see the shots from the other perspective. Give your students the option of using a Filmstrip graphic to write down or sketch relevant visual elements in each shot. Notice how these shots create a contrast between the pain on Jamal's face and the reaction shots (i.e., quick cuts to the reactions) of the laughing, taunting students.

**Step 6:** Have students present their results and jot down information they learn from their classmates.

**Step 7:** Finally, show the entire scene from the beginning through the discussion of gangs and Nazis, ending with Ms. G left alone in the classroom. Make sure you have time to show the whole thing, or save the scene for the next class period.

## VISUAL GRAPHIC INSTRUCTIONS

Divide the class into two groups. Have each group use their side of Mob vs. Victim graphic to take notes on either the power of the mob or the pain of the victim.

## ASSESSMENT

In Diary #85, a Freedom Writer transcribed the famous poem, attributed to Pastor Martin Niemöller (1892–1984), written about the German intellectuals who mostly failed to stand up to the Nazis rise to power. This version is inscribed at the New England Holocaust Memorial in Boston, Massachusetts:

*They came first for the Communists,*
*and I didn't speak up because I wasn't a Communist.*
*Then they came for the Jews,*
*and I didn't speak up because I wasn't a Jew.*
*Then they came for the trade unionists,*
*and I didn't speak up because I wasn't a trade unionist.*
*Then they came for the Catholics,*
*and I didn't speak up because I was a Protestant.*
*Then they came for me,*
*and by that time no one was left to speak up.*

How does this poem apply to the scene you just studied?

## TAKING IT FURTHER

In your journal, write or draw a "Caricature of Me." How does this caricature make you feel? Now write about or draw yourself as an individual. What qualities of your selfhood have been restored? What does this exercise tell you about trying to get to know another person, especially someone from a different cultural background?

On April 4, 2007, New York City radio and TV "shock jock" Don Imus caricatured the stellar Rutgers University women's basketball team as "nappy-headed hos." After a public outcry from civil rights activists and media leaders, Imus was fired by CBS. How would you have felt if you were a member of the Rutgers women's basketball team and heard Don Imus's comment on the radio? What made his racist caricature so hurtful and damaging?

NCTE Standards: 1, 2, 3, 4, 5, 6, 9, 11, 12

# FACE TO FACE

## OBJECTIVE

From the start of *Freedom Writers* the students of Room 203 have regarded each other according to racist groupings. After standing face-to-face, sharing what it feels like to lose friends to gang violence, they can no longer dismiss one another according to superficial differences. Thus, this scene reinforces one of the key themes in both the film and book: the importance of learning to see beneath someone's mask (or persona) and recognizing that person's true self. This activity asks your students to analyze the Line Game in the film and focus on how the students move from segregation to integration. By analyzing that process on screen, students become better equipped to follow this example in their own lives.

## BEHIND THE SCENES

Richard LaGravenese visited classrooms and watched me conduct the Line Game with real students. It was such an emotional experience for him to watch that he decided to make it one of the pivotal moments in the film and to re-create the students' reactions. The unscripted emotion that he captured from the young actors mirrored that of the original Freedom Writers.

## MS. G'S TIPS

If possible, allow your students to experience their own Line Game before they watch it in the film. It is important for them to value their own experiences, rather than feel like they have to measure up to another class's Line Game.

## WHAT YOU'LL NEED

- DVD of *Freedom Writers*
- DVD player and TV
- Film Vocabulary handout (refer to pp. 155–57)
- Paper and pens or pencils for note taking
- Fill the Vase visual graphic (refer to p. 177)
- Journals

## PROCESS

**Step 1:** Show your students the Line Game scene from *Freedom Writers*. Because this is such a fluid scene and the use of sound is important, it may work best just to let the scene run through multiple times instead of going shot by shot.

**Step 2:** Ask students to look for how visual elements, such as where the camera is positioned, reveal how characters communicate and recognize one another's truths, without their having to say a word out loud. Your students will perhaps notice moments of eye contact between students who have been bitter enemies: Eva and Sindy, Jamal and Tito, and André and Jamal. They may also notice how the film score is used to heighten the emotion in this scene.

**Step 3:** Have students share what they have observed. Ask them what has changed for the students of Room 203 by the end of class?

## VISUAL GRAPHIC INSTRUCTIONS

Put your students into pairs and give each small group a Fill the Vase visual graphic. The picture, a famous optical illusion, can be viewed as either two faces looking at each other or a vase. Have your students "fill the vase" with anything and everything they have in common. You can give them ideas (birthplace? favorite foods or movies? absent parents?) or let them surprise you with what they generate on their own. After everyone is finished, go around the room and allow students to share a couple of the most surprising things they have in common.

## ASSESSMENT

This scene concludes with Ms. G handing out journals to her students. She says, "Everyone has their own story and it's important for you to tell your own story, even to yourself." Ask students to write in their journals about how her comment relates to the Line Game and to the theme of seeing—and being seen—as individuals.

## TAKING IT FURTHER

Have your students find three examples—one each from art, literature, and popular culture—that illustrate the theme of how people sometimes wear "masks" or personas to fit into a certain identity or group. Students should write a paragraph about each example, explaining how this theme is conveyed.

NCTE Standards: 1, 2, 3, 4, 5, 6, 9, 11, 12

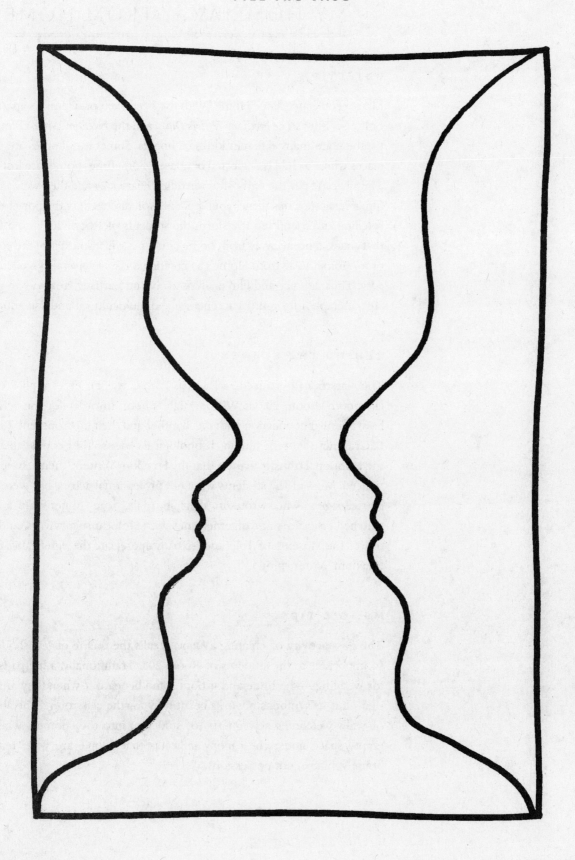

# MY HOME AWAY FROM HOME

## OBJECTIVE

Many people associate "Home" with the safe haven of a family's apartment or house. But as *The Freedom Writers Diary* and the *Freedom Writers* film show us, there are many different kinds of homes. Sometimes homes are unsafe places where a child is neglected or abused. Sometimes homes are lost when a family can't pay the rent. After rereading Diary #24 and then watching the film's version of this scene, your students will discuss how the power of storytelling and friendship transform the students of Room 203 into a family that shares a home away from home. Students will also explore the concept of a "Home Away from Home" by creating a class *huppa* (also spelled *chuppah*). Thus, literary and film analysis evolve into artistic creativity to generate a metaphor for mutual acceptance and multicultural understanding.

## BEHIND THE SCENES

The classroom portrayed in *Freedom Writers* was an exact replica of my classroom, Room 203 at Wilson High School. In order for the actors to have a similar connection with one another and their environment, Richard LaGravenese shot the film in chronological order so they could experience the emotional transformation that the Freedom Writers, themselves, experienced. Most of the students were not professional actors, but were regular teenagers who wrote in their journals, read Anne Frank's diary, watched *Schindler's List* together, met with Holocaust survivors, and even toured the Museum of Tolerance to truly appreciate the significance of the Freedom Writer spirit.

## MS. G'S TIPS

The class activity of creating a *huppa* recalls the theme of Jewish identity so important to the students of Room 203. Traditionally, a huppa is used for weddings—the bride and groom stand beneath it when they are married—but its symbolism works beautifully for the classroom: The absence of walls welcomes new guests (or students) into the "home," while the empty space under the canopy indicates that people are what makes a home valuable, not possessions.

## WHAT YOU'LL NEED

- *The Freedom Writers Diary*
- DVD of *Freedom Writers*
- TV and DVD player
- Squares of paper/card stock with holes punched in each corner
- Colored yarn
- Markers
- Art supplies for decorating huppa squares
- Journals

## PROCESS

**Step 1:** Read aloud or have your students read Diary #24, and then show the scene from the film.

**Step 2:** Have your students discuss the following questions related to editing:

- What parts of the story were left out and why? Is the meaning of the story affected? Would it have worked for the character in the film to read the entire story aloud in the scene? Why or why not?
- In the film, why was this particular story read aloud during the ceremonial Toast for Change? (Hint: To convey the immense power of friendship and acceptance, the audience bears witness to a classroom full of students transformed into a family and a home.)

**Step 3:** On squares of paper or card stock, have students create images of their personal Home Away from Home. These "homes" might range from literal homes (that of a relative, for example, or a best friend), to a special spot, to a hiding place, to an outside place. Students should be sure to include their names on their squares. Teachers may wish to create a center square representing their classroom.

**Step 4:** When finished, students will present their squares to the class and explain what makes this place their Home Away from Home. To complete the project, weave the squares together with strands of yarn for a "quilt" that can be hung on the wall.

## ASSESSMENT

For this assessment, your students will write a descriptive piece in their journals. Have students describe their Home Away from Home. What are its homelike features and what do these features symbolize or represent? For example, a blanket may symbolize warmth and coziness; a secret space may represent safety or uniqueness; a friend's home may represent acceptance; a stash of food may represent nurturing.

## TAKING IT FURTHER

During a meeting with the Board of Education in the film, Ms. G explains that the students want to stay together because "they've become a family to each other" and that Room 203 is "a kind of home." In return, the department chair argues that Ms. Gruwell's methods are hopeless because there are millions of kids in the system: In your journal, write what your response would be to this situation.

NCTE Standards: 1, 2, 3, 4, 5, 6, 9, 11, 12

# TURN ON A LIGHT

## OBJECTIVE

When Marcus calls Miep Gies his hero in *Freedom Writers*, she replies:

> I am not a hero. No. I did what I had to do because it was the
> right thing to do. That is all. We are all ordinary people. But
> even an ordinary secretary, or a housewife, or a teenager can,
> within their own small ways, turn on a small light in a dark
> room.

By telling their stories and sharing their truths—and by touching the lives
of other teenagers who are now reading their book—the students in Room
203 have turned on many lights. In order to adapt *The Freedom Writers Diary*
into a feature film, writer/director Richard LaGravenese faced a daunting
challenge: turn the experiences of a teacher and 150 students at Wilson
High School into a coherent, unified story that can be told in about two
hours. One strategy was to create composite characters by combining
related stories, while other stories were left out due to time constraints. Your
students may feel that some important stories are missing. For this activity,
each student will write a one-page synopsis of a scene based on a diary
entry, then use the Filmstrip graphic to design a series of shots that illustrate the action of their scene. Students thus have an opportunity to "turn
on a light" by returning to a favorite diary entry and creating a movie scene.

## BEHIND THE SCENES

Since there were over twenty drafts of the screenplay, Richard LaGravenese
had a difficult time deciding on which scenes to exclude. Several scenes
were filmed, such as the Freedom Writers climbing out the classroom window with Ms. G and nearly getting arrested, and the students going to see
*Schindler's List*, yet wound up on the cutting-room floor. The basis of every
scene of the film came directly from *The Freedom Writers Diary* and interviews with the Freedom Writers or me.

## MS. G'S TIPS

If students ask to use several diary entries and/or devise multiple scenes
for this activity, remind them that there is a great deal going on in a single
scene and even a single shot. They can always add more material as a
"Taking It Further" activity.

**WHAT YOU'LL NEED**

• *The Freedom Writers Diary*
• DVD of *Freedom Writers*
• Pens or pencils
• Paper
• Film Vocabulary handout (refer to pp. 155–57)
• Lightbulb visual graphic (refer to p. 94)
• Filmstrip visual graphic (refer to p. 60)

**PROCESS**

**Step 1:** Begin by having your students review the book and choose a favorite entry.

**Step 2:** On a piece of paper, students should identify the entry's main characters and list chronologically the main events of the story. From this list, students choose one scene on which to focus. This scene should be pivotal to the story, perhaps a turning point for the character.

**Step 3:** Underneath the Lightbulb on their visual graphics, students will identify the diary entry they are using. Inside the Lightbulb, students will brainstorm ideas for what to include in their scenes. When they are ready, they should write down (underneath the Lightbulb) the theme or message they wish to communicate through their scene.

**Step 4:** Students write a one- to two-page synopsis of their scene. The synopsis should describe the characters and actions, and if possible include a few sample lines of dialogue.

**Step 5:** Next students will use their Filmstrip visual graphics to sketch a sampling of shots from their scene. Stick figures are fine.

**Step 6:** To accompany the Filmstrip graphic, students should submit a numbered list that briefly summarizes the content of each shot (similar to the list of shots included with the Who Am I? activity). Remind your students to consult their Film Vocabulary handouts for help in thinking about things like where the camera will be and what the lighting will be like.

**VISUAL GRAPHIC INSTRUCTIONS**

Underneath the Lightbulb, students will identify the diary entry they are using and the theme or message they wish to communicate through their scene. Inside the Lightbulb, students should write down ideas for what the scene will include. Inside the Filmstrip graphic, students will sketch a sampling of shots from their scene.

## ASSESSMENT

Collect an anonymous compilation of your students' work—written synopses, Filmstrip graphics, and accompanying shot lists—in a portfolio. When everyone has had an opportunity to review the results, organize a class vote on which project best deserves to be turned into a short film. Discuss what made that project work so well.

## TAKING IT FURTHER

Organize the class into a film company and produce the winning script. You may not have access to a video camera, but you can still have your students edit the script, cast parts, write dialogue, make costumes, create a set, work on lights and music, and stage the winning scene. The writer of the script will serve as director, but the teacher should oversee everything as producer and run the project as democratically as possible. Ultimately, this project could reach beyond the walls of the classroom. Your students may be inspired to do some fund-raising and rent a camera, or perform the piece for peers and parents.

NCTE Standards: 1, 2, 3, 4, 5, 6, 9, 11, 12

# THAT'S A WRAP

## OBJECTIVE

The Freedom Writers and I selected some of the most frequently asked questions pertaining to the *Freedom Writers* feature film. By answering these thought-provoking questions, it is our hope that your students will have a deeper appreciation of the movie and the characters that portrayed us.

## BEHIND THE SCENES

The access the Freedom Writers and I had creating this film was unprecedented. We were treated like partners, and our input was always validated. We were involved in the screenplay, were able to make casting suggestions, and were even invited to the set.

## MS. G'S TIPS

As a perceptive teacher, I was always conscious that in lieu of reading a book I had assigned, some students would chose to watch the film's adaptation. In the case of *Freedom Writers,* I feel that this film actually enhances *The Freedom Writers Diary* experience. Teaching the film and the book in tandem allows you to juxtapose the Freedom Writers' four year experience chronicled in the book with the two-hour journey spotlighted in the film. Discussing the similarities and differences will make your students astute literary and film critics.

## WHAT YOU'LL NEED

- Journal
- Pen or pencil
- DVD player
- DVD of the movie *Freedom Writers*
- Computer with Internet access (optional)

## PROCESS

**Step 1:** Have your class read the questions generated by Freedom Writer teachers and their students and discuss the answers provided by the Freedom Writers and me.

**1. How did the Freedom Writers' story become a movie?**

On April 15, 1998, ABC's *Primetime Live* aired a segment about the

Freedom Writers. A couple years later, the producer of Primetime Live shared her ABC piece and *The Freedom Writers Diary* with the screenwriter Richard LaGravanese. He was so inspired by our story that he decided to turn it into a major motion picture.

**2. To what extent were the Freedom Writers and Ms. Gs involved with the making of the film?**

Luckily, Richard LaGravenese wanted this movie to be as accurate as possible. Much of the movie's dialogue was taken straight from the pages of *The Freedom Writers Diary,* and the majority of the scenes portrayed came directly from interviews that Richard conducted with the Freedom Writers and me. We had many opportunities to read the script and make suggestions. In fact, there were over twenty versions of the script! Also, Freedom Writers were allowed to not only be on set, but were also placed in various scenes throughout the span of the movie. It was an awesome experience for them to be involved in this process and to leave their mark on history.

**3. How was Hilary Swank chosen to play Ms. G?**

When Richard LaGravenese first asked me, "Who would you like to play you?" I immediately said "Hilary Swank." Hilary got the role two days before she won her second Academy Award for *Million Dollar Baby,* and I was elated. She was the perfect Ms. G. Besides the uncanny resemblance, Hilary mimicked my mannerisms by tucking her hair behind her ears and talking with her hands like I do.

**4. Describe the casting process of the movie?**

The director and the casting crew tried very hard to select "real" kids who had the spirit of the Freedom Writers. They interviewed thousands of teenagers, most of whom had never acted before. Surprisingly, most of the kids had similar life stories and upbringings. In addition, Richard felt it was very important to pay homage to the Holocaust survivors who touched our lives. Renee Firestone and several other survivors were honored to play themselves. Also, several Freedom Writers had cameos in the movie; from court reporters, to school security guards, to toy store employees, to waiters, etc.

**5. Was the setting of the film realistic?**

The set department created an exact replica of my classroom at Wilson High School on the Paramount Studio lot. The first time the Freedom Writers and I visited the set and walked into "Room 203," we all began to cry. It was like holding a mirror to our beloved classroom. Freedom Writers were also involved in scouting locations in their community, and many of the scenes outside of "Room 203" were filmed right in their backyard.

**Step 2:** As a class, continue to discuss additional questions your students may have about the film.

## ASSESSMENT

Using the Internet, have your students research media coverage of the production and release of *Freedom Writers*. In small groups, have them recreate an entertainment TV show (like *Entertainment Tonight* or *Extra*) and have one student be the anchor, while the others can play Ms. G or the Freedom Writers to answer their questions.

## TAKING IT FURTHER

If you were making a sequel to the movie *Freedom Writers*, what diary entries would you like to incorporate into the screenplay from *The Freedom Writers Diary* that are not currently in the movie? Have your students write a scene that includes specific journal entries and uses information directly from the text. After the scene is written, suggest that your students act out the scene to the class.

# EMPOWER YOUR STUDENTS

One of the most rewarding aspects of teaching the Freedom Writers was their interest in the subject matter beyond a test, book report, or essay. Since my students made real-life connections with the academic material, there was a desire to take the lessons directly from the classroom to the streets. It was gratifying to watch my students mature and develop from apathetic adolescents into mature young men and women who were interested in making changes in their communities. Getting to know themselves through the Engage Your Students activities and strengthening their knowledge through the Enlighten Your Students activities truly encouraged the Freedom Writers to empower themselves to change the world around them.

## BEYOND THE CLASSROOM

These activities provide strategies and tips for teachers to continue the learning process outside the confines of the classroom. To help stimulate student involvement, the following activities include visual graphics to help students brainstorm various plans of action: to encourage family and community involvement, to fundraise and garner sponsorship, bring in guest speakers, take class field trips, engage in the mentoring process and participate in community outreach programs.

## CERTIFICATE OF COMPLETION

We suggest giving your students a certificate of completion when they finish reading *The Freedom Writers Diary* and complete the meaningful and rewarding activities from the *Teacher's Guide*.

### SELF-EVALUATION

Evaluating your own achievements and being accountable for your own actions is not easy. But this introspective task can be an immensely productive way for students to reflect upon where they were at the beginning of the unit, how they progressed throughout, and where they ended up. Students who made a real commitment to change will feel gratified by all they accomplished. The personal assessment will also help teachers identify students who undervalue their own efforts and need encouragement.

# LESSON PLANS

The Empower Your Students lesson plans have been streamlined in a consistent format to ease implantation in your classroom. Each lesson plan contains the following components:

- **Objective:** Describes the overall goal and tasks of the activity.
- **Backstory from Room 203:** Provides the context and the anecdotal evidence from my classroom experience.
- **Ms. G's Tips:** A bullet list of guidelines based on my personal experience.
- **Visual Graphic Instructions:** Brief summary of how to use our student-generated visual graphics.

Each lesson in the Empower Your Students section also comes with a sidebar that contains comments from the Freedom Writers, *The Freedom Writers Diary* and the Freedom Writer Teachers.

- **Freedom Writer Feedback:** Comments from the Freedom Writers recalling the impact these lessons had on them.
- *Freedom Writers Diary* **Quotations:** A passage from the book illustrating the Freedom Writers' experience.
- **Teacher Talk:** Comments and useful advice from our Freedom Writer Teachers in the field who have implemented these activities with their students.

## DESIGN YOUR OWN BOOKMARK

**Directions:** Create your own *Freedom Writers Diary* bookmark. Find a quote from the book, write it on the book-mark, and design it however you would like. Remember to have fun and be creative. If you want, you may draw, use magazine clippings, or use words to help describe what the quote means to you. Cut out your bookmarks when you are done and tie a piece of ribbon, yarn, or string through the hole. Shown below are two examples.

"In spite of everything I still believe that people are truly good at heart."
—Anne Frank

"I feel like I finally have a purpose in this class and in life. That purpose is to make a difference and stand up for a cause."
—Diary #75

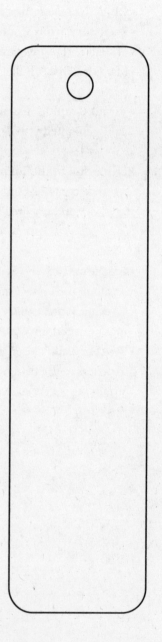

Name: _____ Class: _____

**SELF-EVALUATION**

**IMPRESSIONS OF THE FREEDOM WRITERS DIARY UNIT**

What were your thoughts when you first learned that the class was going to be doing this unit?

_____

_____

_____

_____

Now that the unit is over, what are your impressions? Have they changed? If so, how?

_____

_____

_____

_____

**INDIVIDUAL LEARNING**

What do you believe are your areas of academic strength?

_____

_____

_____

_____

In what academic areas do you believe you need to improve?

_____

_____

_____

_____

What aspects of *The Freedom Writers Diary* unit benefited you the most and how can you apply those lessons to your everyday life?

_____

_____

_____

_____

## GROUP LEARNING

How would you assess your contributions to the group activities?

_____

_____

_____

_____

## ACADEMIC GOALS

What are your short-term academic goals?

_____

_____

_____

_____

What are your long-term academic goals?

_____

_____

_____

_____

## ASSISTANCE

What kind of assistance (if any) do you need in this class? How can I, as your teacher (or a tutor, or counselor), help you?

_____

_____

_____

## GRADE

What grade do you believe you deserve for this unit, and why?

_____

_____

_____

_____

# FAMILY AND COMMUNITY INVOLVEMENT

## OBJECTIVE

Parents and guardians can be the best advocates for their children, so create opportunities for them to get involved with your class. Create a non-threatening, inclusive environment that welcomes and validates other adults.

## BACKSTORY FROM ROOM 203

Many parents were hesitant or unable to come to my first back-to-school night. In an act of desperation, I engaged one mother who seemed especially interested in her child's education. I say "especially" because she was the only parent who actually showed up at my first back-to-school night (Yes, that's right. One hundred and fifty students and only one parent). I asked her to help and she quickly became engaged by my willingness to include her. She explained to me that many parents avoid school functions or PTA meetings because of work, language barriers, and transportation difficulties. She shared that some parents may even have negative or minimal school experience, so visiting a teacher can be intimidating. Feeling empowered, she solicited the help of her friends and members in the community. My students eventually nicknamed her and the other volunteers, the "Dream Team Moms." The Dream Team Moms did all kinds of things to help, such as organizing phone trees, introducing me to their community, sharing their Rolodexes, chaperoning field trips, soliciting donations, providing goodies for our potlucks, and nurturing my students.

## MS. G'S TIPS

- Be willing to ask for help.
- Give parents meaningful jobs, not just busywork.
- Align parents' strengths, interests, and passions with ways to help your students.
- Be open to other members of the community who are willing to volunteer.
- Involve your own family. Since parents weren't lining up at my door in the beginning, I turned for help to my own family first. I invited my father to be a chaperone for some of our class field trips and he soon became a fixture in the lives of my students. They even nicknamed him "Papa G."

**Freedom Writer Feedback**

"Sharing Anne Frank's diary or attending Zlata's dinner allowed me to get my parents involved in my education one step at a time."

**Freedom Writers Diary Quotation:**

"Our day began with a breakfast by the 'Dream Team Moms.' These are the dedicated moms who have adopted our class as their kids."
—Diary #49

**Teacher Talk**

"Family involvement is the key, the missing link . . . we must make it a priority, to take the students and their families out of their environments/comfort zones enabling them to heal, develop and offer their gifts to themselves, each other and the community at large."

NCTE Standards: 2, 4, 9, 11, 12

## VISUAL GRAPHIC INSTRUCTION

The Family Portrait visual graphic is for your students to brainstorm creative ways to get family and community members involved. The frame symbolizes that "family" is what you make it and with its support, what's inside stands out more!

FAMILY PORTRAIT

# FUNDRAISING AND SPONSORSHIP

## OBJECTIVE

The Freedom Writers and I were fortunate enough to find a benefactor who was interested in supporting our cause in whatever way he could. John Tu donated money and computers and helped sponsor field trips for the students. But the most valuable contribution that he gave the Freedom Writers was in serving as a role model, mentor, and someone who cared deeply for them. I encourage you to find people who are committed to helping your students, who will in turn, inspire your students to participate in the process. By making the relationship reciprocal, your students will give as much as they receive.

## BACKSTORY FROM ROOM 203

Some of the most valuable learning experiences that I've been able to provide for my students have come from field trips, guest speakers, and other beyond-the-classroom activities. Let's face it, these things cost money. Although I picked up extra jobs to pay for these activities, I realize that it is totally unrealistic and unnecessary for a teacher to get a part-time job to pay for the full-time job. Below are some ideas for how you and your students may raise funds for your class.

## MS. G'S TIPS

- Try and find a benefactor or a private sponsor in your own community—oftentimes they will donate funds, materials or in-kind contributions.
- Find out if sponsorships or gifts can be tax-deductible for donors through your school. This provides an added incentive to give.
- Utilize your network.
- Host a multicultural concert where students perform and serve as MC's and DJ's.
- Organize a raffle where students auction off their time and skills; a car wash, house cleaning, baby sitting, painting a room, etc.
- Send sponsors samples of the effects of their donations, have your students write thank-you notes, and send photos.

## VISUAL GRAPHIC INSTRUCTIONS

Using the Piggybank visual graphic, have your students generate a list for sponsors or fundraising activities that they can do to generate funds for their supplies and future projects.

# GUEST SPEAKERS

## OBJECTIVE

Bringing guest speakers to class is one of the most effective ways to bring history and literature to life. Writing letters to Miep Gies in Amsterdam and Zlata Filipovic in Sarajevo was one of the most empowering activities my students engaged in because they felt their letters would actually be read by each of these women. When they actually agreed to come for a visit, the students became the hosts of a very memorable experience. While my students were able to meet Miep Gies and Zlata Filipovic, some of our most unforgettable visitors were right in our own backyard. I encourage you to have your students bring the outside world into their classroom by hosting a meaningful event.

## BACKSTORY FROM ROOM 203

When I did a unit on the Holocaust, I was able to find survivors and their descendants living in our community. Many Freedom Writers declared that meeting the Holocaust survivors really brought history to life for them. Other great resources are veterans of the civil rights movements and the military. Every community has a myriad of resources that often go underused. One example is the senior citizen community. I have had the best success in getting senior citizens to interact with students and serve as inspirations for them. Seniors often love to share their pasts with today's young people. The Freedom Writers and I also hosted diversity panels with community members whose backgrounds reflected the topics we were studying in class.

## MS. G'S TIPS

- Empower the students to take responsibility for these events.
- Choose student ambassadors to host each event.
- Arrange for students to decorate the room or space where the event will be held.
- Provide food.
- Encourage your students to participate and ask questions.
- Encourage the hosts to present their guest with something special (flowers, a book, a group photo).
- Take the lessons forward by sharing them with families and friends.
- Write the speaker a thank-you letter.

## VISUAL GRAPHIC INSTRUCTION

Have your students brainstorm on the Guest Speaker visual graphic about whom they would like to invite to visit, and how they can make the visit a rich classroom experience.

### Freedom Writer Feedback

"Renee Firestone actually put a face, a name, and a personal testimony to a historic event like the Holocaust. Meeting her made it real for everyone."

### *Freedom Writers Diary* Quotation

"To a fifteen-year-old, the only heroes I ever read about ran around in tight underwear and threw buildings at each other for fun. But today, that all changed. A true hero leapt off the pages of a book to pay my class a special visit. Her name is Miep Gies, and she is the lady Anne Frank wrote about in her diary. I can't believe that the woman responsible for keeping Anne Frank alive in the attic came to speak to us in person! . . . Now after meeting Miep, I can honestly say that my heroes are not just made-up characters—my hero is real." —Diary #42

### Teacher Talk

"Classroom lessons, lectures, discussions, readings, and writings come to life with a guest speaker. You can choose a big name, famous person, or it can be the police officer who worked his way through college with the goal of growing up to catch the bad guys . . . real people tell real stories, and that is what inspires our very real kids!"

NCTE Standards: 2, 4, 5, 6, 8, 9, 11, 12

# FIELD TRIPS

## OBJECTIVE

Field trips extend beyond the walls of the classroom and undoubtedly expose students to a whole new world. Field trips are a powerful way to show students that learning is not relegated to the hours between 7 A.M. and 3 P.M., book-ended by bells and buzzers. It's important for students to realize that learning is not restricted to #2 pencils and chalkboards, confined in the cluttered spaces between classroom walls. Field trips help bring learning to life. One minute they could be reading about a historical location in their book, and the next moment, they may visit it. Essentially, the world can become their classroom.

## BACKSTORY FROM ROOM 203

The most effective field trips are purpose driven and embedded in an assignment or class activity. For example, before my students attended the Museum of Tolerance, they completed a writing assignment about overcoming adversity. By the time we arrived at the museum, the students were already engaged in the learning process.

## MS. G'S TIPS

- Obtain clearance from your principal and/or administrators.
- Create a permission slip that explains any and all sensitive content of the field trip or use a district permission slip.
- Keep a running list of places of interest from students.
- Develop assignments that correspond to the field trip (such as a journal entry, history project, or poem) that your students can do before, during, and after the trip.
- Delegate additional tasks to your "Dream Team" parents and community volunteers, such as securing necessary chaperones and collecting permission slips.

## VISUAL GRAPHIC INSTRUCTION

Use the Field Trip graphic to brainstorm with your students everything it's going to take to get where you want to go. Where would they like to go and what do they need to do to get there? How does the field trip tie in with their curriculum?

---

**Freedom Writer Feedback**

"Venturing outside Room 203 to places like the Museum of Tolerance made me understand that learning isn't limited to the confines of a desk or a chalkboard."

**Freedom Writers Diary Quotation**

"God! I can't believe what I saw at the US Holocaust Museum. I tried to hold back the tears as I walked through the museum, but I couldn't help it. As I walked through the entrance . . . I couldn't stop thinking of the pain and suffering they went through." —Diary #85

**Teacher Talk**

"I used to have a student who said, 'The worst field trip is better than the best day at school.' Since doing my Freedom Writer lessons and field trips, I can say that this is not true, because the lessons and the field trips are the best of BOTH worlds . . . enhancing and deepening the learning and bonds within, creating endless possibilities for us."

NCTE Standards: 2, 4, 8, 9, 11, 12

---

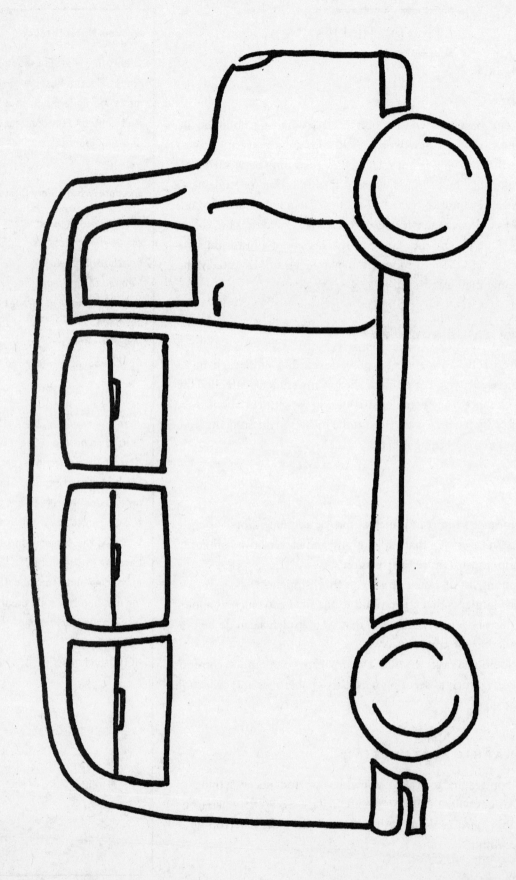

# MENTORING

## OBJECTIVE

The Freedom Writers represented a population of students who stood to benefit from positive adult role models. Many came from broken homes and endured acute hardships in their personal lives. My goal was to find members of the community who could expose them to careers and help to find direction in their lives.

## BACKSTORY FROM ROOM 203

The Freedom Writers were lucky enough to have a mentor named John Tu. Many students were surprised that John Tu chose to be a mentor, considering the fact that he didn't have a son or a daughter at their school and didn't live in their community. When asked about why he invested so much time, energy, and resources on the Freedom Writers, he told us a parable about a starfish:

> A young man walking down the beach observed an old man picking up starfish that had washed up on the shore. As he got closer, he saw the old man throwing them back into the ocean. He approached the old man and asked, "What are you doing?" The old man replied, "If I don't throw the starfish back in the water, they're going to die." "But there must be thousands of beaches and millions of starfish. You can't save them all. Don't you know you'll never make a difference?" The old man reached down and simply replied, "I'll make a difference to this one."
> —Acknowledgments, page 278

It is important to note that the mentoring relationship is reciprocal, with benefits for all participants—the mentors and the mentee. (The Freedom Writers successfully used many of the Engage activities with the children at Butler Elementary School, one of the most challenged schools in Long Beach. By saving "starfish," they, too, were making a difference.)

## MS. G'S TIPS

- Get clearance from your principal and/or administrator.
- Solicit mentors from corporations, law firms, or nonprofits in the community.

## Freedom Writer Feedback

"Being mentored by John Tu made me want to mentor kids who look like me, talk like me, and come from a place where I come from."

## *Freedom Writers Diary* Quotation

"*Today at Butler Elementary School the Freedom Writers mentored the kids. I feel so happy right now because we made a difference that will probably change some lives. These children are like lotus plants. A lotus flower doesn't grow in a swimming pool, but grows in a muddy pond. It lives in a dirty environment, but amid the muddy pond lies a beautiful flower emerging from the water. I hope with guidance, these kids can become as beautiful as the lotus flower.*"
—*Diary #107*

## Teacher Talk

"Having my students meet up with university students to help with their writing has been a wonderful experience for everyone involved. If you work anywhere near a college, you will likely find a willing group of collaborators. Service to the community is very much on the minds of college students, and they are looking for ways to help others. College students often have extra hours each week to get involved in meaningful organizations."

NCTE Standards: 2, 4, 5, 7, 11, 12

- Encourage your students to mentor younger students, by partnering with a local elementary school or bookstore.
- Partner with a local book store. (The Freedom Writers partnered with Barnes & Noble to promote literacy in their community by setting up readings from their journals and holding slam poetry performances.)

### OBJECTIVE

In the Starfish visual graphic, have your students brainstorm about different ways they can engage in the mentoring process.

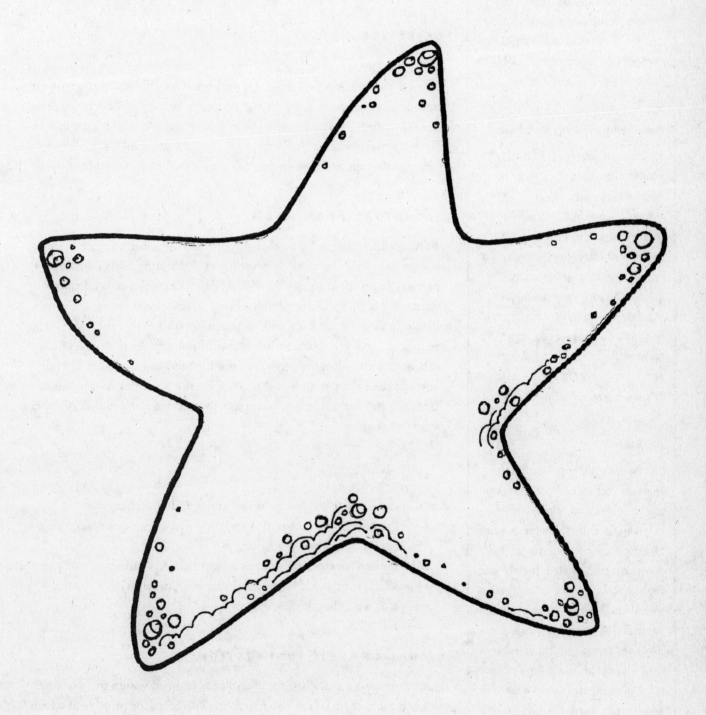

# SERVICE LEARNING PROJECTS

## OBJECTIVE

The goal of service learning is to encourage your students to give back to their communities with a sense of purpose. One of the most gratifying aspects of my experience with the Freedom Writers has been watching them become local activists and bring about positive changes in their community. I would like to challenge your students to follow in the Freedom Writers footsteps and make a positive impact in their community as well.

## BACKSTORY FROM ROOM 203

"Basketball for Bosnia" was probably the most exciting service learning project that the Freedom Writers took part in. Meeting Zlata Filipovic was the catalyst for them to raise funds and donate items to refugee camps in Bosnia. Many of the donated items came directly from their own homes. Zlata provided my students with so much inspiration that they wanted to reciprocate and give back to her war-torn country. In the process, they were able to truly live the motto of "teach one to teach another," because they educated their friends and families on the atrocities in the Balkans. Suddenly, they were able to teach others the relevance and impact of other people's struggles.

## MS. G'S TIPS

- Get clearance from your principal and/or administrators.
- Use the Internet to explore outreach opportunities in your community, such as www.servicelearning.org.
- Use the Internet to look at other nonprofits and charities to gain ideas.
- Model in examples of effective service learning projects.
- Align to what they are learning in class.

## VISUAL GRAPHIC INSTRUCTION:

Have your students brainstorm about areas of need within their community and fill in their Globe visual graphic with ideas for projects in which they can make a difference. Have your students write the Gandhi quote "You must be the change you want to see in the world" on the top of their handout to help plant a seed about what that change may actually be.

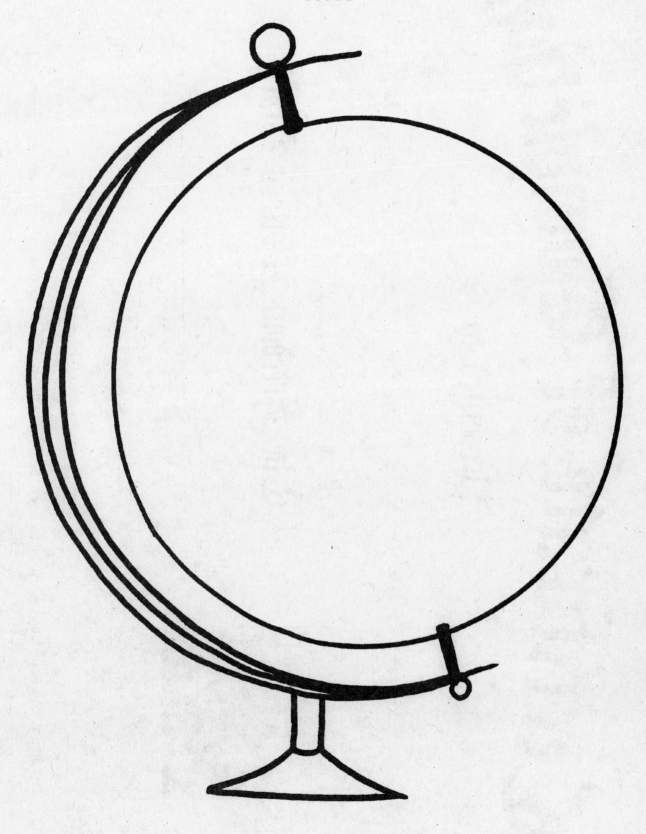

# Certificate of Completion

## Presented to

_____
(NAME)

For Completing

## The Freedom Writers Diary

on

_____
(DATE)

_____
(TEACHER)

Foreword by Zlata Filipović

THE
FREEDOM WRITERS
DIARY

How a Teacher and 150 Teens
Used Writing to Change Themselves
and the World Around Them

THE FREEDOM WRITERS
with ERIN GRUWELL

Freedom Writers Foundation • Post Office Box 41505 • Long Beach, CA 90853 • www.freedomwritersfoundation.org

# HELPFUL RESOURCES

## SOCIAL SERVICES

### Suicide

Teen Line
800-TLC-Teen
www.teenlineonline.org

### Pregnancy

Planned Parenthood
800-230-PLAN
www.plannedparenthood.org

America's Crisis Pregnancy
Helpline
888-4-OPTIONS

### AIDS/ STDs Hotlines

National Aids Hotline
English: 800-342-AIDS
Spanish: 800-344-7432

AIDS/ HIV Nightline
800-273-2437

National Sexually Transmitted
Diseases (STD) Hotline
English: 800-227-8922
Spanish: 800-344-7432

### Gay/ Lesbian

Human Rights Campaign
800-777-4723
www.hrc.org

PFLAG
202-467-8180
www.pflag.org

GLAAD
212-629-3322
www.glaad.org

### Alcohol/ Drugs

Al-Anon Meeting Information
888-4AL-ANON
www.al-anon.org

Narcotics Anonymous
www.na.org

Alcoholics Anonymous
www.aa.org

U.S. Substance Abuse Treatment
800-662-HELP

### Domestic Violence/ Child Abuse

Friends of Battered Women and
Their Children
800-603-HELP

National Domestic Violence
Hotline
800-799-SAFE
www.nduh.org

RAINN (Rape, Abuse, Incest,
National Network)
800-656-HOPE
www.rainn.org

### Eating Disorders

EDAP (Eating Disorders
Awareness and Prevention)
800-931-2237
www.edap.org

The Renfrew Center (Eating
Disorders)
800-736-3739
www.renfrew.org

Overeaters Anonymous
www.oa.org

## MENTORING GROUPS

**Boys and Girls Club of America**
404-487-5700
www.bgca.org

**Big Brothers Big Sisters**
215-567-7000
www.bbbs.org

**Children's Defense Fund**
800-233-1200
www.childrensdefense.org

**Mentor**
703-224-2200
www.mentoring.org

**National Association for the Advancement of Colored People (NAACP)**
877-NAACP-98
www.naacp.org

**National Conference for Community & Justice (NCCJ)**
718-783-0044
www.nccj.org

**National Urban League**
212-558-5300
www.nul.org

**YMCA of the USA**
800-872-9622
www.ymca.net

**YWCA of the USA**
202-467-0801
www.ywca.org

## MUSEUMS

**Museum of Tolerance**
Simon Wiesenthal Plaza
9786 West Pico Blvd.
Los Angeles, CA 90035
310-553-8403
www.museumoftolerance.com

**New York Tolerance Center**
226 East 42nd Street
New York, NY 10017
212-697-1180
www.wiesenthal.com

**United States Holocaust Memorial Museum**
100 Raoul Wallenberg Place, SW
Washington, DC 20024-2126
202-488-0400
www.ushmm.org

**Oklahoma City National Memorial**
620 N. Harvey
Oklahoma City, OK 73102
405-235-3313
888-542-HOPE
www.oklahomacitynational
memorial.org

**The King Center**
449 Auburn Avenue, NE
Atlanta, GA 30312
404-526-8900
www.thekingcenter.org

**Japanese American National Museum**
369 East First Street
Los Angeles, CA 90012
213-625-0414
www.janm.org

**National Civil Rights Museum**
450 Mulberry Street
Memphis, TN 38103
901-521-9699
www.civilrightsmuseum.org

**National Museum of the American Indian**
One Bowling Green
New York, NY 10004
212-668-6624
www.nmai.si.edu

**The Anne Frank Center, USA**
38 Crosby Street, Fifth Floor
New York, NY 10013
212-431-7993
www.annefrank.com

**The Latino Museum of History, Art and Culture**
514 South Spring Street
Los Angeles, CA 90013
213-626-7600
www.thelatinomuseum.com

## TOLERANCE GROUPS

**100 Black Men**
141 Auburn Avenue
Atlanta, GA 30303
404-688-5100
www.100blackmen-atlanta.org

**Anti-Defamation League**
P.O. Box 96226
Washington, DC 20090-6226
www.adl.org

**Facing History and Ourselves**
16 Hurd Road
Brookline, MA 02445
617-232-1595
www.facinghistory.org

**Mexican American Legal Defense Education Fund (MALDEF)**
634 S. Spring St., 11th Floor
Los Angeles, CA 90014
213-629-2512
www.maldef.org

**Southern Poverty Law Center: "Teaching Tolerance"**
400 Washington Avenue
Montgomery, AL 36104
334-956-8200
www.splcenter.org

**Tools for Tolerance at the Museum of Tolerance**
1399 South Roxbury Drive
Los Angeles, CA 90035
310-772-7620
www.toolsfortolerance.com

**USC SHOAH Foundation Institute**
650 W. 35th Street, Suite 114
Los Angeles, CA 90089
213-740-6001
www.usc.edu/vhi

## EDUCATION GROUPS

**Advancement Via Individual Determination (AVID)**
8301 East Prentice Avenue, Suite 303
Greenwood Village, CO 80111
303-741-0134
www.avidonline.org

**Ruby Payne: "Framework for Understanding Poverty"**
P.O. Box 727
Highlands, TX 77562
800-424-9484
www.ahaprocess.com

**Scholastic Inc.: "Read 180"**
175 Hillmount Road
Markham, Ontario, Canada L6C 1Z7
800-268-3860
www.scholastic.ca/education/read180/

**Teach for America**
315 West 36th Street, 6th Floor
New York, NY 10018
800-832-1230
www.teachforamerica.org

**Teacher Curriculum Institute: "History Alive"**
P.O. Box 1327
Rancho Cordova, CA 95741
800-497-6138
www.historyalive.com

## RECOMMENDED BOOK AND FILM LISTS

### Recommended Books Used in Room 203
- *The Catcher in the Rye*, J. D. Salinger
- *The Color Purple*, Alice Walker
- *The Diary of a Young Girl*, Anne Frank
- *Farewell to Manzanar*, Jeanne W. Houston and James D. Houston
- *The Joy Luck Club*, Amy Tan
- *Living Up the Street*, Gary Soto
- *Night*, Elie Wiesel
- *Romeo and Juliet*, William Shakespeare
- *The Wave*, Todd Strasser
- *Zlata's Diary: A Child's Life in Sarajevo*, Zlata Filipovic

### Recommended Films Used in Room 203
- *The Color Purple*, directed by Steven Spielberg (1985)
- *The Diary of Anne Frank*, directed by George Stevens (1959)
- *To Kill a Mockingbird*, directed by Robert Mulligan (1962)
- *The Killing Fields*, directed by Roland Joffé (1984)
- *Mississippi Burning*, directed by Alan Parker (1989)
- *The Outsiders*, directed by Francis Ford Coppola (1983)
- *Schindler's List*, directed by Steven Spielberg (1993)
- *The Shawshank Redemption*, directed by Frank Darabont (1994)
- *Twelve Angry Men*, directed by Sidney Lumet (1957)
- *The Wave*, directed by Alexander Grasshoff (1981)

### Recommended Documentaries Used in Room 203
- *Anne Frank Remembered*, directed by Jon Blair (1985)
- *Dying to Tell the Story*, directed by Kyra Thompson (1998)
- *Eyes on the Prize*, directed by Henry Hampton (1987)
- *Eye of the Storm*, directed by William Peters (1970)
- *Hoop Dreams*, directed by Steve James (1994)
- *The Last Days*, directed by James Moll (1998)
- *Lost Children of Berlin*, directed by Elizabeth McIntyre (1997)
- *One Survivor Remembers*, directed by Kay Antholis (1995)
- *Romeo and Juliet in Sarajevo*, directed by Jon Zaritsky (1994)
- *Survivors of the Shoah*, Visual History Foundation (1997)

# APPENDIX A

## THE FREEDOM WRITERS DIARY VOCABULARY LIST

The following is a list of 100 vocabulary words that are found in *The Freedom Writers Diary.*

**Absurdity** (page 39) — something that is irrational, incongruous, or illogical

**Accelerated** (page 57) — course of study that is completed in less time than usual

**Accolades** (page 109) — praise and public recognition of somebody's achievements

**Accumulating** (page 37) — gathering something together or collecting something over a period of time

**Advocate** (page 206) — to support or speak in favor of something; somebody who supports or speaks in favor of something; somebody who acts or intercedes on behalf of another

**Alibi** (page 44) — an explanation offered to justify something

**Alienate** (page 144) — to make somebody feel that he or she does not belong to or share in something

**Alleged** (page 115) — claimed to have taken place

**Amendment** (page 56) — a revision or alteration to a document or procedure

**Animosity** (page 110) — a feeling or spirit of hostility and resentment

**Apprehensive** (page 257) — worried that something bad will happen

**Assumption** (page 270) — something that is believed to be true without proof

**Audacity** (page 134) — lack of respect in somebody's behavior toward another

**Barrack** (page 40) — a building or set of buildings used as lodging for soldiers or prisoners

**Belittle** (page 58) — to cause a person to seem little or less

**Blatant** (page 60) — obvious offensive manner

**Camaraderie** (page 161) — a feeling of close friendship and trust among a particular group of people

**Caricature** (page 2) — a drawing that exaggerates somebody's physical features for humorous or satirical effect

**Circumstances** (page 84) — factors that lead up to a situation or event

**Commiserate** (page 271) — to express sympathy or sorrow

**Confines** (page 2) — the limits or borders of a space or area

**Contemplate** (page 48) — to debate or consider

**Contour** (page 38) — the outline of a figure, body, or mass

**Conventional** (page 108) — conforming to socially accepted behavior or style that lacks imagination

**Deliberately** (page 68) — done on purpose or by intention

**Delusional** (page 138) — to have a false or mistaken belief or idea about something

**Demographics** (page 2) — characteristics of human populations and population segments

**Dependable** (page 21) — able to be trusted in the way required or expected; reliable

**Depict** (page 1) — to describe or portray something

**Derogatory** (page 19) — expressing a low opinion or negative criticism

**Destiny** (page 251) — the inner purpose of a life that can be discovered and realized

**Deteriorate** (page 267) — to become or make something worse in quality, value, or strength

**Discrimination** (page 93) — unfair treatment of one person or group, usually because of prejudice about race, ethnic group, age group, religion, or gender

**Disingenuous** (page 223) — not straightforward or candid; insincere or calculating

**Doctrine** (page 246) — a rule or principle that forms the basis of a belief, theory, or policy; a body of ideas, particularly in religion, taught to people as truthful or correct

**Embellish** (page 140) — to make an account or description more interesting by exaggerating details

**Empathize** (page 83) — to understand or be sensitive to a person or situation

**Emulate** (page 261) — to try hard to equal or surpass somebody or something, especially by imitation

**Engulf** (page 257) — to overwhelm somebody or something with a great amount or number of something; to surround, cover over, and swallow up somebody or something

**Entourage** (page 81) — friends or associates

**Eradicate** (page 261) — to destroy or get rid of something completely, so that it can never recur or return

**Exhilarate** (page 258) — to cause to feel happy, refreshed, and energetic

**Expectation** (page 4) — a confident belief or strong hope that a particular event will happen

**Façade** (page 85) — false, superficial, or artificial

**Fatigued** (page 68) — extremely tired or weak

**Frantic** (page 261) — in a state in which it is impossible to keep feelings or behavior under control, usually through fear, worry, or frustration

**Ghastly** (page 94) — terrifying; horrible

**Harassed** (page 75) — persistently approached to the point of hostility

**Hereditary** (page 67) — characteristics passed to or received from family member

**Heritage** (page 247) — something, such as a way of life or traditional culture, that passes from one generation to the next in a social group

**Humane** (page 103) — having consideration for humans or animals

**Humility** (page 109) — the quality of being modest or respectful

**Hypocrisy** (page 40) — the false claim to or pretense of having admirable principles, beliefs, or feelings

**Inhibited** (page 258) — unable to behave spontaneously or express feelings openly

**Integral** (page 6) — being an essential part of something or any of the parts that make up a whole

**Internment** (page 40) — imprisonment; the confinement of somebody in a prison, concentration camp, or other place, especially during a war

**Intimidate** (page 29) — to threaten, frighten, bully

**Intrigue** (page 115) — to make somebody greatly interested or curious

**Irony** (page 39) — form of speech in which the real meaning is concealed or contradicted by the words used

**Loiter** (page 140) — to stand around without any obvious purpose

**Mayhem** (page 139) — absolute chaos or severe disruption

**Mediocre** (page 260) — adequate but not very good

**Meticulous** (page 3) — extremely careful and precise

**Misogyny** (page 125) — the hatred of women

**Muse** (page 139) — to think about something in a deep and serious or dreamy and abstracted way

**Nonchalant** (page 113) — calm and unconcerned about things

**Overwhelmed** (page 47) — overcome by strong emotions

**Perish** (page 16) — to die; to come to an end or cease to exist

**Permeating** (page 139) — entering something and spreading throughout it, so that every part of it is affected

**Perpetuating** (page 49) — a continuation; everlasting

**Persecuted** (page 92) — punished or harassed to the point of suffering

**Plight** (page 114) — a difficult or dangerous situation, especially a sad or desperate predicament

**Poignant** (page 112) — particularly penetrating and effective or relevant

**Potential** (page 46) — the capacity or ability for future development or achievement

**Predominantly** (page 254) — mainly; in the greatest number or amount

**Prestigious** (page 249) — having a distinguished reputation

**Propaganda** (page 2) — deceptive or distorted information that is systematically spread

**Prophecy** (page 80) — prediction of something to come

**Prosecution** (page 56) — to bring legal action against a person

**Regime** (page 245) — a particular government or managing group, especially one that is considered to be oppressive

**Regulate** (page 107) — to control or rule over people

**Reiterate** (page 48) — to repeat or explain again

**Reminisce** (page 108) — to talk or write about events remembered from the past

**Remorse** (page 263) — a strong feeling of guilt and regret

**Restitution** (page 26) — compensation for a loss, damage, or injury

**Segregate** (page 161) — to separate one person or group from the rest; keep things separate

**Seniority** (page 192) — a state of being older than others or higher in rank than another

**Solicit** (page 82) — to request or obtain favors

**Spontaneous** (page 165) — arising from natural impulse or inclination

**Stereotype** (page 30) — an oversimplified standardized image or idea held by one person or group of another; to categorize individuals or groups according to an oversimplified standardized image or idea

**Stigma** (page 30) — the shame or disgrace attached to something regarded as socially unacceptable

**Stipulate** (page 141) — to make a specific demand for something, usually as a condition in an agreement

**Strewn** (page 140) — scattered, especially carelessly or untidily

**Suffice** (page 113) — to be enough for somebody or something

**Surreal** (page 222) — having an oddly dreamlike quality

**Tedious** (page 210) — boring because of being long, monotonous, or repetitive

**Tradition** (page 34) — a long-established custom or belief; a body of long-established customs and beliefs viewed as a set of precedents

**Transformation** (page 251) — a complete change, usually into something with an improved appearance or usefulness

**Treacherous** (page 231) — marked by betrayal of fidelity, confidence, or trust

**Unorthodox** (page 47) — not conventional; untraditional

# APPENDIX B

## THE FREEDOM WRITERS DIARY WRITING PROMPTS AND THEMES

The following is a list of writing prompts for your students, that are designed for a variety of academic levels. We invite you to adapt them as necessary. The list also serves as a guide to the topic and theme of each diary entry.

### Entry 1: Ms. Gruwell

Ms. Gruwell is frustrated by the labels given to her students. Put yourself in her shoes. What could Ms. Gruwell have done in the first days of school to show her students that she didn't believe in those labels?

### FRESHMAN YEAR

### Diary 1: First Day of School

This student passes judgment on Ms. Gruwell and the other students in the class without waiting to get to know them first. Why do people label one another? How would you have been labeled if you'd been sitting in that classroom?

### Diary 2: Racial Segregation at School

This student describes how strictly segregated the high school quad is at lunchtime. Choose an area of your own school or community and describe how certain crowds "own" different spaces. Explain what would happen if someone from one crowd tried to join another. What would be the positive and negative consequences?

### Diary 3: Getting "Jumped"

This Freedom Writer got jumped by five other students. Why did they go after her? Why does she vow to get revenge on these five even though they are "just like" her?

### Diary 4: Race Riot on Campus

The writer of this diary fled from the scene of a fight, worried about being blamed for the actions of friends. Think of a time when you or someone you know was blamed for something for which they weren't responsible. Explain what happened and how the person reacted to the blame.

### Diary 5: Buying a Gun

This Freedom Writer describes how buying and carrying a gun provided a sense of strength and protection even though it was dangerous. Think of the troubles you face in your life. Describe what provides you strength and protection. Is it something physical or a part of your personality?

### Diary 6: Death of a Friend

The writer of this diary describes witnessing the death of a friend. Examine how this death affects the way the Freedom Writer feels about people and life. What other changes might someone experience after the loss of someone close?

### Diary 7: Gang Initiation

This writer describes getting jumped into a gang as "worth it." What have you or someone you know done that was "worth it" that someone else may not understand? Explain why it was important.

### Diary 8: Rushing a Sorority

The Freedom Writer in this diary joined a sorority because she "wanted to fit in just like every other high school freshman." How important is it for you to fit in? Have you ever done something as part of a crowd that you later felt bad about when you were alone? Why do you think fitting in is so important?

### Diary 9: Tagging

This writer states, "What goals do I aim for? I don't aim, because I don't have any goals; instead I deal with what comes." Think about yourself and your view of the future. How far do your plans extend? One day? One year? Five years? Ten? What are they, and how do you plan to achieve those goals?

### Diary 10: Proposition 187: Discrimination

This Freedom Writer chose not to take part in a school walkout, deciding to seek sanctuary in Ms. Gruwell's room instead. Describe a place or activity that provides you safety or peace when you are feeling stressed or pressured. What does it offer you that no other place or activity can?

## Diary 11: Dyslexia

The writer in this entry reveals animosity toward school and anxiety of reading aloud: "Everyone would laugh at me and call me stupid." He describes how he struggled in school and compensated by developing his abilities in baseball. What is a major challenge that you or someone you know has faced in life? What did or could you do to cope or overcome that challenge?

## Diary 12: Juvenile Hall

This student writes about getting in trouble and even spending time in Juvenile Hall. This Freedom Writer's life has since turned around. Describe a time when you got into a situation you should not have. What do you do now to attempt to stay clear of this type of trouble?

## Diary 13: The Projects

The writer explains his struggles of not having a father as he grew up and his realization that his friend also had to grow up without a father figure: "I felt sorry for him. I knew how hard it was to grow up without a father." Have you or someone close to you grown up missing a parent? Describe how this has affected you or a person close to you.

## Diary 14: Russian Roulette

In this diary entry, a group of people who are present during an accidental shooting change the crime scene and make it look like a suicide. Why did they do this? Have you or someone you know ever chosen to change a version of events rather than tell the truth?

## Diary 15: Romeo and Juliet: Gang Rivalry

This Freedom Writer considers gang rivalry: "It's stupid because I don't even remember why we are rivals. That's just the way it is." Think of a past grudge, rivalry, or problem you have had with another person. Explain the root of the problem and how you chose to solve it.

## Diary 16: Teenage Love and Running Away

In this entry, the writer describes how her parents' reactions to her boyfriend made her realize that she wasn't as deeply in love as she thought. Describe a time when someone warned you about something and you didn't listen. How did things work out? Explain how you would persuade a friend not to make the same mistake.

## Diary 17: Coping with Weight

The writer of this entry describes being fiercely picked on due to her appearance: "I heard people shouting, 'Hey Fatso!' 'You big buffalo!'" Think of a time when you or someone you know was the victim of a bully. How did you react? What advice would you give this Freedom Writer?

### Diary 18: Learning about Diversity

This student is amazed that people will let the others' differences in appearance and beliefs keep them separated. Think of a time when someone else let your appearance or background keep you from being heard. Explain how you dealt with the situation.

### Diary 19: Oklahoma Bombing

This Freedom Writer describes people who commit acts of violence by stating: "They are just like walking time bombs waiting to go off. . . ." Think of a time when you experienced yourself or someone else "going off." What happened? What were the consequences?

### Diary 20: Farewell to Manzanar: Japanese Internment Camps

In this diary, the student describes how her life compares to that of a character in a book her class is reading. Who is a character from a book, movie, TV show, or song to whom you can relate? How are you similar?

### Diary 21: Overcoming Adversity Panel

The writer of this diary entry recalls a panel discussion that showcased individuals who overcame obstacles in their lives and became successful. Think of the obstacles in your life and your own set of strengths. What strengths do you possess that will best help you to meet with similar success?

### Diary 22: John Tu: Father Figure vs. Absent Father

This Freedom Writer writes about feeling like Cinderella at the ball. She also states the thing she's missing out on the most is not the "fancy stuff" but bonding with her father. Think of the adults in your life. Describe the one to whom you feel closest. Explain the relationship.

### Diary 23: Freshman Turnaround

The student in this entry writes about choosing to ditch school and then feeling guilty for letting down her mother and Ms. Gruwell. Think of a time when you let someone down. Explain what you did or can do to change the consequences of your actions.

### SOPHOMORE YEAR

### Diary 24: Homelessness

The writer of this entry describes feeling as though he has lost everything that matters, but then finds hope in returning to Ms. G's class and his classmates. Think of a person in your life who symbolizes the same hope Ms. G and her students offered this student. Explain what that person means to you.

### Diary 25: Cystic Fibrosis

This Freedom Writer explains a portion of what life is like for someone living with a chronic illness. Through all of the complications of the illness, this student wants nothing more than to return to school and Ms. Gruwell's class. Write to explain why returning to the routine is so important to this student.

### Diary 26: Shyness

The student in this entry is desperate to avoid being noticed. Think of a time when you or someone you know wanted to blend in like this student. Describe the situation, the feelings, and the "moment." Help the reader relive the scene with you and what it felt like to want to disappear.

### Diary 27: Twelve Angry Men

This Freedom Writer whose brother has just been sentenced to go to jail for a crime he didn't commit states: "They proved that justice doesn't mean the bad guys go to jail, it just means someone pays for the crime." Do you agree or disagree with this statement? Explain why.

### Diary 28: Honors English

This student felt uncomfortable in the Distinguished Honors Program and moved to Ms. Gruwell's class. Put yourself in this Freedom Writer's shoes. Would you have stayed on "the road to the brightest of the bright" or chose to forgo it to be part of the Freedom Writers? Explain your answer.

### Diary 29: Medieval Times

In this entry, the writer describes a situation where he suffered discrimination because of the way he was dressed. Think about how other people react to your own appearance. Describe a time when you or someone you know was treated differently from others because of what you were wearing.

### Diary 30: Lesson on Tolerance

In this entry, the writer describes a ceremony Ms. Gruwell and her students held called the "Toast for Change." If you were able to have a fresh start in one part of your life, what would you change?

### Diary 31: Toast for Change

This student writes, "I was always known as the person that was going to be a druggie, or get pregnant before I turned fourteen and dropped out. Now I have the chance to prove them wrong." What expectations are put on you because of your past actions? How do you feel about this? Explain what you will do to improve those expectations.

### Diary 32: Change for the Better

The Freedom Writer in this entry talks about choosing different paths in life and acting as a role model. Think about the paths available to you in life. Which path leads you to becoming someone others could look up to? What must you do to make certain you stay on that path?

### Diary 33: Testifying in Murder Case

The writer of this diary entry describes being torn between loyalty to her people and telling the truth to save an innocent man. Think of the reasons for making either choice. Which would you have done if you were in this writer's place? How do you make difficult choices in your life?

### Diary 34: Teenage Alcoholism

In this entry, a female student describes how she seemed a "goodie goodie" on the outside, yet was really an alcoholic. She showed the world one persona and kept another to herself. Think about your own life. How is the person you show the world different from the person you keep to yourself? What could keep a person from showing the world who they truly are?

### Diary 35: Shoplifting

In this entry, the writer describes shoplifting some makeup to prove to her friends that she wasn't a "goodie two shoes." Think about peer pressure in your own life. How do other people's opinions of you shape your actions? Why is this?

### Diary 36: Anne Frank's Diary

The writer of this entry asks, "Why should I read books about people that don't look like me? People that I don't even know and that I'm not going to understand because they don't understand me!" Why is it important to read books by, listen to, and learn from people who are different from us? What might be some dangers of ignoring those people?

### Diary 37: Teen Diarists

The writer of this entry compares his/her life to Anne Frank and Zlata Filipovic and states: "My cage is my own house." Think of a time in your life when you felt trapped, without a choice. How did you cope with that situation?

### Diary 38: Zlata's Diary—Bosnia vs. L.A. Riots

In this entry, the author says that he/she has a lot in common with Zlata because "while Zlata was living through a war in Sarajevo, I was living through a different kind of war—the L.A. riots." Think about the problems and choices in your own life. Describe how other students from around the country and around the world could relate to those dilemmas and choices.

### Diary 39: Peter Maass: Article on Bosnia

This Freedom Writer finds a connection with other women through a tragic event in her life. Think of your own life or the life of someone you know. What is the potentially painful or negative experience that you could turn around and use the same way this Freedom Writer does to connect to someone who is feeling lost or alone?

### Diary 40: Zlata

The student in this entry describes joining Ms. Gruwell's class and finding a close connection with Zlata. Think of an author, actor, or musician to whom you look up. Write a letter to that person explaining the connection you feel and describing how they have affected your life.

### Diary 41: Meeting a Holocaust Survivor

In this entry, the Freedom Writer's neighborhood is compared to the world of those people trapped during the Holocaust. Think of a time when you've felt trapped or limited by your surroundings or something about yourself you could not change. Describe the situation and what you did when faced by these difficulties.

### Diary 42: The Woman Who Sheltered Anne Frank's Family

In this entry, the writer tells of a visit from Miep Gies, who tells the students, "You, my friends, are the true heroes." Come up with a definition for the word "hero" and describe how you or someone you know fits that definition.

### Diary 43: "Moment"

After meeting Miep Gies, this Freedom Writer states, "They wanted us to seize the moment. Ms. Gruwell wanted us to realize that we could change the way things were. …That's when it all became crystal clear. Anne's message of tolerance was to become our message." Think of chances and opportunities in your life. What is a moment that you have seized or could seize? What did you do to seize it?

### Diary 44: Zlata Accepts Our Invitation

This student writes about expecting Zlata to decline the Freedom Writer's invitation to visit and then being surprised when it is accepted. Think of your own experiences. Describe a time when someone or something exceeded your expectations. What did it feel like? Have you ever exceeded someone else's expectations?

### Diary 45: Dinner with Zlata

This entry describes one Freedom Writer's experience meeting Zlata Filipovic and how Ms. Gruwell promises there is more to come. Think back to the beginning of the Freedom Writers' freshman year. Describe how the students in Ms. Gruwell's class have changed since then. What was the catalyst for their change?

### Diary 46: Diverse Friendships
In this entry, the writer's father doesn't like her best friend because of her race. Think of race relations in your community. Write to explain how people of different races interact in your community.

### Diary 47: "I am a human being . . ."
The writer of this entry recounts how Zlata Filipovic was asked what her racial identity was during a presentation. Zlata's response was "I'm a human being." Describe a time when you wish you could drop your racial, cultural, or gender identity. Explain a time when you felt proud of that same identity.

### Diary 48: Terrorism
This Freedom Writer recounts how Zlata wrote about "Bosnian children becoming 'soldiers' and the soldiers becoming 'children.'" Think of your own life. Write to explain a time when you felt pressure to be more of an adult or when you saw adults behave more like children.

### Diary 49: Day of Tolerance: A Field Trip
The writer of this entry describes how negative thoughts can turn into violence. Consider examples of violence in the world today. What types of negative thoughts inspire these acts? What can you do to persuade people to release their negative thoughts?

### Diary 50: Doing Speed
The author of this entry has an addiction to drugs and states, "In some sick way I wish I could get caught so all this lying could be behind me." Why would someone wish to get caught doing something they constantly try to hide?

### Diary 51: Basketball for Bosnia: Weight
The author of this entry writes that she has "always been the oddball" and "never felt accepted" because of her weight. Have you ever felt like an "oddball" or that you didn't fit in? Can you think of a time when you might have made someone else feel that way? How would you handle it if you heard someone making fun of your sister, brother, or friend?

### Diary 52: Divorce
This Freedom Writer shares the experience of having to keep a family secret. Reflect on a time when you were responsible for keeping a secret.

What was that like for you? Did you keep the secret or share it with someone?

### Diary 53: Friends Join Class

The student in this entry shares the joy of being able to return to Ms. Gruwell's class the following year and having new friends join the class. Think of a time when you felt very lucky to have a teacher or mentor you clicked with, was able to do a project that really meant something to you, or went to a school that fit you. Describe why and how it made a difference in your life.

## JUNIOR YEAR

### Diary 54: Racist Teacher

The writer in this entry describes some of the labels that she feels are attached to the African American race. Think of positive or negative labels that have been attached to your race(s). Write to describe the ways you have accepted or ignored these labels and whether or not they've come to define the way you see yourself.

### Diary 55: A Grandmother's Death

This student ends the entry by writing, "No one really understood what I was feeling. They were so caught up in what they thought about me that they didn't really care." Reflect on a time when you felt misunderstood. Write to explain why others did not understand you. What did you or could you do to help them have a better picture of who you were?

### Diary 56: Race Riot

The writer in this entry who witnessed a boy being beaten wrote, "Even though I could have been hurt, I wish I had done something." Put yourself in this writer's shoes. Share what you would have done in a similar situation. Did you ever face a comparable choice?

### Diary 57: Grade Accountability

The writer of this entry states: "A truly self-reliant person finds his weak link and strengthens it." Everyone has unique strengths and weaknesses. Think of one of your "weak links." Plan the steps you will take to strengthen it.

### Diary 58: Suicide

This Freedom Writer shares a family battle with clinical depression and suicidal thoughts. What moves many teenagers to think about suicide? How can they be helped? What would you say to someone who showed signs of suicide?

### Diary 59: Running Away

The writer in this entry states, "I just need to get away." Describe a time when you wanted to get away from your life but didn't or couldn't. What held you back? How would your actions affect your friends, family, teachers, etc.?

### Diary 60: Getting a Job

Some people would say that this Freedom Writer was "lucky" by landing a job with John Tu. However, what had the Freedom Writer done leading up to that moment that influenced John Tu's job offer? Describe a time in your life when you worked to earn something you wanted. How did it feel to reach that goal?

### Diary 61: Misogyny

The writer of this entry describes how double standards exist and how girls are treated differently from boys just because they are girls. Describe a time when you felt you were treated differently just because of your gender. What influences how women and men are treated in society? What expectations do you have for men and women?

### Diary 62: Molestation

The writer of this entry recalls how she was molested by a family member she trusted. Describe a time when you were betrayed by somebody you trusted. What was your reaction?

### Diary 63: Boyfriend Abuse

This Freedom Writer describes physical abuse at the hands of her boyfriend. She writes, "Unfortunately, we gave each other what we were both missing." There are many theories as to why women stay with men who mistreat them physically, emotionally, or both. Why do you think people who are being abused stay with the abuser? What can be done to stop and prevent abusive situations?

### Diary 64: Domestic Violence

The writer of this entry feels the need to act as protector to an abused mother. Think of times in your life when you needed help or protection. Who was there to offer you safety? Describe a time when you were called upon to protect someone else.

### Diary 65: Child Abuse

This Freedom Writer describes feeling liberated after purging the emotions that have been bottled up as a result of continuing domestic abuse. Consider your own life. To whom or what do you turn when you need to unload the stresses you are facing? Describe the feeling you have afterward.

### Diary 66: Death of a Brother

In sharing the loss of a brother, this Freedom Writer states, "No matter how bad the situation got, and how many times the doctors told me he was going to die, it just didn't sink in." It's very difficult to deal with a friend's or loved one's serious illness. How would you handle a similar situation? What advice or questions would you have for someone who is currently going through a similar situation?

### Diary 67: Anne Frank's Friends Visit

This student writes, "My mom always says, 'Silence will get you nowhere in life.'" Think of opportunities you've had in your life to speak up for yourself or someone you know. Have you spoken up or remained silent? What inspired your choice?

### Diary 68: Masking Fears

The Freedom Writer in this entry is new to Ms. Gruwell's class and nervous about opening up. Compare the situation to your own life. When you have a new experience or meet new people, do you open yourself up or hide your true self? What might be possible reasons for either decision?

### Diary 69: Living in the Projects

This student writes, "It's easier to pretend I don't live where I live or see what I see." We all have a need to escape our reality from time to time. Describe a time when you had to escape the reality of your life.

### Diary 70: Dyslexia

The writer of this entry explains how technology made it easier to cope with a learning disability. Think of a time when something or someone taught you something that made your schoolwork or life situation easier to deal with. How can you pass those tools on to others with similar problems?

### Diary 71: Letter from Miep

Miep Gies inspires this Freedom Writer to write the story of a friend who was shot and killed. Think of the people who have affected your life. Write the story of a person who has had an impact on you and deserves to live on in writing.

### Diary 72: Student Editing

This student writes about dealing with a painful truth from her past. Consider your own life. What would you do if given the chance to write your own truth and share it with others? What would inspire you to share your truth? What reservations would you have about making it public?

### Diary 73: Abortion

A dark secret returns to haunt this Freedom Writer. Think about choices you have made in the past. Which choices would you change if given the chance? How would that affect your life today?

### Diary 74: Catalysts for Change

In this entry, the writer quotes his/her mother having said, "One person can make a difference that can change the whole world." Think of a famous person or someone you know who has changed or is in the process of changing the world and describe their achievement.

### Diary 75: Freedom Riders

This Freedom Writer found a sense of purpose in learning about the Freedom Riders, stating, "That purpose is to make a difference and stand up for a cause." Reflect on the world around you. What causes could use your help? Which do you believe in strongly? What will you do to help further those causes?

### Diary 76: An American Diary . . . Voices from an Undeclared War

This student writes about how Ms. Gruwell and the other Freedom Writers put in extra hours and effort to tell their stories. It was not enough for the Freedom Writers to have written their stories; they wanted to share them with someone in power. Think about the stories you have to tell. What are you willing to do to make sure they are heard? Who would benefit most from hearing them?

### Diary 77: Fund-raiser Concert

In this entry, the writer talks about how the Freedom Writers held a fund-raiser called Echoes of the Soul to raise money for their trip to Washington, D.C. Think of your own heritage and culture. Write and describe what you would share of your culture to contribute to an event like Echoes of the Soul.

### Diary 78: Freedom Writer Poem

In this entry, the author describes himself as "an innocent boy now twelve years of age [who] finds himself locked up in a human-sized cage." When do you feel alone, confined, afraid? Whom do you turn for support? What do you need to feel comfortable reaching out?

### Diary 79: Freedom Writers Unite

The writer of this entry describes how the Freedom Writers are going to meet with the U.S. Secretary of Education because "we want people who are adults to take the time to listen to teenagers and respect what we have to say." What important information about being young would you want to explain if you had a similar opportunity?

## Diary 80: Strict Father

In this entry, the author describes the pain of feeling "left out." Think back to a time when you felt disconnected from a group or friendship. Describe the experience in detail. Looking back, what could you have done to feel more empowered? What can you do in the future to ensure others do not feel abandoned or alone?

## Diary 81: Arlington Cemetery

The writer of this entry recalls his friends who have died and states: "To me, my friends are soldiers, not soldiers of war, but soldiers of the streets." Think about how the friends of this writer were treated in death as compared to the soldiers buried in Arlington Cemetery. Why were these two types of soldiers treated so differently? Should they have been honored equally?

## Diary 82: Lincoln Memorial: Freedom Writers Have a Dream

In this entry, the author commemorates the power of dreams, citing Martin Luther King, Jr., and the Freedom Writers. What are your dreams for your future? Have you told anyone? Why or why not? What are you willing to sacrifice to make your dream a reality?

## Diary 83: Covering Up the Swastika

In this entry, the author makes a trip to Washington and is astonished to see a swastika on a wall, "just blocks away from the White House and the Holocaust Museum." After this experience, he explains that his "judgment about Washington being perfect was wrong." We often stereotype people based on their exterior appearance. Think of a time when you were either a victim or perpetrator of a stereotype. Describe the situation and answer the question: What matters more, the outside appearance or the inside heart?

## Diary 84: Hate Crimes

In this entry, the writer describes how watching a movie makes him relive an attack that members of the Ku Klux Klan made against him. The entry concludes with the words "I guess some things never change . . ." Consider what you know about hate and intolerance throughout history. Do you believe people's treatment and understanding of others is improving or not? Support your thoughts with specific examples.

## Diary 85: Holocaust Museum

In this entry, the author has an epiphany when saying she used to think, "If it doesn't affect me, why bother?" Have you ever felt this way? What would motivate you to take action?

### Diary 86: Dr. Mengele's Experiment with Twins

Through her experiences at the Holocaust Museum, this Freedom Writer comes to realize how much she values her twin sister and their ability to work toward the dream of their futures. Consider the people who are close to you in your life. What can you do to show them how much they mean to you and how much you value your relationships with them?

### Diary 87: Dinner with U.S. Secretary Riley

This Freedom Writer is surprised to realize the value of education. Think of where you want to be five or ten years from now. How can you best take advantage of your education to reach your goals?

### Diary 88: "Stand"

In this entry, the writer shares a poem he/she wrote entitled "Stand." List the things in your life of which you are proud. Describe a time when you took a stand for your beliefs.

### Diary 89: Secretary Riley Receives *The Freedom Writers' Diary*

This Freedom Writer tells of being called a hero for taking action to save a brother. Think of a time when you did something that could be considered "heroic" or witnessed a "heroic" act. What was it and how did it happen?

### Diary 90: Candlelight Vigil

The student in this entry reflects on overcoming many roadblocks to achieve success and admits there were ample opportunities to give up. Did you ever contemplate giving up in your life? What kept you from giving up? Describe the factors in your life that make it easier or more difficult to persevere.

### Diary 91: Departing D.C.

This Freedom Writer describes finding hope in Ms. Gruwell after being raised to believe none existed on the horizon. Think of a time when someone thought you couldn't do something but you proved them wrong. What did you do, say, think, or accomplish that they didn't think you could? Explain how it felt and if it motivated you to try to do more with your life.

### Diary 92: Returning a Family Hero

The writer of this entry is welcomed home by family and friends as a hero. When have you felt that your family or friends were the most proud of you and loved you the most? What did you do and how did they show you?

### Diary 93: Jeremy Strohmeyer: Murder

This Freedom Writer explains the difficulty of speaking up in the face of evil. Consider times when others have had the chance to speak up but didn't. What factors make speaking up difficult to do?

### Diary 94: David Cash

In this entry, a Freedom Writer argues that people should "rock the boat" when they witness an injustice. Have you observed an unjust action or behavior? What did you do? If you could go back in time and revisit that moment, would you handle it differently?

### Diary 95: Peace March for Sherrice Iverson

In this entry, the Freedom Writers and other students decided to take a stand for peace, to remember the victim of violence. Though they stood together in peace, the media ignored them. Is it important to stand up for what you believe even if no one else acknowledges your stand?

### Diary 96: Senior Class President

The student in this entry decides to become involved in her school and make a change. Think of a time when you ran for an office or tried out for something? How did the election or audition turn out? What did you learn from the experience? Would you do it over again? Why or why not?

### Diary 97: Separation Anxiety

This writer describes finding a family in the Freedom Writers that she lacked at home. Think about the people you consider your family. What makes a group of people a family? What do you do to make other people feel like they are family?

### Diary 98: Staying Together

The student in this entry describes how she dealt with divorce and the arrival of her stepmother. What are the qualities that make a good mother? A good father? What type of parent do you want to be? Describe where you want to live with your family and the type of home you hope to have.

## SENIOR YEAR

### Diary 99: Cheryl Best: Inspiration

This Freedom Writer's mother uses the cliché "What doesn't kill you makes you stronger." When have you found this phrase fitting for a situation you have been in? What was it that almost "killed" you? What were your different options for ways to respond? How did you respond? Did you make the right choice?

### Diary 100: "Eviction Notice"

After being evicted, this writer states, "It seems like hope is the only thing

I have to hold on to." What is meant by this? Explain a time when you felt like hope was the only thing you had to hold on to.

### Diary 101: Financial Problems
This Freedom Writer talks about being an A and B student until he/she was left alone to run a house and take care of a younger sibling. Describe how you have felt when someone has been too busy or did not take the time to listen to you when you were in need of help. Describe your feelings and what you did to move forward.

### Diary 102: Illegal Immigrant
In this entry, the writer talks about how his status as an illegal immigrant hinders her ability to continue her education. Write about roadblocks that you've had to overcome that made reaching your dreams more satisfying than if they were handed to you.

### Diary 103: The First Latina Secretary of Education
This Freedom Writer shares her plans to become the first Latina Secretary of Education. Think about all that needs to be done in the world. What "first" would you like to claim for yourself? How can you set yourself on the course to succeed in this goal?

### Diary 104: Pursuing Filmmaking
The author of this diary thought about four or five careers before finally writing down what he thought would be more realistic. Why do you think the author did not believe his goal was realistic? What other careers can you think of that might not be considered realistic? Write down what you would like to do for a career and explain why this is interesting to you.

### Diary 105: Road Not Taken: Contemplating College
The parents of the author of this story pressure her to get an education, even though neither of them finished grade school. Why do you think education is important to her parents? What benefits do you think you will gain by graduating from high school and college?

### Diary 106: Finding a Mentor
This student shares how meeting a mentor opened doors to her future. Consider what you want to do with your future. How could having a mentor assist you in reaching those goals?

### Diary 107: Being a Mentor
In this diary, the author has a chance to help other students by finding out about their lives and listening to what they have to share. Think about what you have been through in your life. What experiences and skills could you use to help a child who needs someone to look up to?

### Diary 108: *Los Angeles Times* Article

In this diary, the author mentions that he was surprised by how many people reacted to one newspaper story. Consider how many other people could benefit and identify with your own story. Describe how you could make connections and share your truth with others.

### Diary 109: A Letter from Prison

In this journal entry, the author describes how she lost her father because he would not rat on his homeboys. Put yourself in the place of the author. Write a letter to her father to convince him to tell the truth and return home.

### Diary 110: Deadbeat Dad

In this entry, the writer describes how his father was too much of a coward to meet his son for the first time, so he had the writer's grandmother send the writer away. Describe a time when you or someone you know was so afraid of facing someone or something that they ended up blowing it off. Explain why this was or was not the correct decision.

### Diary 111: Sorority Hazing

In this entry, the writer talks about how she was a member of a popular sorority and watched on as new "pledges" were hazed. Think about what people are willing to endure to become popular. Explain what people have to gain by being part of the "popular" crowd. What do they stand to lose?

### Diary 112: Fear of Losing a Father

In this entry, the writer tells of a tragedy, his dad being shot in the head, and "living with a scar" from that experience. Reflect on your own life. Describe the "scars" you are living with. Do you try to hide them or wear them proudly?

### Diary 113: Death of a Mother

This Freedom Writer must confront a mother's death and the speed with which it came. Rather than turning to friends to help with the grieving process, the writer chooses to shut down and turn away from the outside world. Think of a time when you wanted to turn to others for support but couldn't. What kept you from doing so? How can you choose to open up in the future?

### Diary 114: GUESS? Sponsorship

This student writes, "Now that I am a part of something like the Freedom Writers, I don't have to try to fit in or to buy my way into acceptance. Material things are no longer a top priority in my life. Of course, I want nice things, but I don't feel as if I have to have them to feel complete. It's funny how material things mean so much to adolescents." Describe the importance you place on material things. What would life be like if you had nothing?

### Diary 115: Spirit of Anne Frank Award

This Freedom Writer explains concerns over joining Ms. Gruwell's class, but describes being welcomed without hesitation: "I was totally ecstatic about being a part of something that I'd heard so many wonderful things about. But I was completely terrified." Think of your own class or school. Describe what you can do to make sure a new student feels accepted and welcome.

### Diary 116: New York City Roommates

The writer of this entry describes how her father's racist views made her feel uncomfortable sharing a room with girls of other races. Think of a time when you were uncomfortable around another person you hardly knew. Explain what it was about the experience that made you uncomfortable.

### Diary 117: Celebrating Anne Frank

In this entry, the writer shares what happened when they received the Spirit of Anne Frank Award. The last line of the entry reads, "I want to go on living even after my death." Describe a person that you know or know of who has gone on living after their passing. How have the person and their message been remembered?

### Diary 118: Abuse of Power

This Freedom Writer's father inflicts abuse on the writer and the writer's siblings. The author ends the entry by saying that they will break the cycle of abuse. We learn many things from the positive role models around us and sometimes even more from negative role models. Write about a person that you view as a negative role model and what they taught you.

### Diary 119: Peter Maass: The Role of a Journalist

In this entry, the writer talks about meeting Peter Maass and what that felt like. The writer asked a "tough" question of Peter Maass—about whether he "just stands there watching people die" or if he does something. Have you ever had to act like Peter Maass and observe a dangerous act?

### Diary 120: Book Agent

This Freedom Writer says that Carol does not fit the description of what a pimp should look like. Think of all the good qualities you possess. Would another person recognize those qualities at first glance? Explain what you do to make sure the good in you is noticed by others.

### Diary 121: Getting Published

In this entry, the writer tells about getting *The Freedom Writer's Diary* published and being "added to the short but ever growing list of African American female writers" so that she can leave behind something of which she is proud. Consider all you have to offer. For what would you like to be remembered when you are gone?

### Diary 122: Basketball Playoffs: Teamwork

In this entry, the writer describes how feeling too much pressure caused her basketball team to lose a game. Describe a time when you were under so much pressure that you didn't do as well as you had hoped. What techniques have you learned that help you decrease the pressure in stressful situations?

### Diary 123: A Lesson from *Animal Farm*

In this entry, the writer talks about how some Freedom Writers are not doing their part. Reflect on a time when you needed others to come together to accomplish a goal. Explain what happened that led to your group's success or failure. What will you do in the future to inspire others to work toward a common goal?

### Diary 124: Attitude Adjustment

This Freedom Writer describes the frustration of being kicked off her basketball team, but she writes that she never gave up on the team. Think of an incident from your life where the world seemed to be turning against you. Describe how you dealt with it. Did you give in, or did you hold on to hope that things would work out?

### Diary 125: Introducing U.S. Senator Barbara Boxer

In this entry, the writer shares how he/she feels they are undeserving to speak on behalf of the Freedom Writers to a state senator. Describe a moment when you have felt undeserving of a gift, praise, or honor. Explain how it felt for others to think more of you than you thought of yourself. How can you use that feeling in the future?

### Diary 126: Attention Deficit Disorder

In this entry, the writer talks about life with ADD, medication, and speaking in front of college professors that resulted in a standing ovation. Consider the lengths to which this student had to go in order to gain attention and acceptance. Explain why a person would "act up" to make friends and give examples of times that you did something you would not normally have done to gain acceptance from others.

### Diary 127: Homosexuality

In this entry, the writer discusses her fears about not being accepted by friends and family because of her sexual orientation. Think of an instance in your life where you were not sure whether you would receive the support and respect of those you love. How did they end up reacting? Explain how you dealt with their reactions.

### Diary 128: Prom Queen

In this entry, the writer describes the sacrifices her mother made to ensure the safety of her family. Think of someone you know personally or from a book or movie who sacrificed a lot for the sake of others. What decisions or sacrifices would you have made if you were in this other person's shoes?

### Diary 129: "Whoever saves one life saves the world entire."

In this entry, the author reflects on a powerful statement: "Whoever saves one life, saves the world entire." Think of the experiences of the Freedom Writers and the people they have met. Explain whether or not one person can make a difference to the world.

### Diary 130: Breaking the Cycle

This Freedom Writer explains the importance of the quotation "History repeats itself." Think of the tools and experiences the Freedom Writers have gained. Describe whether or not they have the resources to break the cycles of which they are a part. Think of a cycle you are a part of. What will it take for you to break that cycle?

### Diary 131: Football All-American

In this entry, the author talks about a transformation that occurred in his life. How was he able to change his life in such a positive way? Describe a time in your life when things drastically changed, either for better or for worse.

### Diary 132: Baseball Dilemma

This Freedom Writer struggles with a decision that will affect the rest of his life. Describe a time when you were forced to make an important decision. What considerations did you think about when making your decision? Was the outcome of your decision what you hoped for? Looking back, is there anything you would do differently?

### Diary 133: A College Acceptance

This writer shares her good news with several people and is let down by each of their reactions. Finally, she shares her news with Ms. Gruwell and the Freedom Writers and they cheer. Consider the people in your life. To whom would you turn if you had news you were excited about? What would be their reaction?

### Diary 134: Fear of Abandonment

This author talks about being abandoned by her father, then feels that she will be abandoned by her friends after graduation. Think about a time when you felt abandoned. How did you deal with those kinds of feelings and what advice would you give a friend who was experiencing similar feelings?

### Diary 135: Teenage Pregnancy

In this entry, the writer talks about a situation that will change her life. At first she sees her life falling apart (unable to attend college, losing her job, etc.), then she is able to create a plan to follow through with her goals and dreams. Reflect on a moment when you have had to face jarring news. Discuss the situation and describe how you dealt with what happened. Did things go as badly as you first thought they would?

### Diary 136: Southwest Airlines

This Freedom Writer talks about feeling like a caged bird. The writer tells us that only caged birds sing because they have lost their freedom. Consider the different kinds of freedom in life. Now describe the freedoms you value most and how you would react if you lost those freedoms.

### Diary 137: Computers for College!

This writer describes John Tu, an entrepreneur, who contributed much to the Freedom Writers. Think about why John Tu felt it was important to give to the Freedom Writers community. Describe what you can do now to give back to your community and help to improve it.

### Diary 138: The Giving Tree: Crackhead Parents

In this entry, the writer talks about Shel Silverstein's *The Giving Tree* and plans to break the cycle of taking and become a giver instead. Describe a person (family member, community member, or entertainer) who is a giver and continues to give even though they receive only self-satisfaction in return. How can you emulate this person and become more of a giver?

### Diary 139: Graduation Class Speaker

This writer dreams of becoming the first in her family to graduate from high school. The writer talks about inspiration coming from both positive and negative influences. We are inspired by people around us through either their positive actions or their negative actions. Describe someone whose actions inspire you to become a better person.

### Diary 140: From Drugs to Honors

This Freedom Writer hated going to rehab but came to realize it was the right decision. Describe a time that you had to do something that you "hated" but looking back later realized that it was the best thing for you.

### Diary 141: Overcoming the Odds

Though cystic fibrosis is debilitating, it did not stop this writer from achieving a goal; it merely forced the writer down a different path. There are many people who overcome their physical or medical issues to achieve. Describe a person you know or know of who has overcome a physical or medical issue to achieve their goal and thus become an inspiration.

### Diary 142: Graduation

This Freedom Writer looks back on four years with Ms. Gruwell and admits no one could have predicted the success of the Freedom Writers from the first day of freshman year. The writer talks about Room 203 as the focal point for bringing a group of people together who normally would not socialize with one another. Describe a place or group that you are a part of where you connect with people who are different from you. How did those connections form?

### Epilogue

In the final paragraph of Ms. Gruwell's Epilogue, the book is described as "the third leg of a relay race." Describe something specific you are willing to do to act as the fourth leg of the relay race and be a catalyst for change and acceptance in your own community.

# APPENDIX C

### 1. Reading for Perspective

Students read a wide range of print and nonprint texts to build an understanding of texts, of themselves, and of the cultures of the United States and the world; to acquire new information; to respond to the needs and demands of society and the workplace; and for personal fulfillment. Among these texts are fiction and nonfiction, classic, and contemporary works.

### 2. Understanding the Human Experience

Students read a wide range of literature from many periods in many genres to build an understanding of the many dimensions (i.e., philosophical, ethical, aesthetic) of human experience.

### 3. Evaluation Strategies

Students apply a wide range of strategies to comprehend, interpret, evaluate, and appreciate texts. They draw on their prior experience, their interactions with other readers and writers, their knowledge of word meaning and of other texts, their word-identification strategies, and their understanding of textual features (i.e., sound-letter correspondence, sentence structure, context, graphics).

### 4. Communication Skills

Students adjust their use of spoken, written, and visual language (i.e., conventions, style, vocabulary) to communicate effectively with a variety of audiences and for different purposes.

## 5. Communication Strategies

Students employ a wide range of strategies as they write and use different writing-process elements appropriately to communicate with different audiences for a variety of purposes.

## 6. Applying Knowledge

Students apply knowledge of language structure, language conventions (i.e., spelling and punctuation), media techniques, figurative language, and genre to create, critique, and discuss print and nonprint texts.

## 7. Evaluating Data

Students conduct research on issues and interests by generating ideas and questions, and by posing problems. They gather, evaluate, and synthesize data from a variety of sources (i.e., print and nonprint texts, artifacts, people) to communicate their discoveries in ways that suit their purpose and audience.

## 8. Developing Research Skills

Students use a variety of technological and information resources (i.e., libraries, databases, computer networks, video) to gather and synthesize information and to create and communicate knowledge.

## 9. Multicultural Understanding

Students develop an understanding of and respect for diversity in language use, patterns, and dialects across cultures, ethnic groups, geographic regions, and social roles.

## 10. Applying Non-English Perspectives

Students whose first language is not English make use of their first language to develop competency in the English language arts and to develop understanding of content across the curriculum.

## 11. Participating in Society

Students participate as knowledgeable, reflective, creative, and critical members of a variety of literacy communities.

## 12. Applying Language Skills

Students use spoken, written, and visual language to accomplish their own purposes (i.e., for learning, enjoyment, persuasion, and the exchange of information).

# ACKNOWLEDGMENTS

**THE FREEDOM WRITERS**

**The Freedom Writer Teachers**

Sefakor Amaa – Dunbar Middle School
(Fort Worth, TX)

Gail Anderson – Will J. Reid High School
(Long Beach, CA)

Scott Bailey – North County / South County
Community School (Oroville, CA)

Booker T. Washington High School
(Atlanta, GA)

Darwin Chan – McCrimmon Middle School
(Mississauga, Ontario, Canada)

Zac Chase – Phoenix Academy (Sarasota, FL)

Jamie Coburn – McCrimmon Middle School
(Mississauga, Ontario, Canada)

Kelly Dhatt – McCrimmon Middle School
(Mississauga, Ontario, Canada)

Bill Feaver – Worsley School / Fresno County
Juvenile Justice Campus (Fresno, CA)

Michael Galbraith – Grover Washington, Jr.
Middle School (Philadelphia, PA)

Kate Hogg – Richmond High School
(Richmond, IN)

Jenn Laskin – Renaissance High School
(La Selva Beach, CA)

Erin Mangahis – Patrick Henry High School
(San Diego, CA)

Megan McDonough – MATCH School
(Boston, MA)

Dave McKay – Chico High School (Chico, CA)

Robin Meehan – Fletcher's Meadow Secondary
School (Brampton, Ontario, Canada)

Heather Meldrum – Western Village Academy
(Oklahoma City, OK)

Marcia Nelson – Crossroads Alternative High School
(Coon Rapids, MN)

Jon Paul Pedergnana – Frederick Douglass
Academy VI (Far Rockaway, NY)

Mike Ross – McCrimmon Middle School
(Mississauga, Ontario, Canada)

Debbie Sidler – Mission Viejo High School (Mission
Viejo, CA)

Darence Shine – Bremerton High School
(Bremerton, WA)

Monalisa Siofele – Waipahu High School
(Waipahu, HI)

Karen Sojourner – DeLaSalle Education Center
(Kansas City, MO)

Joseph Thornton – Hermiston High School
(Hermiston, OR)

Robert Waller – Charles R. Drew Charter School
(Atlanta, GA)

Jan Werner – DeLaSalle Education Center
(Kansas City, MO)

Katie Williams – T. Dewitt Taylor Middle-High
School (Pierson, FL)

Ken Williams – Warm Springs Middle School
(Murrieta, CA)

## Contributors

Robyn Marotta
Sonia Pineda
Faye Walsh
Shelley Olson
Naja Hayward
Sue Ellen Alpizar
Maria Reyes
Dr. Sabrina Barton
Dr. Daniel J. O'Connor
Dr. Marilyn Korostoff
Dr. Carl Cohn
Dr. Karin Polacheck
Dr. Lynn Winters
Dr. Kristin Powers
Marcia Nye
Dave Beard
Horace Hall
John Tu
Wing Lam
Don Ayres III
Renee Firestone
Mel Mermelstein
The Dream Team Moms (Debbie Mayfield,
   Marilyn Tyo, Mary Rozier, Fran Sawdei)
Richard LaGravenese
Carol Schild and Marvin Levy
Michael Palgon
Janet Hill
Christian Nwachukwu
Clarence Haynes
Kira Fluor-Scacchi

Antoine Wilson
Brett Ferguson
Maggie Kayne
California State University, Long Beach
Common
will.i.am
Paramount Pictures
Brad Grey
Hilary Swank
Danny Devito
Stacey Sher
Michael Shamberg
Dan Levine
Tracey Durning
Connie Chung
Anna Quindlen
Zlata Filipovic
Miep Gies
Tina Henderson
MTV Films
Kayne Foundation
Kilpatrick Stockton, LLP
Righteous Persons Foundation
Museum of Tolerance
Southwest Airlines
Marriott Hotels
Supporters and Donors of the Freedom Writers
   Foundation
Readers of *The Freedom Writers Diary*

The next generation of Freedom Writers everywhere . . .

# ABOUT THE AUTHORS

## ERIN GRUWELL

Erin Gruwell, better known to her students as "Ms. G," has been credited with giving her students a "second chance," but it was perhaps she who changed the most during her tenure at Woodrow Wilson High School in Long Beach, California. With every new challenge, Erin learned a little more about how to teach her "unteachable" students. She listened to their voices. She adapted her curriculum. With Erin's support, her students shattered stereotypes to become critical thinkers, aspiring college students, and citizens for change.

Erin is a graduate of the University of California, Irvine, where she received the Lauds and Laurels Distinguished Alumni Award. She earned her master's degree and teaching credentials from California State University, Long Beach, where the School of Education honored her as a Distinguished Alumna. Erin taught at California State University, Long Beach, from 1998 to 2004, where she taught educators as a Distinguished Teacher in Residence. Currently, Erin teaches for the Freedom Writers Foundation, a nonprofit organization that promotes the Freedom Writers Method: educational strategies designed to promote diversity, inspire teachers and students, and decrease high school dropout rates. With the publication of *The Freedom Writers Diary: Teacher's Guide*, Erin furthers her goal of channeling her experiences toward a world of educators and learners beyond the walls of Room 203, her classroom at Wilson High in Long Beach, California, the place where the Freedom Writers were born.

## FREEDOM WRITERS

In the fall of 1994, 150 students walked into Erin Gruwell's freshman English class at Woodrow Wilson High School. They began writing in their journals as an English assignment, not knowing that their journal entries of hardship, discrimination, and loss would one day be collected and published in a book that would become a number-one-ranked *New York Times* bestseller, *The Freedom Writers Diary: How a Teacher and 150 Teens Used Writing to Change Themselves and the World Around Them* (Broadway Books, 1999).

In 1997, the Freedom Writers made a trip to Washington, D.C., and delivered a copy of their unpublished manuscript to Richard Riley, the U.S. Secretary of Education, and in 1998 they received the Spirit of Anne Frank Award for their commitment to combating discrimination, racism, and bias-related violence. The same year, 150 Freedom Writers walked across a graduation stage to claim their high school diplomas, a feat few people had thought possible. Since then, many of the Freedom Writers have graduated with college degrees, thanks to the scholarships provided by the Freedom Writers Foundation; some have earned master's degrees; and some are even pursuing Ph.D.s. The Freedom Writers continue to contribute to the day-to-day running of the Foundation, help to lead and organize teacher training workshops, and visit schools to spread the Freedom Writer message of hope.

Throughout this *Teacher's Guide,* you will find "Freedom Writer Feedback," a collection of comments and reactions about the activities they experienced during their four years in Room 203.

## FREEDOM WRITERS FOUNDATION

Erin Gruwell and the Freedom Writers established The Freedom Writers Foundation, a nonprofit 501(c) 3 organization, in an effort to replicate the Freedom Writers' success in classrooms throughout the country. The Foundation has encouraged, inspired, and motivated thousands of teachers and students with the same methods Erin Gruwell used with the Freedom Writers in Room 203.

The Freedom Writers Foundation positively impacts a growing number of communities through school visits, scholarship awards, and teacher training workshops. The Foundation trains teachers with innovative teaching tools, such as the lessons included in this *Teacher's Guide.* Teachers from across the United States and Canada have participated in the Freedom Writers Institute taught directly by Erin Gruwell and the Freedom Writers, and have returned to their classrooms with renewed energy and focus.

## FREEDOM WRITER "PILOT" TEACHERS

The Freedom Writer Teachers were the first two pilot groups of educators to complete the Freedom Writers Institute training in Long Beach, California. These dynamic teachers come from urban, rural, and suburban regions of the country and represent a myriad of classrooms reflecting various socioeconomic and academic levels. The Freedom Writer Teachers have a breadth of experience that includes working with at-risk students, honors students, English language learners, and incarcerated youth, ranging from middle school through high school.

These teachers have used *The Freedom Writers Diary* in their classrooms and have tested the activities in this guide. They have played an integral role in the creation of this guide, contributing ideas and suggestions, sharing their students' reactions to the activities, and passing along their own comments, which can be found in the "Teacher Talk" sections of the *Teacher's Guide*.

Freedom Writers Foundation
P.O. Box 41505
Long Beach, CA  90853
562-433-5388 ph
562-433-5367 fax
www.freedomwritersfoundation.org

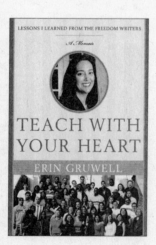